Text and design © Carlton Books Ltd 2021

First published in 2021 by Welbeck
An imprint of Headline Publishing Group Limited

8

Apart from any use permitted under UK copyright law, this publication may only be reproduced, stored, or transmitted, in any form, or by any means, with prior permission in writing of the publishers or, in the case of reprographic production, in accordance with the terms of licences issued by the Copyright Licensing Agency.

Cataloguing in Publication Data is available from the British Library

ISBN 978 1 78739 924 2

Printed and bound in China

Headline's policy is to use papers that are natural, renewable and recyclable products and made from wood grown in well-managed forests and other controlled sources. The logging and manufacturing processes are expected to conform to the environmental regulations of the country of origin.

All trademarks, images, quotations, company names, registered names, products and logos used or cited in this book are the property of their respective owners and are used in this book for identification, review and editorial purposes only. This book is a publication of Headline Publishing Group Ltd and has not been licensed, approved, sponsored, or endorsed by any person or entity and has no connection or association to Ferrari S.p.A. and/or Scuderia Ferrari S.p.A.

Editor: Ross Hamilton
Design: Eliana Holder & Luana Gobbo
Picture Research: Paul Langan
Production: Arlene Alexander

HEADLINE PUBLISHING GROUP LIMITED
A Hachette UK Company
Carmelite House
50 Victoria Embankment
London EC4Y 0DZ

The authorised representative in the EEA is Hachette Ireland,
8 Castlecourt Centre, Dublin 15, D15 XTP3, Ireland (email: info@hbgi.ie)

www.headline.co.uk
www.hachette.co.uk

THE STORY OF
Ferrari

THE STORY OF
Ferrari

A TRIBUTE TO AUTOMOTIVE EXCELLENCE

STUART CODLING

CONTENTS

Birth Of A Legend 6

E La Macchina? 18

Sale Of The Century 40

Glory And Power 60

The Price Of Progress........................... 80

The Schumacher Years 98

World Domination 118

Ferrari In Popular Culture.................... 140

Index 156

Credits 160

BIRTH OF A LEGEND

BUILDING THE DREAM

Il Commendatore. Il Drake. L'Ingegnere ("the Commander", "the Drake", "the Engineer"), "Agitator of men." Enzo Anselmo Ferrari gratefully assumed many titles, ranging from grandiose to enigmatic, over the course of a long and eventful life. Fittingly, perhaps, the myths surrounding that life even shroud the date his given name was inked into the records: Ferrari's own official origin story has it that Enzo was born in Modena on 18 February 1898 but, owing to a blizzard, this fact wasn't registered with the authorities until two days later.

Then as now, compliance with such niceties as official paperwork was a low priority for the average citizen of what was a young kingdom, unified within the lifetime of Enzo's parents, Alfredo and Adalgisa. Turmoil continued to be a fact of life in a nation which had once been home to one of Europe's defining civilisations and then, after that empire's fall, become a seething hotbed of rival city states defined by great artworks and rampant infighting, frequently invaded by neighbouring dynasties. Nationalism fuelled the movement towards unification and, by the end of the 19th century,

OPPOSITE: The young Enzo Ferrari dreamed of being an opera singer, journalist, or a racing driver

BIRTH OF A LEGEND 9

rapid industrialisation in the north of Italy would make the country one of Europe's powers – without fully addressing the inequalities which would fuel ongoing social fractures in the century to come.

It was a world of chaos and poverty, but also of great opportunities for the likes of Enzo Ferrari, ambitious men who learned very quickly how to make the right connections. Above all, Enzo Ferrari was a different man to different people, an empire-builder who came to relish his role as the spider in the centre of an elaborate tangle of intrigues.

During the glory days of the Roman Empire, the Emilia-Romagna region was colonised by former legionaries who were granted parcels of land upon completing 25 years' service to the empire. Modena was one of many settlements which grew up along the *Via Aemilia*, the Roman road connecting Piacenza to Rimini. Enzo's mother hailed from Forli, the walled city on the other side of Bologna snatched by the Borgias in the 15th century. Enzo's father's trade was one which had not only survived, but thrived in the transition to industry: metalwork. Modena rang to the sound of hammers in the many workshops around the town, manufacturing such items as once formed the underpinnings of carts and which now clothed and sprung the motor car. In time this area would become a hub of artisan design and coachbuilding for the automobile industry.

Enzo's father ran such a workshop, facilitating the family with the trappings of the middle class. In his autobiography *My Terrible Joys*, Enzo wrote of sharing a bedroom over the workshop with his older brother, Alfredo Jr, and being woken each morning by the ringing of hammers below. He took note of his father's organisational fastidiousness, acting as company secretary as well as the manager, designer and salesman.

Unlike his brother, Enzo was an indifferent and unmotivated scholar, frequently beaten by his father upon

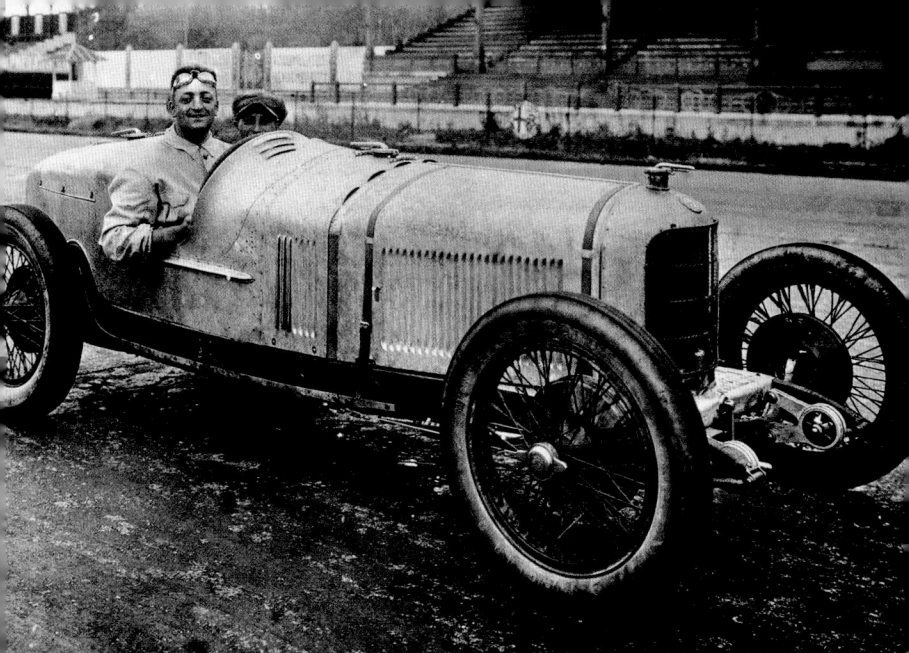

ABOVE: Enzo Ferrari's driving talent and gift for making connections enabled him to secure a job with Alfa Romeo.

receipt of critical school reports. Enzo would never become the engineer his father desired him to be, though he willingly adopted the honorific title *L'Ingegnere*, He would, in time, become something rather greater, but his father did not live to see it. Alfredo Sr died of pneumonia in 1916, shortly after Enzo's 18th birthday. Alfredo Jr was away, having enlisted in the air force, and before the year was out he too was dead, of an illness which went unrecorded.

Enzo had dreamed of becoming a racing driver ever since his father took him to watch the 1908 Coppa Florio road race in Bologna; and if not that, perhaps an opera singer, or a sports journalist – a handful of his football reports were published in the *Gazzetta dello Sport*. But those lofty ambitions seemed gone as, in his father's absence, the family business collapsed and Enzo was drafted into the army, where he was tasked with shoeing mules in an artillery regiment. His one lucky break was that he survived the deadly 1918 flu pandemic, though it left him severely debilitated.

Returning to civilian life after the armistice, Enzo faced the prospect of building a life without the traditional family support network. "I was back where I had started [in Modena]," he wrote in his autobiography. "No money, no experience, limited education. All I had was a passion to get somewhere."

Turned down for an engineering job with Fiat in Turin, Enzo nevertheless demonstrated his knack for making connections, living modestly and securing work with CMN, one of many engineering companies making the transition from putting together military-industrial machinery to assembling passenger cars. Enzo's job was to test-drive and deliver these cars, and it enabled him to revive his dream of becoming a racing driver.

BELOW: Tazio Nuvolari and his Scuderia Ferrari mechanics push his Alfa Romeo onto the grid for the 1935 French Grand Prix.

ABOVE: German teams were dominant in the 1930s, but in the 1935 German GP Tazio Nuvolari beat them resoundingly on home ground in his Ferrari-run Alfa Romeo.

This was to be a short but instructive phase of Enzo's life. Thrilled by initial tastes in the Parma–Poggio di Berceto hillclimb and the Targa Florio road race aboard a CMN, he acquired a more powerful car, an ageing Isotta Fraschini 4.5-litre beast, for his return to the hillclimb, finishing third overall. For his second crack at the Targa Florio he looked to Milan and Alfa Romeo, then Italy's pre-eminent manufacturer of racing cars, as well as more humble machinery. Here he would lay the foundations of his future empire.

Alfa Romeo took on Enzo as a driver and he energetically expanded his role as a salesman and networker, helping the company recruit engineering and driving talent from the ailing CMN, as well as raiding Fiat for promising personnel. Most notably he was instrumental in the poaching of leading racecar engineer Vittorio Jano when Alfa's P1 grand prix car proved underwhelming. The work proved lucrative enough for Enzo to establish an Alfa Romeo dealership in his home town while still racing occasionally.

BIRTH OF A LEGEND 13

ABOVE: Tazio Nuvolari is a blur in his Alfa Romeo, occupying first position at the Nürburgring in 1935 on the way to a memorable victory.

The turning point came in July 1924. Enzo had won minor races but was not considered good enough to rank among Alfa's stars. In the high-profile Coppa Acerbo road race he won in a second-string car after team-mate Giuseppe Campari, driving Jano's mighty new P2, stopped with a burst tyre. This was enough to persuade Alfa competitions manager Giorgio Rimini to field Enzo in a P2 at the forthcoming French Grand Prix. The car was too powerful and unpredictable even for one so determined as Enzo, who suffered a panic attack and beat a retreat back to Italy. He would race again, but not at this level.

Three years later, Alfa Romeo also withdrew from grand prix racing, providing Ferrari with the germ of an idea. He now enjoyed connections with wealthy customers who nurtured a passion for racing, and with talented mechanics who knew their way around a racing car. Enzo put together a deal to create his own racing company, Scuderia Ferrari, with seed capital from two wealthy customers, plus a buy-in from Alfa Romeo – who understood the marketing value of retaining an involvement with motor racing – and Pirelli. Enzo would run the cars and all his customers had to do was turn up on the day to race.

This arrangement proved so successful that Scuderia Ferrari survived Alfa Romeo's return to grand prix racing, and its nationalisation by Benito Mussolini's fascist government in the early 1930s. In 1932 Ferrari adopted the prancing horse motif although, as with so many elements of the Ferrari story, scepticism surrounds the official account that it was the personal emblem of a fighter ace who served in the same squadron as Enzo's older brother.

What *is* well-documented is that the 1930s grand prix racing scene was co-opted by Nazi Germany as a prestige project. Hitler's government ploughed resources into Mercedes and Auto Union's advanced racing cars and Mussolini felt under pressure to do the same. Having taken responsibility for running Alfa's works racing machines

BELOW: A packed crowd watches Louis Chiron (leading) in his Alfa Romeo Tipo-B P3 during the 1934 French Grand Prix. He would go on to win the race.

post-nationalisation, Ferrari was outgunned on the track despite the valiant efforts of some of the best drivers of that generation, including Tazio Nuvolari. While Jano fell out of favour as a result, and was obliged to leave, Enzo's solution to the money-no-object German speed machines was to build cars which would race in a different class, thereby avoiding the humiliation of direct competition.

That notion didn't cut it with the echelons above. As Enzo's proposed car took shape, drawn by Jano's assistant, Gioachino Colombo, the political wheels continued to grind. Alfa Romeo bought Scuderia Ferrari in 1938, rendering Enzo an employee, then brought in a new design team led by an outsider, Wilfredo Ricart, for whom Enzo quickly developed an outright loathing.

Scuderia Ferrari ceased to exist, becoming Alfa Corse, and Enzo walked away to form a new company, Auto Avio Costruzioni, agreeing with his old employers not to race in opposition to them for four years, but World War II meant this agreement went untested. Ferrari's business churned out machine tools and aircraft parts for the Italian government, a prime example of Enzo *realpolitik*: this area of Italy was a communist stronghold and Enzo was always hard but scrupulously fair with his employees – while serving a regime implacably opposed to communism.

When motor racing spluttered into life after World War II, Ferrari felt the urge to go racing again. He contacted Colombo, then serving a suspension while his membership of the fascist party was investigated.

OPPOSITE: Rudolf Caracciola's Mercedes-Benz W25B (right) leads Tazio Nuvolari's Alfa Romeo during the 1935 French grand prix. Mercedes benefited from a huge influx of funding from the Nazi government during the 1930s.

E LA MACCHINA?

THE CAR'S THE STAR

"[Enzo] Ferrari's expectation of performance exerted a strong force that radiated throughout the organisation, and the drivers were not exempt from it," wrote the 1961 world champion Phil Hill. "Rather than the race being a culmination of a team effort to win, there was a feeling instead as if you, the driver, had been reluctantly entrusted with this gem of a machine, this fruit of genius, and hopefully your natural dunderheadedness would not destroy it."

"When one of us did win I sensed a certain reluctance on Ferrari's part to share the laurels with the driver, to pat him on the back and thank him for a job well done. It was more like Ferrari felt the victory was doubly his – he had not only managed to build a car that was better than all the other cars, but a car that was also good enough to foil even his driver's natural destructiveness."

The key to the Ferrari legend, that x-factor which makes its road cars such objects of desire and seats in its race cars so coveted, is the presence of the creator etched into the DNA.

OPPOSITE: Enzo Ferrari poses with three of the four 290 MMs built specifically to win the 1956 Mille Miglia road race. Number 600 (front), driven to fourth place by Juan Manuel Fangio, fetched more than $25 million at auction in 2015.

ABOVE: Eugenio Castellotti, seen here in a Ferrari 555 in the 1955 Dutch GP, died while testing a Ferrari in 1957.

Enzo's personality, his hopes and dreams, inhabit every car which rolls out of the factory gates.

When he began building cars under the Ferrari name again in 1947 he had already fathered two children: Alfredo, fondly known as Dino, aspired to be an engineer but died young of muscular dystrophy; Piero was born to Enzo's mistress and went unacknowledged publicly during Laura Ferrari's lifetime. Hill believed this left a hole in Enzo's life which he filled with work. Hill wrote, too, that Enzo's cars "were so directly an extension of his own being, to admit fault in them was to admit fault in himself".

Once back in business under his own name, Ferrari had little interest in building road cars, save where it would subsidise his racing activities. This would change as the financial burdens of racing grew, but Enzo had already proved himself a master salesman as well as a successful entrepreneur. As the legend grew, so too did the line of supplicants hoping to buy a piece of it.

There are those who claim Enzo ceased to travel and attend motor races after Dino's death in 1956, but in truth his wanderlust had long since been quenched. Ferrari preferred life in his new workshops in Maranello, just down the road from Modena, where he established his new kingdom. There he would pull strings, stoke rivalries, divide and rule.

BELOW: Ferrari's son Alfredo, known to all as Dino, had muscular dystrophy and died young.

Thanks partly to this kind of internal competition, it didn't take long for Ferrari to supplant Alfa Romeo as Italy's premier exponent of racing and performance cars. Before Gioachino Colombo's suspension was lifted and he returned to Alfa, he designed a diminutive but readily expandable 1.5-litre V12 which would power Ferrari's first racing cars. Reworked over the years with larger displacements and more sophisticated valve-gear, it would also see service in Ferrari road cars until the late 1980s.

ABOVE: The troubled 555 'Super Squalo' took one grand prix win in 1954 but was quickly set aside.

Colombo's presence at Maranello overlapped with that of Aurelio Lampredi, a former scooter and aircraft engine designer who had a different vision: a larger all-aluminium V12 which, unlike Colombo's engine, wouldn't need supercharging to be competitive in what was soon to become known as Formula 1.

Ferrari's first race car, the 125S, took its name from the swept volume (in cubic centimetres) of a single cylinder in the Colombo V12 which powered it. On 11 May 1947, Franco Cortese raced the prototype for the first time at Piacenza,

LEFT: Ferrari won 14 of the 17 races in the world championship's Formula 2 era from 1952-53. Alberto Ascari was responsible for 11 of them.

ABOVE: British drivers Mike Hawthorn and Peter Collins (foreground, left and right) were among Ferrari's star drivers in the 1950s. Hawthorn was the world champion in 1958.

briefly taking the lead before his fuel pump failed. Cortese had sold machine tools for Ferrari's Auto Avio Costruzione and told him he was insane to give that up for motor racing. Now he changed his tune, winning two weeks later in Rome, on a street circuit around the ancient baths of Caracalla. Ferrari also received a visit from his old friend Luigi Chinetti, a double winner of the Le Mans 24 Hours now settled in America – a promised land, home to dozens of wealthy amateurs who, he claimed, would leap at the chance to race an exotic European car.

In a continent shattered by war and still facing shortages of raw materials, motor racing offered precious entertainment for the masses and an adrenaline buzz for a new wave of participants who had seen combat and struggled to adapt to

BELOW: Luigi Musso carried Ferrari's – and the nation's – hopes of being an Italian world champion, but he pushed too hard in the 1958 French GP and crashed fatally.

peacetime life. Most of the cars were pre-war stock which had survived being melted down for munitions.

Not that this meant Ferrari would have an easy ride. The ladder-frame chassis of the early cars were crude and flimsy, not that this mattered greatly to Enzo, who believed the engine to be the greatest performance differentiator (later in life he would dismiss aerodynamics as a science for people who don't understand engines). But this was also a problematic area in the early years of the "new" Ferrari, for Colombo's V12 required considerable development – and much rancour between the engineers – to deliver respectable horsepower.

Perhaps this accounts for Ferrari's initial reluctance to take on his old firm, Alfa Romeo, head-to-head on the grand prix scene. Ferrari chassis powered by 1.5-litre and 2-litre versions of the Colombo engine, and clad in neatly sculpted bodies

crafted by local coachbuilders, began to pick up victories in the late 1940s.

Most immediately significant was Chinetti's win at the revived Le Mans enduro in 1949, where he drove the majority of the race after his co-driver Lord Selsdon fell ill. And yet, while the Ferrari company of today enjoys flaunting its long association with Formula 1, Ferrari was a notable absentee from the first ever World Championship round, at Silverstone in 1950.

Whether it was the presence of Alfa Romeo – fielding the surviving 158s Ferrari had commissioned Colombo to construct in the late 1930s – or the meagreness of the prize money on offer, Ferrari preferred to concentrate on the Monaco Grand Prix which followed. There the peaky power delivery of the supercharged V12 and dicey handling of the 125 F1 chassis might be less of a disadvantage. Alberto Ascari, whose father had been a racing contemporary of Enzo and had died at the wheel of an Alfa Romeo in 1925, finished second for Ferrari.

BELOW: Monza's newly rebuilt concrete banking formed part of the circuit layout for the 1955 Italian Grand Prix. Ferrari entered six cars (Maurice Trintignant pictured) but were well beaten by Mercedes.

BELOW: Wolfgang von Trips in Ferrari's iconic 156 'Sharknose'.

OPPOSITE: Pole position, fastest lap and race victory in the 1958 French GP earned Ferrari's Mike Hawthorn (4) several bonus cases of champagne from the race promoter.

OVERLEAF: Victory in a Ferrari 250 TR at Le Mans in 1958 set Phil Hill (driving, with Olivier Gendebien) on course for an F1 drive with Ferrari.

Swapping to the Lampredi naturally-aspirated V12 design enabled Ferrari to overturn Alfa Romeo's supremacy and deliver a first World Championship win in 1951, and when the older company hit financial difficulties and withdrew from grand prix racing, Ferrari only had Maserati and, briefly, Lancia as rival national flag bearers. Enzo's sportscars won eight editions of the challenging 1,000-mile Mille Miglia road race and he enjoyed a profitable working relationship with the coachbuilder Pinin Farina in the manufacture of production cars, potential buyers of which were personally vetted by Enzo himself.

ABOVE: Phil Hill won the 1961 Italian GP and the world championship, but the race was overshadowed by the death of Hill's team-mate Wolfgang von Trips.

The cars continued to be the stars, while those who designed and raced them were expendable. Perhaps Enzo had developed his armour-plating on the pre-war racing scene as friends and rivals fell. Once engineers had given of their best and began to fail, they fell from favour immediately.

Even Lampredi, whose four-cylinder 2-litre engine enabled Ferrari to dominate the World Championship in 1952–53 – when a shortage of F1 cars led race promoters to court F2 entrants instead – was cast out in 1955, when a larger version failed to cut it as F1 embraced 2.5-litre unblown engines. Enzo had a ready-made replacement in the form of pre-war Alfa Romeo engineer Vittorio Jano, who came part and parcel with the assets of the Lancia D50 project when insolvency forced

Lancia out of racing. Jano contributed a V12 engine which would claim two sportscar world championships and a V6 that would do the same in F1.

Drivers, too, came and went without sentiment, sometimes to their graves. Ascari died testing a Ferrari sportscar at Monza in 1955, bringing Enzo the first of several waves of condemnation from the Vatican and the Italian media. Other deaths, including Alfonso de Portago during the 1957 Mille Miglia and Wolfgang von Trips in the 1961 Italian Grand Prix, brought lengthy legal wrangles as well as further opprobrium

BELOW: The aftermath of the fatal accident on the second lap of the 1961 Italian GP in which Ferrari driver Wolfgang von Trips and 14 spectators died.

OPPOSITE: A tyre blow-out at high speed in the 1957 Mille Miglia had fatal consequences for Alfonso de Portago, co-driver Edmund Nelson, and nine spectators.

from the Pontiff. Trips was Phil Hill's team-mate and rival for that year's Championship and his recollection was that the cars "were never fragile".

"There was, though, something about the ambience at Ferrari that did, indeed, seem to spur drivers to their deaths," recalled Hill. "Perhaps it was the intense sibling-rivalry atmosphere Ferrari fostered, his failure to rank the drivers and his fickleness with the favourites. Luigi Musso died at Rheims, while striving to protect his fair-haired boy status against the encroaching popularity of the Englishmen – Peter Collins and Mike Hawthorn.

"And Peter Collins, a firm favourite… began to get a Ferrari cold shoulder when he married Louise King and went to live aboard a boat in Monte Carlo. Peter was dead within a year."

It's Collins who contributed what is perhaps the most telling piece of eyewitness testimony to Enzo Ferrari's lack of sentimentality towards the people who carried his standard into battle. Collins was in Ferrari's office in March 1957 when the phone rang to inform "The Old Man" that Eugenio Castellotti had died testing a Ferrari F1 car at Modena. Enzo himself had summoned Castellotti from holiday to re-establish a lap record recently broken by Jean Behra in a Maserati.

Enzo – according to Collins – went pale and expressed shock at the news. There then followed a slight pause before he enquired after the health of the car: "*E la macchina?*"

SALE OF THE CENTURY

THE ROAD TO SUCCESS

Racing consumed Enzo Ferrari but it had to be paid for, whether through the arcane and unreliable system of negotiating "starting money" (essentially an appearance fee) with promoters, prize money, selling race cars to private entrants… or by selling road cars based on racing underpinnings. In 1948 Ferrari took a stand at the Turin Motor Show and demonstrated two models which electrified both the industry and the public at large.

Collaborating with the Milanese coachbuilder Carrozzeria Touring to append super-light bodywork and luxurious trim to a tube-frame race chassis, Ferrari offered two variations on the 166, a model taking its name from the swept volume in cubic centimetres of a single cylinder in its two-litre Gioachino Colombo-designed V12 engine.

Touring had pioneered and patented the *Superleggera* construction technique of light aluminium panels laid over a web of small-diameter tubing, used to great effect in the Italian aeronautical industry. The open-top 166MM, named after the Mille Miglia road race, connected explicitly with Ferrari's

OPPOSITE: John Surtees (right) frequently complained that sportscar racing diverted resources and focus from Ferrari's Formula 1 programme.

OPPOSITE: To see off the challenge of Ford, Ferrari had 12 cars entered in the 1965 Le Mans 24 Hours. John Surtees (19) co-drove the 330 P2 Spyder with Ludovico Scarfiotti, but gearbox failure ruled the new car out. Masten Gregory and Jochen Rindt won in a Ferrari 250 LM (21) which had qualified 12 seconds off pole position.

BELOW: Surtees won his 1964 world title in a blue and white Ferrari entered by Luigi Chinetti's NART organisation after a dispute between Enzo Ferrari and the Italian sports federation.

successful racing models and its svelte shape compelled the Italian press to describe it as a *barchetta*, meaning "little boat". A year later, Clemente Biondetti drove one to victory at the Mille Miglia, followed by Luigi Chinetti's victory at Le Mans, crystallising the racing connection. Among those rushing to acquire a 166MM was Gianni Agnelli, heir to the Fiat empire among the Agnelli family's other industrial interests.

Alongside the 166MM Ferrari wowed showgoers with another milestone car, the coupé-bodied 166 Inter. Extending the wheelbase enabled the cabin to accommodate a second row of seats for occasional use and it was this, together with the luxuriously appointed interior, which emphasised its intended purpose as a grand tourer rather than a racer. Around 38 were built via Ferrari's customary method, typical of the day, whereby naked chassis were delivered to a coachbuilder and finished in a body of the client's choice.

Enzo, mindful of his enterprise's mystique, vetted each potential buyer personally; such gatekeeping merely encouraged

ABOVE: The 250 GT Coupé Pinin Farina was the first road-going Ferrari to be built in substantial numbers.

the wealthy, famous and well-heeled to his door. Among the first customers was Prince Igor Troubetzkoy, fourth of Woolworth heiress Barbara Hutton's seven husbands. He co-drove with Biondetti in an Allemano-bodied 166 to win the Targa Florio in May 1948.

Perhaps the most prolific Ferrari purchaser of the 1950s was Porfirio Rubirosa, a polo player and racing driver whom many believe to have been involved in political black-bag operations – including assassinations – on behalf of Dominican dictator Rafael Trujillo. He was also Hutton's fifth husband, albeit for only 53 days, and dated a string of stars including Marilyn Monroe, Rita Hayworth, Eartha Kitt, Joan Crawford, Ava Gardner and Zsa Zsa Gabor (who accompanied him to Le Mans in 1954, only for Rubirosa's team-mate to crash their 375 MM on the fifth lap). Rubirosa met his maker after wrapping his 250 GT around a tree in the Bois de Boulogne, having spent the evening celebrating a polo

BELOW: Though built for the road, the 250 GT Coupé Pinin Farina had enough in common with racing Ferraris to be put through its paces in competition.

victory. Associations with famous rogues did Ferrari's profile no harm at all.

Ferrari's most profitable collaboration with a coachbuilder, before gravitating from the artisan construction model, came with Pinin Farina. Founded in Turin in 1930 by Battista "Pinin" Farina, and renamed with a single-word spelling in 1961 after his sons Sergio and Renzo took over the business, the company established its credentials with a series of smoothly sculpted Alfa Romeo and Lancia-based specials in the pre-war era. Farina-bodied Ferrari road cars powered by the F1-derived long-block Aurelio Lampredi V12 helped launch the marque in America.

48 SALE OF THE CENTURY

From the early 1950s through to the 1960s, a succession of models featuring a three-litre version of the Colombo V12 and bearing the 250 designation (each cylinder being 250cc) seamlessly blended hand-crafted elegance with race-bred technology. Racers including the 250 TR won the Le Mans 24 Hours four times and clocked up three victories in the 12 Hours of Sebring. On the road, the likes of the 250 GT California gained traction with movie stars, while the 250 GT Coupé was the first Ferrari to be built in any great number – more than 350 left the factory.

But the sudden ramping up of production offered a clue to the turbulence behind the scenes if one cared to look deeper. By the early 1960s, the company was being pulled in many different directions. Enzo's policy of ruling his empire from the centre, relying on trusted lieutenants to feed him information, left him open to manipulation and meant he lost touch with what was really happening at the cutting edge. In Formula 1, rival British teams Enzo dismissed as "mere garagistes" profited by relocating the engine to the rear of the chassis for better balance, and following more modern aerospace construction practice to save weight.

Thanks to the power of the "Dino" V6 engine (named after Enzo's deceased son, who is said to have proposed it), Ferrari's Mike Hawthorn narrowly won the F1 drivers' championship in 1958. Ferrari won both drivers' and constructors' titles in 1961 – but only because a smaller version of the Dino engine was ready when racing's governing body slashed the maximum displacement to 1.5 litres.

LEFT: The Le Mans 24 Hours, one of the most arduous and prestigious races in the world, offered a great sales platform for Ferrari sportscars.

SALE OF THE CENTURY 49

LEFT: Through the 1960s Ferrari offered a range of mid-engined cars powered by modest V6 engines, badged as "Dino" after his dead son. The Dino 246 GT was a very capable rival for Porsche's 911.

None of the British teams had an answer until later, whereupon they left Ferrari standing. Innovative low-weight, high-strength chassis design and low-profile aerodynamics would define the competitive order in this era and Ferrari's "Sharknose" 156, while pretty, had little going for it apart from its looks and its engine. The 1961 Monaco Grand Prix, where Stirling Moss danced clear in an obsolete Lotus from the pursuing 156s of Phil Hill and Richie Ginther, should have been taken as an augury.

At the end of 1961, a group of senior staff, including engineer Carlo Chiti and team manager Romolo Tavoni, walked out en masse. Since Dino's death in 1956, Enzo's wife Laura had taken to attending the factory more regularly and staging interventions in matters of policy. Her forthright manner put noses out of joint; Enzo, Chiti would recall, "allowed her to get away with a great deal – possibly too much – because she was the mother of his son". Other behind-the-scenes issues contributed to a souring of the atmosphere, and the death of Wolfgang von Trips in a Ferrari at the Italian Grand Prix led to the inevitable thunder of disapproval from the Vatican.

Widespread industrial unrest in Italy meant supply shortages, and this held back Ferrari from increasing production at a time when the company's finances were under pressure. Laura's presence in the factory jeopardised the careful separation Enzo had established between his different lives, including supporting his mistress and their son. Little wonder that, having passed his 60th birthday, he took refuge in entertaining the desires of his famous customers while considering a partial sale of his company to an outsider.

This was the scene which greeted John Surtees when Enzo recruited him in 1963. Already a champion on two wheels and possessing a willpower as steely as his knuckle-crushing

OPPOSITE: As he entered his 60s, Enzo Ferrari began to consider selling the company that bore his name.

handshake, "*Il Grande John*" spoke Italian and was well-versed in the political nature of the country's industry having ridden for MV Agusta. Nevertheless he immediately cultivated a dislike for Tavoni's replacement, Eugenio Dragoni, while forming a good working relationship with new chief engineer Mauro Forghieri.

Dragoni was already wealthy from other business interests and the chief item on his manifesto was to provide Ferrari – and the country – with an Italian-born world champion. 27-year-old Forghieri's internship at the company had been facilitated by his father, Reclus, a longtime Ferrari employee who had installed the first foundry at Maranello. Now Forghieri junior was persuaded to set aside his hopes of working for Lockheed in the US, and focus on chassis as well as engine development at Ferrari.

Forghieri's youthful energy proved vital in this febrile period while resources were stretched. He led the design on the spaceframe-chassis P-series sports prototypes which finished 1–2–3 at Le Mans in 1964, laid out a new 1.5-litre flat-12 F1 engine, and overhauled the troubled 156. While the latter had mixed results, Forghieri's "Aero" chassis concept aped certain elements of the British cars, such as placing the driver in a more reclined position and using areas of bodywork as load-bearing parts of the structure.

Surtees claimed the F1 world title – just – at the final round of 1964 in Forghieri's new 158, but bugbears continued to abound. The Englishman felt that no meaningful work on the F1 cars was done until after Le Mans, and that Dragoni was forcing him to use new and unproven developments, while the Italian drivers got the best machinery available. The simmering rancour came to a head at Le Mans in 1966 against a broader canvas of Ferrari facing off against Ford.

OPPOSITE: When Formula 1 adopted three-litre engines in 1966, Ferrari lacked resources to build a bespoke engine and had to use a sportscar-derived V12 which was heavy and lacked power.

RIGHT: Ford finally toppled Ferrari at Le Mans in 1966. The highest-placed Ferrari, in eighth, was a privately entered 275 GTB driven by Piers Courage and Roy Pike (29).

During 1963, the US giant had come within a few key contractual paragraphs of acquiring a major stake in Ferrari. Unfortunately, the offending sentences concerned who would have control over the racing budget. Enzo was prepared to abdicate control over his road cars, but not his beloved racing division and walked out on the Ford delegation, prompting Henry Ford II to declare war. Le Mans was the chosen battleground.

Come 1966, Surtees was fuming that his new F1 car wasn't up to scratch; the formula had changed again, to three-litre engines, but there was no budget to develop a new one, so the F1 project had to make do with a sleeved-down version of the sportscar engine. It was too heavy and not powerful enough. Then, at Le Mans, Dragoni partnered Surtees with Ludovico Scarfiotti – Gianni Agnelli's nephew – and directed that Scarfiotti take the first stint behind the wheel. It was a clear

BELOW: Lorenzo Bandini's fatal accident at Monaco in 1967 put an end to the practice of using straw bales as trackside impact protection.

OPPOSITE: Powered by a new flat-12 engine, the 312B briefly revived Ferrari's F1 fortunes in 1970.

political play, since Agnelli was in attendance and Fiat was now the leading candidate to buy Ferrari.

"Do you want to win this race or not?" thundered Surtees, who stormed out, never to race a Ferrari again. Scarfiotti crashed out during the night and Ford cantered to a 1–2–3 finish.

This was a troubling period indeed for Ferrari as Ford's success in sportscar racing jeopardised one of the company's most lucrative profit centres, and the F1 project continued to disappoint. Lorenzo Bandini's death at Monaco in 1967 cast a further pall over Ferrari's fortunes. In June 1969 Enzo agreed to sell 40 per cent of the business to Fiat, which granted his wish of retaining control over all racing activities.

The following years would bring many challenges, but now keeping the company alive would not be among them.

GLORY AND POWER

REBUILDING THE LEGEND

Fiat's investment in 1969 stabilised Ferrari's finances and provided large-scale manufacturer expertise which would prove vital to the company's growth in the road car market. It also enabled Enzo Ferrari to provide for his illegitimate son, Piero, who was given a 10 per cent shareholding; Enzo retained control over sporting matters as well as a 50 per cent holding which would revert to Fiat upon his death. But difficult decisions lay ahead on track, where the Ferrari legend was born, nurtured and sustained.

These decisions would involve confronting an uncomfortable truth John Surtees had voiced years earlier: that Ferrari were trying to compete on too many fronts and lacked the resources to do so, especially when building engines as well as cars.

Changes on the sportscar racing scene were beginning to starve Ferrari's table of its bread and butter. During the 1960s iconic cars such as the 250 GTO proved marvellously lucrative, winning in the hands of Ferrari's own works team and selling to wealthy private entrants. But race promoters increasingly wanted more spectacle and star quality, demanding more

OPPOSITE: Niki Lauda brought technical savvy and a no-nonsense attitude to the F1 team – and claimed two world championships.

GLORY AND POWER

ABOVE: Ferrari fitted a long tail section to the 512 S at Le Mans in 1970 to reduce drag. Ronnie Bucknum and Sam Posey finished fourth, behind three Porsches.

of the high-powered sports-prototypes whose cost and performance were too much for most gentlemen racers. GT cars were declared ineligible for the world championship. The sports-prototype scene became a battle of manufacturers, one in which Ferrari was regularly bested by Ford and Porsche, despite the governing body's attempts to cap performance by insisting each car maker had to build a set minimum number of examples for sale.

Before yielding to the inevitable and quitting sportscars in 1973, Ferrari took the battle to Porsche and its mighty – if hairy – 917. Among the first beneficiaries of the Fiat deal was the 512 S, developed by Mauro Forghieri's engineering team in just a handful of months with the aim of beating the 917s at Le Mans in June 1970.

That January, Ferrari presented the necessary 25 finished cars to FIA officials at Maranello: powered by a five-litre V12

BELOW: A transversely mounted gearbox which improved weight distribution helped make the 312T a winner in Formula 1.

cradled in a semi-monocoque steel-and-aluminium chassis, it was a slightly heavier proposition than the 917 with its air-cooled flat-12 and spindly spaceframe. The balance of power remained with Porsche, although Mario Andretti scored a memorable victory in the Sebring 12 Hours, reeling in and passing an older Porsche 908 driven by Peter Revson and movie star Steve McQueen after the 917s failed. McQueen then acquired one of the modified "M" models of the 512 for his film *Le Mans*.

Fiat's money also lubricated final development on Forghieri's new three-litre flat-12 engine, enabling it to progress from promising failure into a unit which would carry the Maranello torch at the top level of motorsport for a full decade. It would be a faltering path back to greatness, though. Armed with the new flat-12-powered 312B, Jacky Ickx won three grands prix in 1970 and finished second in the World Championship despite retiring from six rounds. Team-mate Clay Regazzoni also delighted the home fans with victory at Monza but, thereafter, Ferrari began to slip back into a trough.

Why was this? As well as the division of resources to sportscar racing, there was the reporting structure which enabled Enzo to enjoy his philosophy of being "an agitator of men", fostering creative tension, but which also kept him remote from reality.

British teams had long since embraced full monocoque construction in which the car's bodywork is integral to the structure rather than a cosmetic addition and Ford's DFV V8 made it possible for the engine to be bolted directly to the chassis and form part of the structure after 1967. Ferrari, however, persisted with a semi-monocoque chassis in which the engine, gearbox and rear suspension were supported by subframes, a

heavier and less efficient configuration.

The DFV's affordability made it almost ubiquitous in Formula 1 in the 1970s, forcing teams to innovate in aerodynamics and chassis technology to find an edge. Tyre manufacturers got in on the act; Ferrari were the first F1 team to use treadless "slick" rubber, in 1971. After going up a number of blind alleys, Forghieri was briefly banished to "special projects" as Enzo lost faith in him, the tipping point coming when Ickx turned his nose up at the unusual-looking 312B3 in testing and the Italian press hooted with derision at the *spazzaneve* – literally "snowplough".

BELOW: Designer Mauro Forghieri tried a short wheelbase and side-mounted radiators in the 1973 312B3, but the car – likened to a snowplough by the press – went unraced.

ABOVE: Ferrari's new sporting director, the urbane, educated, ambitious Luca di Montezemolo (left) formed a strong working partnership with Niki Lauda (right).

As a measure of the desperation involved, Forghieri's replacement Sandro Colombo began a new 312B3 from a clean sheet, approaching the specialist British metalworking company TC Prototypes to construct a monocoque because the expertise to do this did not exist at Maranello. It was a brave move, but the car failed to deliver results. The crunch came at the 1973 British Grand Prix where Ickx qualified 19th, more than two seconds off the pole position time, and finished only eighth even though nine other cars were eliminated in a crash on the opening lap.

The farce prompted rapid changes. Enzo withdrew his cars from the following rounds, recalled Forghieri, and charged new sporting director Luca di Montezemolo with the task of finding a new star driver to replace Ickx, who had indicated he no longer wished to race a Ferrari again. Niki Lauda emerged as the prime candidate although, upon sampling the B3 for the first time, the straight-talking young Austrian had to be coached by Piero not to tell Enzo that his car was a basket case.

Like Surtees before him, Lauda gelled with Forghieri and had a gift for car development. Together they chiselled away at the B3 and Forghieri totally remodelled the cooling system along the lines of the recent championship-winning Lotus and Tyrrell cars, putting the radiators ahead of the rear wheels to concentrate weight in the middle of the car. In 1974 it was a

LEFT: Enzo Ferrari (left) delighted in the turnaround in form on track after recruiting Lauda (centre) and Clay Regazzoni (right).

BELOW: Weeks after suffering severe burns at the Nürburgring, Niki Lauda (right) declared himself fit to race again at Monza… but found Ferrari had hired Carlos Reutemann (left) to replace him, requiring the team to enter a third car.

race-winner again and only a series of retirements eliminated Lauda from the title chase. Team-mate Clay Regazzoni finished a narrow second to McLaren's Emerson Fittipaldi.

For 1975 Forghieri designed an all-new chassis, the 312T, with a transverse gearbox to yield even better weight distribution. After initial reservations – why change when the old car was competitive enough? – Lauda won five races and the world title.

He might have won again in 1976 but for a fiery accident at the Nürburgring in which he nearly died. Six weeks after receiving the last rites, Lauda was back in the cockpit at the Italian Grand Prix to the surprise of everybody, not least Carlos Reutemann, who had been hired to replace him. Lauda was still in contention for the title when he withdrew from the final

ABOVE: The 126C2 was Ferrari's first monocoque car to be built in-house. At Long Beach in 1982 it featured this unusual double rear wing – Ferrari's means of protesting at British teams getting away with what they saw as cheating.

round in Japan, deeming the wet conditions suicidally unsafe. He was castigated as a coward by the Italian press but not by Enzo, who remembered his own crisis of confidence at the wheel more than 60 years earlier.

The 1976 F1 season was the first to be widely televised and the dramatic title battle between Lauda and James Hunt seized the imagination of the global public. Forghieri's 312T series delivered two more world championships, one for Lauda and one for Jody Scheckter, although aerodynamic innovations enabled the British teams to take the initiative once again in a way Ferrari were unable to follow.

To cope with the changing times Ferrari would have to embrace turbocharging, monocoque construction and carbonfibre – seismic changes for a company whose ethos sprang from artisan metalwork. The company's first in-house monocoque, the 126C2, earned Ferrari the constructors' title in 1982, a season marred by off-track politics and on-track tragedy. Enzo delighted in the former, cementing himself in a

position of influence as the British teams formed a negotiating bloc against the governing body; but he was grievously wounded by the latter.

The incandescent driving talent of Gilles Villeneuve made him a fan favourite and Enzo's darling. The Old Man had long since developed an armour plating where driver injury and death was concerned, and yet he was hit hard by Villeneuve's death in an accident during qualifying for the Belgian GP. "He made Ferrari a household name and I was very fond of him," he said. One round earlier, Villeneuve and team-mate Didier Pironi had clashed over team orders at San Marino, where Pironi passed Villeneuve late on to win. They were still not speaking when Gilles met his end. Later in the season Pironi broke both legs in a crash in Germany and never drove an F1 car again.

OPPOSITE: French-Canadian ace Gilles Villeneuve delighted Enzo Ferrari and the team's fans with his bravura approach to racing.

BELOW: Ferrari's first turbo car, the 126CK, was slow and handled badly, but Villeneuve scored a memorable victory in it at Monaco in 1981.

ABOVE: Built to celebrate Ferrari's 40th anniversary, the F40 brought F1 technology to the road and remains one of the company's most desirable and iconic cars.

In 1983 Ferrari again won the constructors' championship but not the drivers' crown. As McLaren rose to prominence with a series of highly advanced and fuel-efficient cars, Enzo decided to make their designer, John Barnard, an offer he couldn't refuse. And yet refuse Barnard did, until granted a remarkable concession: that he could set up a new design and construction facility in England.

Ferrari celebrated 40 years in business in 1987 with the

remarkable limited edition F40 supercar – designed at the behest of Enzo, who felt the company's road car range was growing stale and pedestrian. The F40 was a four-wheeled response to Porsche's 959, a brutally minimalist race car for the road. It was also the last Ferrari to be signed off for production by Enzo before his death in August 1988.

Enzo's final months were turbulent. It's said that what he most feared as his health declined was losing his memory.

OVERLEAF: McLaren dominated the 1988 season, but Ferrari's Gerhard Berger and Michele Alboreto finished 1-2 at the Italian Grand Prix three weeks after Enzo Ferrari's death.

And yet he was trenchant to the last. When it was discovered that Barnard's new F1 car, aimed to be a technological tour de force, had been put behind schedule because a rival faction, led by Piero, had been using Maranello's windtunnel resources to design a car of their own, Enzo came down on the side of his superstar engineer and banished Piero to the road car division.

McLaren won every grand prix in 1988 except one. Three weeks after Enzo's death, Gerhard Berger and Michele Alboreto finished 1–2 for Ferrari – at Monza, of all places, amidst the whispering trees of the royal park where it's said the spirits of departed Italian racing greats walk. Nuvolari, Ascari, and now Enzo Ferrari.

OPPOSITE: Enzo Ferrari suffered from diabetes in later life and died at the age of 90.

BELOW: Monza was the scene of a remarkable win for the Scuderia after Ferrari's death in August 1988.

THE PRICE OF PROGRESS

FORWARDS, NOT BACK

"*Non mi piacciono i monumenti*", Enzo Ferrari once said. "I don't like monuments." And yet the marque which continues to bear his name is precisely that, a moving symphony in *Rosso Corsa*, for all that it tries to look forwards, not back.

That was always the Ferrari way. Very few of the racing cars from the 1950s and 1960s survive, except those which made their way into private hands. Works cars, even the magical, championship-winning ones – the ex-Lancia D50s, the Dino 246s, the "Sharknose" 156s – were unsentimentally cannibalised, modified and/or recycled. Always the focus was on the next race. While there are those who say that in his waning years Enzo took less interest in the business – and perhaps on the road car side, Fiat's bailiwick, that was so – he continued to attend his office in the centre of the Fiorano test track until he was no longer strong enough to stand.

It's this passion which has made Ferrari virtually a second religion in Italy, and enabled the company to survive while

OPPOSITE: The 641 was beautiful as well as ground-breaking – one is on display at New York's Museum of Modern Art.

THE PRICE OF PROGRESS

OPPOSITE: Poached from McLaren and given a free hand, John Barnard brought an uncompromising technical vision to Ferrari.

similar enterprises have failed. Enzo's death was a pivotal moment in Ferrari's history, a moment of existential crisis – but, amid the chaos of the aftermath of his passing, skilled and strong-willed characters emerged to preserve the magic while looking to the future.

What Ferrari needed was success on the track and more volume in road car sales. In Formula 1, Enzo had hired the most gifted and visionary engineer of his generation: John Barnard, "*Il Mago*" (the magician) to the Italian press, "prince of darkness" to those who tested his patience. The working arrangements – Barnard's team designing and prototyping from an office near Godalming and faxing schematics to Maranello for manufacture – were imperfect. Michele Alboreto likened it to performing brain surgery down the telephone.

For all the politics and Maranello sabotage, though – largely quashed after Enzo purged the dissidents, including his own son – Barnard's new Ferrari would turn out to be a work of art. While the engine department disliked being dictated to by an outsider, especially a perfectionist one with a short fuse, the idea of going back to a naturally aspirated V12 wasn't unwelcome.

Motor racing's governing body, the FIA, sealed the deal by outlawing turbocharged engines ahead of the 1989 season. Barnard's key innovation, one present in the majority of Ferraris today as well as countless other cars, was born of imagining how to eliminate one of a race car designer's principal bugbears: how to package the gearshift mechanism.

In 1964, John Surtees cured the problem of his hand being too big to slip between the gear lever and the chassis by whacking the bulkhead out with a lump hammer. In the late 1980s, the problem facing Barnard was that aerodynamic priorities called for a narrow cockpit, and there was very little space to accommodate the gearshift comfortably alongside the

BELOW: Gerhard Berger was a race winner, and a fan favourite, during two stints with Ferrari in the 1980s and 1990s.

driver. Creating a "blister" to leave room for the gear lever to move – essentially doing via a moulding what Surtees did with a hammer – was considered inefficient and inelegant. There was also the perennial problem of routing the shifting mechanism out through the back of a load-bearing structure, past the engine, to the gearbox. Changing gears electro-pneumatically, via levers mounted behind the steering wheel, did away with all that and enabled the driver to change gear without taking their hand off the wheel.

Unfortunately, the semi-automatic system was bedevilled by reliability glitches which proved hard to pin down. Barnard's gorgeously sculpted 640 car would run competitively quickly for a handful of laps before halting. At the first grand prix of the 1989 season, in Rio, team manager Cesare Fiorio wanted drivers Gerhard Berger and Nigel Mansell to start with barely any fuel on board so they could at least lead the race before

ABOVE: Alain Prost brought the number one to Ferrari in 1990 but fell just short of the drivers' title.

they inevitably stopped. Seemingly against the odds Mansell won, even though the bolts holding his steering wheel in place worked loose.

It would be another three months and six grands prix before either Ferrari finished a race again, during which time the theory that the gearbox was the source of the problems became inked into the public consciousness. In fact, vibrations through the engine's crankshaft threw off the alternator belt and killed the electrics.

In 1990 Alain Prost joined Ferrari from McLaren and pushed his old nemesis Ayrton Senna closely for the championship, until Senna had a moment of madness in Japan and drove Prost (and himself) off the road at 180 mph. After Barnard had left for another team, his successors struggled to develop the concept, so 1991 was a disappointing season, and

Prost was fired before the end of it for making critical remarks about the car. Some aspects of life at Ferrari never change…

For all Ferrari's yo-yo performances on track, mystique continued to inhabit its road cars even though some models – the front-engined V12 grand tourers in particular – lacked appeal to the younger demographic. Others, while iconic, were unattainable and already long in the tooth as the 1980s drew to a close.

The mid-engined flat-12 Testarossa, for instance, was essentially a rebodied and re-engineered version of the 512 BB, which had first seen the light of day in 1973. Customers hadn't liked the way the ducting for the front-mounted radiators made the cockpit hot; in relocating the radiators to the flanks and

feeding them with dramatic-looking side streaks, the engineers and stylists perfectly captured the emergent "look-at-me vibe" of the 1980s. While the Testarossa was too wide, and its handling at the limit too unruly, to be considered a proper performance car by purists, sheer desirability ensured demand outstripped Ferrari's production capacity.

Similarly the pretty, Pininfarina-styled and V8-powered 328, though a big seller, was an evolution of the 308 first introduced in 1975, and the influential motoring press was beginning to point out that rival manufacturers' cars were better. The 348, launched in 1989, offered little that was new, except Testarossa styling cues.

Global economic recession, rising oil prices and changing

BELOW: While many of the 348 Spider's underpinnings dated from the 1970s, its streaked sides perfectly caught the ostentatious vibe of the 1980s.

ABOVE: A world champion with the Scuderia in 1975 and 1977, Niki Lauda returned as a consultant in the 1990s.

social attitudes had an ossifying effect on performance car sales. Conspicuous consumption briefly ceased to be fashionable. The waiting list for the Testarossa – one which speculators were willing to pay up to double the asking price in order to jump – melted away like April snow. Debts began to accumulate as the F1 team's wobbly performances impacted the balance sheet.

Enzo's death had left a power vacuum, with all the petty manoeuvrings that entailed. Another strong leader was required and, to that end, Fiat magnate Gianni Agnelli installed former sporting director Luca di Montezemolo as president, with the twin aims of restoring sales and rebooting the flagship F1 racing programme.

When the suave, urbane Montezemolo first arrived at Maranello in 1973, fresh out of university, there were those who wondered what family connections he enjoyed to have been elevated so quickly to a position of such responsibility. Now, after a successful career in Italian industry and sport – including a role in the Italia '90 football World Cup – there was no doubting his credentials.

Montezemolo rehired Niki Lauda, twice a world champion with Ferrari, as a consultant, and they quickly realised change was needed in the F1 project. The radical but flawed F92A car was evidence of a chaotic design programme: the aerodynamic benefits of its twin-floor design were highly theoretical and untested in the field. Sure enough, the aero loads were super-sensitive to changes in pitch under acceleration and braking.

BELOW: The F92A looked fantastic, but its daring twin-floor aerodynamic concept didn't work in practice

With an active suspension system like the one on the rival Williams car, it might have worked, but Ferrari's equivalent was late and unreliable, and added weight to the car. The new V12 engine lacked power and was prone to oil starvation in corners, something new recruit Ivan Capelli pointed out, only to be directed to shut up – because team-mate Jean Alesi was raving about how great the engine was.

The enormity of the task ahead was brought home in 1992. Realising the jobs of revitalising the racing and road car division was too much for one person, Montezemolo hired

ABOVE: John Barnard's 412T1 made Ferrari winners again but its cooling architecture required a lot of debugging first.

former rally co-driver Jean Todt from Peugeot's sportscar programme to head up Ferrari's *Gestione Sportiva*. Lauda, who won his last world title at the wheel of a Barnard-designed car, set to work luring the legendary engineer back into the fold.

Barnard's svelte 412T1 car wowed the excitable Italian media, which likened it to "a pebble washed by the sea". Its innovative cooling system proved troublesome, though, since – according to Barnard – the engine department had got its calculations wrong. Several months were lost to mutual recriminations but, after several revisions, the car returned

BELOW: Though its looks harked back to previous mid-engined V8 Ferraris, the F355 was a huge improvement on its predecessors in terms of quality and everyday driveability.

Ferrari to the winners' circle at the German Grand Prix in 1994.

That year was also significant on the road for Ferrari, as the F355 replaced the moribund 348. Styled again by Pininfarina, its shape and detailing evoked the classic 288GTO and 308GTB without lapsing into pastiche. Multi-valve heads and advanced materials enabled the high-revving 3.5-litre V8 to produce more power per litre than any of its rivals and yet the car had impeccable manners on the road. It was the most civilised Ferrari yet, despite its incredible performance potential. More than 11,000 units had hit the road by the time it was superseded five years later.

Ferrari also established a profitable sideline in US sportscar racing as it designed and built – with the aid of subcontractors – the 333SP sports prototype. Proposed by Gianpiero Moretti, founder of the MOMO aftermarket components company, championed by Enzo's son Piero, and part-realised by former Ferrari engineer Gian Paolo Dallara's company, the 333SP won 12 significant sportscar championships in its lifetime.

And yet consistent success in Formula 1 continued to prove elusive, prompting Jean Todt to begin sweeping changes – both in the cockpit and in the design office.

RIGHT: Ferrari's first sports-prototype in over 20 years, the 333SP, was a great success in US sportscar racing.

THE PRICE OF PROGRESS 97

THE SCHUMACHER YEARS

THE MASTER ARRIVES

From the mid-1990s onwards, the elements which would bring about a renaissance in Ferrari's fortunes on road and track began to slot into place. On the second Sunday of June 1995, plucky Jean Alesi – a favourite of the Ferrari *tifosi*, and seen very much as the heir to Gilles Villeneuve – won the Canadian Grand Prix in John Barnard's handsome 412T2 F1.

Superstitiously inclined fans saw it as an augury: Alesi was celebrating his birthday and carrying the number 27, Villeneuve's race number, on his car – at a circuit named in honour of Villeneuve. Sadly, it would be Alesi's only F1 victory.

Less sentimental, more pragmatic business was brewing behind the scenes. Newly hired engine chief Paolo Martinelli was thinking the unthinkable, plotting the end of the V12 engine synonymous with Ferrari's brand. Amid a host of changes introduced to cut car performance in the wake of Ayrton Senna's tragic death at Imola in 1994, the FIA had reduced the maximum engine displacement from 3.5 litres to three. Exotic materials, more advanced lubricants and high-

OPPOSITE: Michael Schumacher's ability and work ethic proved transformative when he arrived at Maranello.

BELOW: Jean Todt had been a rally co-driver and his early years with Ferrari were just as much of a white-knuckle ride

tech design resources now enabled V10 engines to rev as highly as V12s and match them for power, while weighing less and having fewer moving parts to fail or suffer frictional losses.

And on the very weekend of Alesi's triumph, rumours began to circulate that reigning world champion Michael Schumacher was on his way to Maranello. The rumours were somewhat premature, but turned out to be correct. Team principal Jean Todt, along with Schumacher and his manager and Ferrari's lawyer, met in a Monte Carlo hotel a month later. Fearful of being observed, they furtively relocated to Schumacher's apartment and it was there, hidden away from prying eyes, they put pen to contractual paper for the 1996 season.

ABOVE: Schumacher was remarkable in the 1996 Spanish Grand Prix, circulating three seconds a lap faster than his nearest rivals in the wet.

Being a Ferrari driver exerts a special pull. For Schumacher this was both a new challenge and an opportunity to put space between himself and his soon-to-be-former team, Benetton, who were widely believed to have cheated during 1994, his first championship year. FIA investigations had discovered illegal traction control functions hidden in Benetton's software, but the governing body hadn't been able to establish beyond doubt that they had actually been used.

Reliability continued to be a disappointment and Alesi's victory plus a handful of other podium finishes were all Ferrari could take from the season. Schumacher was coming on the promise that change was around the corner but, when the first batch of V10 engines proved fragile, as an insurance policy a V12-engined 412T2 was packed into the truck for a post-season test at Portugal's Estoril circuit. In it, the newly crowned

double world champion lapped a second quicker than either Alesi or Gerhard Berger had managed in the Portuguese Grand Prix at the same venue during the summer. In public he merely acknowledged the car was "very, very good", but in private – according to Barnard – he said, "I could have won the world championship much more easily with this car…"

The first car designed to accommodate a V10, the F310, proved to be something of a misstep as Barnard's design team overlooked a number of obvious regulatory loopholes in their

LEFT: Teething troubles with Ferrari's first V10-powered F1 car, the F310, prompted a significant change in the team's technical philosophy.

search for unusual and radical solutions. New regulations dictated higher cockpit padding to improve driver safety, and the F310's cockpit padding was faithful to the spirit of the rules, while rival designers exploited the wording to minimise potential aerodynamic blockages in this area.

Vibrations from the new engine cracked the gearbox casing, forcing Ferrari to revert to a previous design which had different pick-up points for the suspension wishbones, forcing another compromise. Poor form and reliability

BELOW: Schumacher was stripped of his championship points after hitting title rival Jacques Villeneuve in the 1997 European Grand Prix.

OPPOSITE: Ferrari poached technical director Ross Brawn from Benetton with a mandate to transform operations at Maranello.

early in the season led to calls in the Italian media for Todt to be sacked, and the shrieking abated only briefly when Schumacher claimed a sensational wet-weather victory in the Spanish Grand Prix at the Circuit de Catalunya.

Schumacher made it known that if Todt was forced out, he would follow, but this high-profile backing would only buy a little time. It was time to put an end to the peculiar arrangement in which the car designs were faxed from the UK to Italy one page at a time. Barnard declined to move to Italy, so Todt needed to install a whole new design facility, which he achieved by poaching technical director Ross Brawn and chief designer Rory Byrne from Benetton, courtesy of an introduction furnished by Schumacher.

Lacking substantial resources to begin with, and not just in terms of staff – Ferrari's wind tunnel was well out of date – they developed the F310 into a B-spec for 1997. Schumacher won five grands prix in it and put himself in contention for the title, but was stripped of his points for trying to ram his championship rival, Jacques Villeneuve, off the track in the final round.

The upward trajectory continued as Todt's appointees formed an increasingly powerful fighting unit, with Todt in effect acting as a firewall to shield them from internal politics and the rabid Italian media. One of Brawn's first acts was to ban newspapers from the technical office as he felt too much time and energy was being wasted reading and worrying about what outsiders thought of the job they were doing.

Brawn also acted to remove the parochial thinking and petty inter-departmental rivalries, encouraging round-table discussions in which all attendees were invited to conjure ideas which might provide fractional gains. Taken together, Brawn assured them, these tiny gains would accumulate into big ones.

Throughout 1998 and '99 the revitalised team firmly established their status as F1's second force behind McLaren, who had the fastest car but not always the most reliable one. Schumacher was second to McLaren's Mika Häkkinen in 1998, but missed almost half of the 1999 season after breaking his leg at the British Grand Prix.

Team-mate Eddie Irvine pushed Häkkinen close, and helped Ferrari to win the constructors' title. The key difference between the teams was that McLaren had a competitive car straight out of the box, even if it occasionally broke, whereas Ferrari had discovered durability but required lots of in-season development to match their rivals' speed.

The year of the big push was 2000, aided by the newly built wind tunnel which was installed, in a huge statement of intent, at the eastern gate of the Maranello campus in a grandiose building designed by the celebrated architect Renzo Piano.

Todt was insistent that his team had to redouble their efforts and start strong. After an epic season-long duel with Häkkinen, the balance shifting almost from race to race, Schumacher sealed the title with one round to go in Japan. It was Ferrari's first drivers' championship in 21 years, and Schumacher

OPPOSITE: Schumacher's 'victory leap' on the podium became a common sight in the early 2000s.

ABOVE: The F2002 enabled Schumacher to secure his third consecutive drivers' title with six rounds of the 2002 season remaining.

emphasised that this was no transient fluke by winning the last four rounds from pole position.

Over the next four seasons Schumacher brought his total of championships to a record-breaking seven and Ferrari established an unparalleled and virtually unchallenged position of technical dominance. The F2002 and F2004 rank among the most successful grand prix cars of all time (indeed, more than 15 years later, the F2004 still holds race lap records at Albert Park, Shanghai International Circuit and Monza). Of the 85 grands prix contested between 2000 and 2004, Ferrari won 57 and appeared on the podium of 23 others, as well as claiming 51 pole positions and recording 42 fastest laps.

This relentless success was founded upon an absence of complacency. Even after a resounding victory, Todt and Brawn habitually gathered senior staff to forensically analyse the race and identify possible improvements. They never took anything for granted, as evidenced by the 2002 Austrian Grand Prix, round six of 17, where Schumacher's team-mate Rubens Barrichello was ordered to move over and hand victory to Michael. Every point counted.

Inevitably, this run of success prompted mutterings of disquiet in the corridors of power. Rival teams tried to copy Ferrari's designs but failed to come close, so they lobbied for change, as did the commercial rights holder, who fretted that global TV audiences were becoming fatigued by repetition. Rule changes were introduced to peg Ferrari back.

This period of dominance also sprinkled stardust on the balance sheet as the F1 team became a net contributor to Ferrari's profits rather than a drain on them – and not a moment too soon, since parent company Fiat had hit financial turbulence. The halo effect of burgeoning excellence on track, allied to Schumacher's star power, fed a golden period of

BELOW: Fans booed during the podium ceremony of the 2002 Austrian GP after Rubens Barrichello (centre) was ordered to hand over the lead to Schumacher.

OVERLEAF: The F430 brought a fresh look to Ferrari's model range as well as a lightweight aluminium construction.

THE SCHUMACHER YEARS 111

ABOVE: Returning to the front-mounted V12 template for its grand tourers with the 550 Maranello, Ferrari created a better-handling car than the mid-engined models it replaced.

road car sales as new models decisively blew away some of the lingering weaknesses of old.

The F50, built to celebrate the company's 50th anniversary, was the first road-going Ferrari not to employ the traditional fundamentals of a tube-frame chassis. Based on a carbon fibre monocoque and powered by a 4.7-litre V12 engine derived from the one used in the 640 F1 car, it genuinely brought Formula 1 technology to the road. Ferrari's volume models

BELOW: The 612 Scaglietti offered four seats as well as immense power within a retro-styled bodyshell.

were also transformed: the 360 Modena, which replaced the F355 in 1999, featured a larger V8 engine than its predecessor as well as the optional F1-inspired paddle-shift gearbox, but it was lighter – thanks to mostly aluminium construction – and even more refined.

A new flagship, front-engined V12 grand tourer, the 550 Maranello, blew away the lingering dust of the 1980s while stylistically nodding to the legacy of the iconic Daytona. In the year Schumacher claimed his final world title Ferrari launched the 612 Scaglietti, a four-seater whose name and style was a homage to the 1950s' 375MM, for which film director Roberto Rossellini commissioned a bespoke coupé body from Modenese coachbuilder Sergio Scaglietti.

On the track, the Schumacher era came to a close with a changing of the guard as rival teams rose to challenge Ferrari's dominance. A moment of madness during qualifying in Monaco, when Schumacher spun and blocked the track while Renault's Fernando Alonso was on a faster lap, prompted Ferrari president Luca di Montezemolo to muse that his superstar was reaching his sell-by date. Schumacher was duly nudged into retirement at the end of the season in favour of young Finn Kimi Räikkönen. Jean Todt moved aside in favour of sporting director Stefano Domenicali, and Ross Brawn announced that he would take a sabbatical to go trout fishing.

RIGHT: While the 248 F1 car was a return to form, Schumacher had a fight on his hands in 2006 in the form of newly crowned champion Fernando Alonso (following).

WORLD DOMINATION

THE ROAD TO INDEPENDENCE

> From the outside, the transition from one era to the next appeared seamless. Michael Schumacher retired from the Formula 1 frontline but energetically took up a new role as an ambassador and development driver for Ferrari's road-going cars.

Jean Todt moved "upstairs" as chief executive officer, handing the F1 team principal role to his chosen successor, Stefano Domenicali. Aldo Costa, Ross Brawn's understudy, became technical director of the F1 programme as Brawn embarked on a year's sabbatical. Costa's new car, the F2007, won from pole position first time out in the hands of Schumacher's replacement, Kimi Räikkönen.

Still, those schooled in Maranello politics caught a whiff of thwarted ambition in the air. Brawn, it was said, had wanted to be team principal – and, indeed, post-sabbatical, he returned in that role with the Honda F1 team. But the rumblings went deeper than that, and Ferrari were not the only team in which ambition was about to lead to folly.

OPPOSITE: In 2013 Ferrari launched the LaFerrari, bringing F1-derived hybrid engine technology to the road for the first time.

BELOW: Kimi Räikkönen (centre) beat Fernando Alonso (right) to the world championship at the final round in 2007

After two relatively quiet seasons by their standards, Ferrari were back near the top of their game in 2007 thanks to a technically advanced car and the end of the tyre war between rival suppliers Michelin and Bridgestone. The Japanese company won the right to exclusively supply the entire grid, a situation which played conveniently into Ferrari's hands since the Scuderia had been designing their cars around the characteristics of Bridgestone's tyres for the previous eight seasons. Michelin's departure caused Renault, which had delivered Fernando Alonso to the drivers' title in 2005 and 2006, to fall off the proverbial cliff.

ABOVE: The F2007 was among the most competitive cars of the 2007 season.

Having moved to McLaren, Alonso had a competitive car in which to fight Räikkönen and Felipe Massa for the world championship. But he also had to contend with a young upstart in the garage next door, one whose career had been supported by McLaren since he was a teenager: Lewis Hamilton. As a peculiar and increasingly rancorous dynamic evolved between Alonso and Hamilton, a four-way battle for the title developed between the McLaren and Ferrari drivers. In racing terms this was a vintage year.

Politically, too, it delivered in even more highly charged intrigue. The row, which became known as "Spygate", began in May with the discovery of white powder on the floor of the Ferrari garage in Monaco, and escalated from week to week as new revelations surfaced.

The powder was detergent, believed to have been added to the cars' fuel systems as sabotage by former chief mechanic

Nigel Stepney. A key figure in transforming Ferrari's occasionally slapdash trackside operations from 1997 onwards, Stepney supposedly coveted a more senior engineering role – perhaps even technical director – in the recent shake-up but had been parked in a factory job instead.

Subsequent revelations connected Stepney with McLaren chief designer Mike Coughlan, similarly frustrated by lack of opportunities to move onwards and upwards in his own organization. The whistleblower was a Woking copy shop employee who had been given a tranche of Ferrari technical documents, 780 pages no less, to duplicate by Coughlan's wife.

By September the slow drip of revelations had caused toxic levels of paranoia and suspicion to accumulate. Though it became apparent that Stepney and Coughlan planned to use their haul of Ferrari intellectual property to approach other

ABOVE: Ferrari replaced the 360 Modena with the F430, an even more potent junior supercar powered by an all-new V8 engine design.

teams for senior technical positions, questions remained over who knew what, and how much, within McLaren. On September 13 – two days after a smiling Schumacher pulled the covers off the brand new F430 Scuderia at the Frankfurt motor show – racing's governing body handed McLaren a record $100 million dollar fine and deleted their constructors' championship points. Ferrari therefore ran unchallenged to the constructors' title, while Räikkönen claimed the drivers' crown with victory at the season-ending Brazilian Grand Prix.

A year later Brazil would host another thriller, albeit in different circumstances. The political temperature had subsided slightly as McLaren's new car passed a forensic technical investigation to determine if any Ferrari design DNA was present. Räikkönen's title defence got off to a bad start with an engine failure at the Australian Grand Prix, and he won

BELOW: Failure to finish the 2008 Singapore Grand Prix after a pitlane miscue cost Felipe Massa dearly.

just two races as team-mate Massa emerged as the most likely championship contender.

Massa's hopes hit a setback in the infamous Singapore Grand Prix in which Renault's Nelson Piquet Jr crashed deliberately to engineer a Safety Car period which benefitted his team-mate Fernando Alonso. When Massa, leading the race, came into the pits, his flustered team signalled him to go while the fuel hose was still attached to his car. The retirement proved costly and, three rounds later, Massa needed to win the final race of the season with Hamilton no higher than sixth to take the drivers' title.

On a gloomy and intermittently wet day Massa won from pole position and the celebrations began in the Ferrari garage as

he crossed the line – only for Hamilton to make the vital pass for fifth place at the final corner of the last lap. From the top step of the podium, Massa tearfully acknowledged his home crowd in a poignant display of sportsmanship.

The development war between McLaren and Ferrari in the final months of 2008 exhausted both teams and distracted from the pressing matter of new rules to come the following season. Both teams entered a competitive slump in 2009 from which it took several seasons to recover.

Ferrari lost the guiding hand of Todt when he left to run for the presidency of the FIA. Massa also suffered an alarming accident in Hungary when a spring detached from the car in front and struck him on the head, fracturing his skull.

BELOW: Felipe Massa (centre) won the 2008 season-ending Brazilian Grand Prix from pole but lost the drivers' title by a single point.

LEFT: The 2008 title fight drew resources from the design programme for the following year, and the 2009 F60 was disappointingly uncompetitive.

ABOVE: Fernando Alonso (left) quit in 2014 after a series of rows with new team principal Marco Mattiacci.

Old habits crept in as technical director Aldo Costa was scapegoated for the on-track failures. He moved on to Mercedes, becoming a key figure in that team's domination during the era to come. Signing Alonso as lead driver brought a certain level of intensity and the cars were good enough to win races if not quite championships, and three times Alonso was a frustrated runner-up.

The internal atmosphere soured as F1 transitioned to a new technical formula with turbocharged hybrid engines and Ferrari's solution wasn't good enough. Under pressure from Luca di Montezemolo to fire the head of the engine department, team principal Stefano Domenicali refused and resigned. His replacement, Marco Mattiacci, lasted eight months, during which time he fell out with Alonso, who was so desperate to leave that he went to McLaren, whence he had departed under a cloud seven years earlier.

Why all the sudden scrutiny and politics? Di Montezemolo himself was under considerable pressure, and not even his gilded track record could render him immune from the slump of 2014. This was because moves were afoot to demerge Ferrari from the parent company via a partial stock exchange flotation and it was a poor moment indeed to perform far below the expected level.

At the end of the year Di Montezemolo was shown the door and his place taken by his ultimate boss, Fiat Chrysler Automobiles chairman Sergio Marchionne. Born in Italy and raised in Canada, Marchionne conducted his business affairs with an iron fist which belied his nondescript appearance. Having attained degrees in philosophy, commerce and law as well as an MBA, Marchionne learned the inner workings of business as a tax specialist and chartered accountant at Deloitte & Touche before climbing through a series of executive posts in global companies which brought him to the eye of Fiat's controlling Agnelli family.

As Ferrari rose to self-sufficiency during the Schumacher years, its parent company's fortunes were on the slide, and when Marchionne was placed in overall charge of Fiat in 2004 it had lost $7 billion the previous year. He embarked on a radical – and often unpopular – programme of cost-cutting which turned around Fiat and enabled it to buy into the failing American car manufacturer Chrysler in 2009.

By 2014 the financial renaissance of both companies was complete and they were merged. The next stage of Marchionne's plan was to set Ferrari on a "separate path", listing 10 per cent of the company on the New York Stock Exchange, while allocating the remaining shares among the existing investors.

OVERLEAF:
Ferrari kept pace with the times by embracing downsized engines boosted by turbochargers. Launched in 2015, the 488 raised the bar in its class.

OPPOSITE: Mattia Binotto moved from technical director to team principal in 2019.

BELOW: Opened in 2010, the Ferrari World Abu Dhabi theme park features the world's fastest rollercoaster.

The separation acknowledged that these companies were now two very different propositions, one a mass-market car maker which required further investment to carve out market share, the other a prestigious luxury brand as well as a builder of performance cars. Ferrari's prancing horse logo now adorns countless lines of merchandise; indeed, should you visit the Ferrari World Abu Dhabi theme park and, having ridden the Ferrari-themed fastest rollercoaster in the world, you can buy a toy camel emblazoned with the logo.

On the first day of trading in Ferrari shares in October 2015, Marchionne was invited to ring the famous NYSE bell to signify Wall Street had opened for business. Three months later, the Fiat Chrysler Group in effect sold the car manufacturer it had bought in 1969 by floating its 80 per cent share in Milan, though the Agnelli dynasty retained 24 per cent. Piero Ferrari continues to own 10 per cent of the company. Gianni Agnelli's grandson John Elkann took over as Ferrari chairman after Marchionne's untimely death in 2018.

On the track, Ferrari went from strength to strength. Under the technical leadership of the studious Mattia Binotto the F1

team rebounded to become world championship challengers again, though they fell short despite recruiting four-times champion Sebastian Vettel. In the more mass-market fields of motor racing, Ferrari also scored hits, winning the GT class at Le Mans and expanding the Ferrari Challenge one-make series into new territories.

On the road, there is a class-leading Ferrari in virtually every segment of the sportscar market, the appropriately named 812 Superfast having recently supplanted the iconic V12-powered F12, the GTC4 Lusso providing space for four, and the Portofino and Roma offering in twin-turbocharged V8 form what the iconic California delivered in the 1960s.

The mid-engined V8 line has continued to evolve from the 360 Modena through the F430, 458 and 488 to the recently launched F8, Ferrari's most powerful V8-powered car ever thanks to the addition of twin turbochargers. As a pointer to a possible future, the SF90 Stradale augments four-litre twin-turbo V8 with three electric motors, yielding a combined power output of 986bhp.

All of these cars are built only at Maranello, where the window of Enzo Ferrari's old office still overlooks the factory gate.

OPPOSITE: Sebastian Vettel led Ferrari to more race wins but fell short of clinching the world championship.

BELOW: The racing version of the 488 won its class in the Le Mans 24 Hours.

BELOW: Ferrari's flagship car for the new decade is the SF90, the company's first plug-in hybrid – three electric motors and a turbocharged V8 output a combined 986bhp.

FERRARI IN POPULAR CULTURE

AN IMAGE TO DIE FOR

"The 1961 Ferrari 250GT California. Less than a hundred were made. My father spent three years restoring this car. It is his love. It is his passion…"
"…It is his fault he didn't lock the garage."

In the cult classic movie *Ferris Bueller's Day Off,* a popular teen fakes illness to avoid school for the day, joyrides in his friend's father's classic car – and all manner of absurdly improbable scrapes ensue. Come the final reel, the car needs another extensive restoration, though the vehicle which was subjected to the various on-screen indignities was actually a replica which attracted a trademark-infringement lawsuit from Ferrari.

Beneath the entertaining hokum there's an emotional layer to the storytelling in which the car acts as a cypher for the unseen father who loves a valuable object more than his son. And yet the car is also a prisoner, after a fashion: cherished, buffed, kept in an air-conditioned glass box, but rarely used for the purpose for which it was intended.

OPPOSITE: Welcome to the 1980s – the Testarossa perfectly matched the sharp styling of the protagonists in TV's *Miami Vice*.

BELOW: Adolfo Celi (left) played a character clearly inspired by Enzo Ferrari (right) in the movie *Grand Prix*, though Enzo claimed he couldn't see the resemblance.

Such has been the fate of many old and rare Ferraris in recent decades as turbulent global stock markets drive demand for alternative investments. The movie's original script called for a Mercedes, but during pre-production director John Hughes had a moment of clarity: the father is described as loving his classic car "more than life itself". It had to be selected just as carefully as the human members of the cast.

Enzo Ferrari well knew the importance of perception to his marque's mythology, and he cultivated the image of the shadowy figure manipulating events from afar, eyes always

ABOVE: The 250GT California once owned by James Coburn was the first car to sell for over $10 million.

concealed behind dark glasses. In 1966, Hollywood shadowed the Formula 1 circus as John Frankenheimer shot *Grand Prix* in and around the various race events. The Italian actor Adolfo Celi, best known to international audiences as James Bond's nemesis Largo in *Thunderball* played Agostini Manetta, a slippery and Machiavellian team owner clearly modelled on Enzo – who affected a lack of interest in the entire affair and reckoned he couldn't see any likeness, though by all accounts he was quietly delighted when he was shown the rushes.

Cars such as the California were built specifically to appeal to the West Coast market of wealthy socialites and movie stars, for whom European sophistication and exoticism trumped the pure muscle offered by US rivals. James Coburn was talked into buying one by Steve McQueen while in Europe filming *The Great Escape* and, in May 2008, that same car became the first to change hands for more than $10 million.

In the 1980s, Ferrari's appeal crossed over into the mainstream, perfectly appealing to a new, badge-conscious, upwardly mobile generation for whom conspicuous

consumption defined the dream. In some countries during the 1970s, particularly Italy, driving an ostentatiously expensive car had been an open invitation to be kidnapped, and Ferrari's flagship models embodied a suitable level of styling restraint.

Economic growth in the new decade prompted a huge cultural shift. While the likes of the staid, square-rigged 400i remained the province of what one might call the moneyed old European demographic – the cashmere-sweater-over-the-shoulders crowd – more dynamic models such as the Testarossa and 308GTB offered the perfect wealth-flaunting platform for those making a mint in the city.

Underlining this thrusting decade's confidence that everything was attainable, posters of Ferrari models became as *de rigueur* as black ash furniture in teenagers' bedrooms and lit up the screen in popular TV shows. In *Magnum P.I.*, the titular private detective, for all that he seemed permanently on the verge of eviction by his landlord and performed little in the way of paid work, motored around Hawaii in a red 308GTS. Just two owners later, one of the cars used in filming sold for $181,500 at auction in 2018.

But the 308 was already rather long in the tooth as the 1980s got into gear. It was the Testarossa which really rode the consumerist wave and became – literally – Ferrari's poster child. Launched in 1984 it was initially treated with disdain by traditionalists, who felt the swooping waistline and exaggerated strakes on each side flirted with vulgarity. The latter features – necessary because US regulations prohibited an open cooling aperture for the mid-mounted flat-12 engine – became iconic, propelled into the cultural stratosphere by its presence on zeitgeisty crime drama *Miami Vice*,

With its fashionably loud iconography, edgy setting and subject matter (undercover cops masquerading as high-rolling drug dealers) and propulsive, angular electronic soundtrack,

OPPOSITE: Actor Tom Selleck played the titular character in the iconic 1980s TV series *Magnum P.I.*, roaring around Hawaii in a red 308GTS.

OPPOSITE: A Ferrari 641 F1 car is among the exhibits in the New York Museum of Modern Art.

BELOW: The Testarossa became an icon of the 1980s. Posters of it adorned bedroom walls worldwide and Ferrari could barely make enough to fulfil demand.

Miami Vice epitomised an era of style over substance. Co-protagonist James "Sonny" Crockett, played by Don Johnson, drove an open-top 365 GTB/4 in the show's first two seasons, though the vehicles used in filming were actually fibreglass replicas based on Chevrolet Corvette chassis. As the show percolated worldwide the inevitable cease-and-desist order came from Maranello, albeit laced with a remarkable offer: use of genuine Ferraris in the form of two Testarossas. For a company generally not given to providing cars for filming this was truly remarkable; it's said that Enzo was a fan of the show.

Other celebrity owners of the time included Elton John, Rod Stewart, Michael Jordan, OJ Simpson and Mike Tyson. Slightly less celebrated were the drug dealers and city spivs who also found the Testarossa's look-at-me presence irresistible, including the notorious penny-stock scammer Jordan Belfort, who was memorably brought to life by Leonardo di Caprio in Martin Scorsese's *The Wolf of Wall Street*.

OPPOSITE: Notorious for destroying three classic Ferraris and reporting them stolen to claim the insurance money, Lord Brocket exploited his profile to carve out a career on reality TV.

Not that such characters would have been entertained at Maranello: before the boom turned to bust, demand far outstripped supply and many new Testarossa owners sold their cars straight away to queue-jumpers for a healthy cash mark-up. This being the 1980s, plenty of them had acquired the cars specifically for that purpose. Even after the economic winds turned chilly, the Testarossa retained a certain cachet within particular fraternities: in 1993 one of the kidnappers of Kevyn Wynn, daughter of Las Vegas strip casino magnate Steve Wynn, was caught when he used his share of the ransom cash to buy a second-hand 512TR – in white, naturally.

The history of pre-owned Ferraris continues to capture the popular imagination, whether their previous guardians are celebrities or crooks – or both. Charles Nall-Cain inherited a peerage, the title Lord Brocket, and the family's Hertfordshire mansion at the age of 15, when his grandfather died in 1967. As with many relics of aristocracy at the time, the 25-bedroom property and its 1400-acre grounds were subsiding into disrepair. With the aid of loans, Lord Brocket converted it into a luxury hotel and conference centre with a pair of golf courses.

Business boomed during the 1980s and, with the aid of further leverage on the mansion, Lord Brocket began to amass a collection of Italian classics. Soaring interest rates as the economy slammed into reverse gear left him struggling to repay the debts – while the value of his car collection headed south.

Under cover of night in May 1991, Lord Brocket and three employees dismantled four of the most precious cars in the collection – three of them Ferraris – cutting up the bodywork with angle grinders and melting the pieces in a furnace. The dismantled chassis and other components were hidden in various other properties and various items are believed to have been buried – never to be found. Brocket's insurers refused to pay up and he was subsequently arrested and charged with

fraud, to which an obtaining money by deception charge was added when it emerged he had sold Microsoft CEO Jon Shirley a fake 250 GT SWB Berlinetta which had been built from a lesser car and given a bogus chassis number.

One of the Ferraris, a 1951 340 America originally carrying coach-built bodywork by Vignale, was rebuilt after the chassis and engine were recovered. Initially auctioned at $600,000, it has since changed hands several times for increasing values and is now believed to be in Japan. After serving two years of a five-year sentence he was released and parlayed his notoriety into an appearance on the reality TV show *I'm A Celebrity… Get Me Out Of Here!*

The behaviour of celebrity Ferrari owners continues to vex and exercise the guardians of the brand, and the company's press offices worldwide are notoriously choosy regarding whom they lend cars to, particularly musicians and influencers who are wont to court publicity. Rapper A$AP Twelvyy appeared to set an elderly 348 on fire after performing stunts in it during the video for the song "Hop Out". The sheer desirability of the brand is irresistible to those who inhabit the overlapping worlds of reality television and influencer culture, such as *90 Day Fiancé* star Brittany Banks, for instance, whose videos blend rap, highly sexualised dancing, gratuitous product placement, and the occasional wander around luxury car showrooms.

In the 21st century, celebrity carries a potent marketing value, and many individuals with a large social media following shamelessly exploit their appeal to the aspirational youth demographic. In 2019 Ferrari decided enough was enough and, in effect, declared war on influencers. After German fashion designer Philipp Plein posted a number of pictures on his Instagram account of bikini-clad women gyrating atop his 812 Superfast while washing it, along with other images of his own products on the car, he received a stiff takedown order: "This

OPPOSITE: Demi Moore drove a Ferrari Enzo in the movie *Charlie's Angels*.

behaviour tarnishes the reputation of Ferrari's brands," said the letter.

After much public rancour between the two parties the issue was finally resolved in a Genovese court – in Ferrari's favour. It was a landmark ruling which sent a chill through the influencer community. The court upheld Ferrari's claim of trademark infringement, denigration and discredit, as well as unlawful commercial use of the Ferrari logo. Plein's counter-argument, that he was simply sharing elements of his private life and that the images served no commercial purpose, was dismissed. "The Ferrari trademark evokes in the public the characteristics of exclusivity and absence of vulgarity, which are incompatible with the car wash images/videos," was the rather prim summing-up, one which has ramifications for all who seek to piggy-back product placement on others' brands for their own gain.

Thirty-five years after the makers of *Ferris Bueller's Day Off* had their collars felt by Ferrari's trademark police, the message rang loudly once more, like the Modena church bells: "Don't mess with the badge."

LEFT: The 250GT California seen in *Ferris Bueller's Day Off* was actually a replica based on Chevrolet mechanicals. Ferrari sued on the grounds of trademark infringement.

INDEX

Numbers in italics are the pages on which a caption appears.

Agnelli family 131, *131*
Agnelli, Gianni 44, 57, 58, 90
Alboreto, Michele 79, 84
Alesi, Jean 101, 102, 103, 104
Alfa Corse 17
Alfa Romeo 11, *12*, 13, *13*, 14, *14*, 15, *15*, 17, *17*, 24, 30, 31, 32, Tipo 8 *15*
Alonso, Fernando 116, *116*, 122, *122*, 126, 130–1, *130*
Andretti, Mario 65
Ascari, Alberto *27*, 31, 37
Australian Grand Prix 2008 125
Austrian Grand Prix 2002 111, *111*
Auto Avio Construzioni 17, 28
Auto Union 15

Bandini, Lorenzo 58, *58*
Banks, Brittany 153
Barnard, John 74, 84, *84*, 86, 93, *93*, 101, 104, 106

Barrichello, Rubens 111, *111*
Benetton 103, 106, *106*
Berger, Gerhard 79, 86, *86*, 104
Binotto, Mattia 134, *134*, 137
Biondetti, Clemente 44, 46
Brawn, Ross 106, *106*, 108, 110, 116, 121
Brazilian Grand Prix 2007 125
Brazilian Grand Prix 2008 125, 126–7, *127*
Bridgestone tyres 122
British Grand Prix 1950 30
British Grand Prix 1973 68
British Grand Prix 1999 109
Brocket, Lord 150, *150*, 153
Bucknum, Ronnie *64*

Campari, Giuseppe 14
Canadian Grand Prix 1995 101
Caracciola, Rudolf *17*
Carrozzeria Touring 43
Castellotti, Eugenio *22*, 38

Celi, Adolfo *144*, 145
Charlie's Angels 153
Chinetti, Luigi 28, 30, 44, *44*
Chiron, Louis *15*
Chiti, Carlo 52
CMN 12, 13
Coburn, James 145
Collins, Peter *28*, 38
Colombo, Gioachino 17, 24, 25, 30, 43
Colombo, Sandro 68
Coppa Acerbo road race 14
Coppa Florio 1908 11
Cortese, Franco 25, 28
Costa, Aldo 121, 130
Coughlan, Mike 124–5
Courage, Piers *56*

Dallara, Gian Paolo 96
Domenicali, Stefano 116, 121, 130
Dragoni Eugenio 55, 57
Dutch Grand Prix 1955 *22*

Elkann, John 134
European Grand Prix 1997 *106*

Fangio, Juan Manuel *21*
Farina, Pinin 47

Ferrari cars
  125S 25
  126C2 71, *71*
  126CK *73*
  156 "Sharknose" *32*, 52, 55, 83
  158 31, 55
  166 43, 44
  166 Inter 44
  166 MM 43, 44
  250 GT California 49, 137, 143, 145, *145*, *155*
  250 GT Coupé Pinin Farina *46*, *47*
  250 GTO 63
  250 TR *32*, 49
  250 LM *44*
  275 GTB *56*
  288 GTO 96.
  290 MM *21*
  308 89
  308GTB 96, 147
  308GTS 147, *147*
  312B *58*, 65
  312B3 "snowplough" 67, 68, 69
  312T *65*, 71
  328 89
  330 P2 Spyder *44*
  333SP 96
  340 America 153
  348 89, 96
  355SP *96*
  360 Modena *111*, *125*, 137
  365 GTB/4 148
  412T2 101, 103
  458 137
  488 *131*, 137
  512 S 64, *64*
  512 TR 150
  550 Maranello *114*, 115
  555 *22*, *25*
  612 Scaglietti 115, *115*
  641 *83*, *148*
  812 Superfast 137, 153
  1.5L V12 24, 29
  Daytona 115
  Dino 246 GT *51*, 83
  D50s (ex-Lancia) 83
  F8 137
  F12 137
  F40 *74*, 75
  F50 114
  F60 *129*
  F92A 92, *92*
  F310 104, 105, *105*
  F310B 106
  F355 *95*, 96
  F430 125, *125*
  F2002 110
  F2004 110
  F2007 121, *123*
  GTC4 Lusso 137
  LaFerrari *121*
  P-series sportcar 55
  Portofino 137
  Roma 137
  SF90 Stradale 137, *139*
  Testarossa 88, 88, *89*, 90, *143*, *147*, 148, *148*, 150
Ferrari Challenge 137
Ferrari World Abu Dhabi 134, *134*
Ferrari, Adalgisa (mother) 09, 10
Ferrari, Alfredo (Dino, son) 22, 23, *23*
Ferrari, Alfredo (father) 09, 10, 11
Ferrari, Alfredo Jr (brother) 10, 11
Ferrari, Enzo 9–17, *9*, *11*, 21, *21*, 22, 23, 29, 32, 36, 43, 44, 49, *52*, 58, 69, *69*, 71, 73, *73*, 75, 79, 83, 137, 144, *144*, 145
  "agitator of men" 66
  banishment of Piero 79
  birth 09
  death 75, *75*, 79, *79*, 84
  engineers 36
  losing touch 49
  Miami Vice 148
  nicknames 09, 11
  office 137
  racing driver 13, 14
  sale to Fiat 58
  splitting shares 63
  staff walkout 52
  support for Lauda 71
  unsentimentality 38
  working for Alfa Romeo 11, 13

Ferrari, Laura (wife) 22, 52
Ferrari, Piero (son) 22, 63, 69, 96
Ferris Bueller's Day Off 143, 155, *155*
Fiat 13, 44, 63, 83, 111, 131
Fiorino test track 83
Fiorio, Cesare 86–7
Ford 55–6, *56*
Forghieri, Mauro 55, 64, 65, 67, *67*, 68, 71
Frankenheimer, John 145
French Grand Prix 1924 14
French Grand Prix 1934 *15*
French Grand Prix 1935 *12*, *17*
French Grand Prix 1958 *32*

Gendebien, Olivier *32*
German Grand Prix
   1935 *13*
   1976 70
   1994 96
Ginther, Richie 52
Godalming 84
Grand Prix 144, 145
Gregory, Masten *44*

Häkkinen, Mika 109
Hamilton, Lewis 123, 126–7, *127*
Hawthorn, Mike *28*, *32*, 38, 49
Hill, Phil 21, 22, *32*, *36*, 38, 52
Hughes, John 144
Hungarian Grand Prix 2008 127
Hunt, James 71

I'm a Celebrity… Get Me Out of Here! 153
Ickx, Jacky 65, 68
Irvine, Eddie 109
Italian Grand Prix
   1955 *31*
   1961 *32*, 37, *37*
   1976 70
   1988 *75*, 79, *79*
Italy 10

Jano, Vittorio 13, 14, 17, 36
Japanese Grand Prix 1990 87

Lampredi, Aurelio 25, 32, 36
Lancia 32, 36–7
Lauda, Niki *63*, 68, *68*, 69, *69*, 70, *70*, *90*, 91
Le Mans 65
Le Mans 24 Hours 30, *32*, 44, *44*, 49, *49*, 55, 56–7, *56*, 64, *64*, 137, *137*

Magnum P.I. 147
Mansell, Nigel 86–7
Maranello 23, 25, 55, 64, 65, 68, 84, 102, 109, 121, 137
Marchionne, Sergio 131, 134
Martinelli, Paolo 101
Maserati 32
Massa, Felipe 123, 126–7, *126*, *127*
Mattiacci, Marco 130, *130*
McLaren 109, 123–5, 127
McQueen, Steve 65, 145
Mercedes 15, *17*, 130, 144
Miami Vice 143, 147
Michelin tyres 122
Mille Miglia *21*, 32, 36, 37, 38, *38*
Modena 09, 10
MOMO 96
Monaco Grand Prix
   1950 31
   1961 52
   1967 58, *58*
   1981 *73*
Montezemolo, Luca di 68, 90, 91, 116, 130, 131
Monza *31*
Moore, Demi *153*
Moretti, Gianpiero 96
Moss, Stirling 52
Museum of Modern Art, New York 83, *148*

My Terrible Joys (autobiography) 10, 12

Nelson, Edmond *38*
90 Day Fiancé 153
Nürburgring *14*, 70
Nuvolari, Tazio *12*, *13*, *14*, *17*

Parma–Poggio di Berceto hillclimb 13
Piacenza 25
Piano, Renzo 109
Pike, Roy *56*
Pinin Farina company 32
Piquet Jr, Nelson 126
Pirelli 15
Pironi, Didier 73
Plein, Philipp 153, 155
Porsche 64, 65
Portago, Alfonso de 37, *38*
Posey, Sam *64*
Prost, Alain 87, *87*, 88

Räikkönen, Kimi 116, 121, 122, *122*, 123, 125
Regazzoni, Clay 65, *69*, 70
Renault 116, 122, 126
Reutemann, Carlos 70, *70*
Revson, Pete 65
Ricart, Wilfredo 17
Rimini, Giorgio 14
Rindt, Jochen 44

Rossellini, Roberto 115
Rubirosa, Porfirio 46

Scaglietti, Sergio 115
Scarfiotti, Ludovico *44*, 57, 58
Scheckter, Jody 71
Schumacher, Michael *101*, 102, 103, *103*, 106, *106*, 108, *108*, 116, *116*, 121, 125
Scuderia Ferrari (first) 14, 15, 17
Scuderia Ferrari (second) 21, *21*, 22, 24, 25, 28, 29, 38, 43, 44, 52, 55, 58, 73, *73*, 74, 75, 83, 84, 88, 86, 93, 96, 101, 102, *102*, 109, 110, 114, *114*, 122, 123–5, *129*, 130, 131, *131*, 137, 143, 144, 145, 148, 153, 155, *155*
Selleck, Tom *147*
Selsdon, Lord 30
Senna, Ayrton 87, 101
Singapore Grand Prix 2008 126, *126*
Spanish Grand Prix 1996 *103*
"Spygate" 123–5
Stepney, Nigel 124–5
Superleggera construction 43
Surtees, John *43*, *44*, 52, 55, 56, 57, 58, 63, 84, 86

Targa Florio road race 13, 46
Tavoni, Romolo 52, 55
TC Prototypes 68
Todt, Jean 96, 102, *102*, 106, 108, 110, 116, 121, 127
Trintignant, Maurice *31*
Troubetzkoy, Prince Igor 46
Trujillo, Rafael 46
Turin Motor Show 43
12 Hours of Sebring 49, 65
Twelvyy, A$AP 153

Vatican 37, 52
Vettel, Sebastian 137, *137*
Villeneuve, Gilles 73, *73*, 101
Vjlleneuve, Jacques 106, *106*
von Trips, Wolfgang *32*, *36*, 37, *37*, 38, 52

Wolf of Wall Street, The 148
World championship *27*
1950 30, 31
1951 32
1952 *27*
1953 *27*
1958 *28*, 49
1961 *36*
1970 65
1976 70, 71

1982 71	1996 102,	2004 110
1983 74	1997 106, *106*	2006 *116*
1989 86	1998 109	2007 *122*, 123–5, *123*
1990 87	1999 109	2008 125–7, *126*, *127*
1991 87–8	2000 109–10	2009 *129*
1994 103	2002 110	

CREDITS

The publishers would like to thank the following sources for their kind permission to reproduce the pictures in this book.

ALAMY: /Photo 12: 142; /Realy Easy Star/Giuseppe Masci: 149; /Reuters: 145; /Shawshots: 11; /United Archives GmbH: 154-155

GETTY IMAGES: /Barrett-Jackson: 124-125; /Mel Bouzad: 152; /CBS Photo Archive: 146; /Bernard Cahier: 144; /David Cooper/Toronto Star: 115; / Martyn Lucy: 138-139; /Marka/Universal Images Group: 23; /National Motor Museum/Heritage Images: 50-51, 88-89, 114; /Alessia Pierdomenico/ Bloomberg: 4, 120; /Emilio Ronchini/Mondadori: 39; /Sjo: 94-95

MOTORSPORT IMAGES: 58, 62, 73, 106; /Jeff Bloxham/LAT: 66-67; / Ercole Colombo/Studio Colombo: 68, 69, 78, 90; /Steve Etherington/LAT: 102, 108, 116-117; /JEP: 137; /LAT: 12, 13, 14, 15, 16, 22, 24-25, 26-27, 28, 29, 30-31, 32, 33, 34-35, 37, 44, 47, 48-49, 56-57, 59, 65, 70, 72, 76-77, 79, 91, 92-93, 97, 111; /David Phipps: 36, 53, 54; /Rainer Schlegelmilch: 42, 45, 64, 71, 87, 100, 104-105, 110, 123, 126, 128-129; /Sutton Images: 82, 85, 86, 103, 107, 112-113, 122, 127, 136; /Mark Sutton: 135; /Steven Tee: 130

PA IMAGES: /Fabio Fiorani/IPA MilestoneMedia: 8

SHUTTERSTOCK: /Anglia Press Agency Ltd: 148; /Burachet: 134; /ermess: 74-75; /Cameron Laird: 151; /Time & Life Pictures: 20; /yousang: 132-133

WIKIMEDIA COMMONS: /GTHO: 46

Every effort has been made to acknowledge correctly and contact the source and/or copyright holder of each picture any unintentional errors or omissions will be corrected in future editions of this book.

THE STORY OF
Lamborghini

Text and design © Carlton Books Ltd

First published in 2024 by Welbeck
An imprint of Headline Publishing Group Limited

Apart from any use permitted under UK copyright law, this publication may only be reproduced, stored, or transmitted, in any form, or by any means, with prior permission in writing of the publishers or, in the case of reprographic production, in accordance with the terms of licences issued by the Copyright Licensing Agency.

Cataloguing in Publication Data is available from the British Library

ISBN 978-1-80279-851-7

Printed and bound in China

Headline's policy is to use papers that are natural, renewable and recyclable products and made from wood grown in well-managed forests and other controlled sources. The logging and manufacturing processes are expected to conform to the environmental regulations of the country of origin.

Disclaimer:
All trademarks, images, quotations, company names, registered names, products and logos used or cited in this book are the property of their respective owners and are used in this book for identification, review and editorial purposes only. This book is a publication of Headline Publishing Group Ltd and has not been licensed, approved, sponsored, or endorsed by any person or entity and has no connection or association to Automobili Lamborghini S.p.A.

Editor: Conor Kilgallon
Design: Rebecca Hills
Production: Rachel Burgess

HEADLINE PUBLISHING GROUP LIMITED
A Hachette UK Company
Carmelite House
50 Victoria Embankment
London EC4Y 0DZ

The authorised representative in the EEA is Hachette Ireland,
8 Castlecourt Centre, Dublin 15, D15 XTP3, Ireland (email: info@hbgi.ie)

www.headline.co.uk
www.hachette.co.uk

THE STORY OF

Lamborghini

A TRIBUTE TO AUTOMOTIVE EXCELLENCE

STUART CODLING

WELBECK

Contents

THE SIGN OF THE BULL 6

PAID BY THE HORSE 26

COUNTACH! 46

THE SHOW MUST GO ON 66

THE AUDI RENAISSANCE 88

ELECTRIC DREAMS 110

LAMBORGHINI AT THE RACES 122

ON THE BIG SCREEN 142

INDEX 156

CREDITS 160

The Sign of the Bull

Go Your Own Way

> "Lamborghini, you may be able to drive a tractor but you will never be able to handle a Ferrari properly."

Today, the arrival of an ambitious new sportscar manufacturer – launched by a respected businessman with the support of local government rather than vague promises of cash from venture capitalists – would no doubt be promulgated to the world via a slickly produced video hosted by a bellowing influencer. Lamborghini's launch possessed a subtlety that the brand and its cars would subsequently abandon. One of the first items of press coverage in Britain, for instance, came in the back pages of *Autocar* magazine in July 1963, where a rather dull monochrome image of a rolling chassis and engine appeared beside the similarly restrained headline "*Italian 3500cc GT from a new constructor*".

OPPOSITE: Ferruccio Lamborghini poses with an early version of his V12 engine and the 350 GTV prototype at the 1963 Turin show.

Contemporary sources might have documented Lamborghini's birth in drily factual tones but, over 60 years later, the company's history is draped appropriately in the seductive layers of myth essential to any supercar manufacturer in which the customer is buying into the story and image as much as the car. And what a story: a self-made man butting heads with a similarly pugnacious character – Enzo Ferrari – and resolving to beat him at his own trade.

Like any myth, only fragments of it may be true. But, as the newspaperman tells James Stewart's character in the classic film *The Man Who Shot Liberty Valance*, "*When the legend becomes fact, print the legend.*"

Believers in astrology hold that those born under the constellation of Taurus, the bull, are possessed of unusual strength and tenacity, and place great value on material pleasures. The sign itself is historically associated with the worship of bulls. Ferruccio Lamborghini was born in the Italian farming town of Renazzo on 28 April 1916, the week after Easter and a handful of days after the sign of the bull came into the ascendant. The youngest of five children, Lamborghini arrived into a Europe torn apart by war and civil disquiet, a cycle that would repeat during his lifetime.

Farming and artisan crafts have formed the backbone of the Emilia-Romagna region's economy since Roman times, when retiring legionaries were granted parcels of land as a reward for their services to the empire. There they worked the land or took up craft trades; as the decades passed, the region acquired a reputation for fine food, engineering and metalwork.

As a teenager, Lamborghini became more interested in the mechanics of the machines that worked the land than in cultivating the land itself. The modern Lamborghini myth holds that he built his own forge and machine shop on the family farm. It is widely claimed, though no documentation appears to exist, that he enrolled in a technical college – likely the Fratelli Taddia in nearby Bologna – to study engineering. But his date of birth placed him in the prime demographic to be compelled into military services when hostilities flared once more in 1939; a year later, aged 24, he was drafted into the Italian Air Force.

Ferruccio's mechanical skills came into play as a member of the ground crew servicing the aircraft fleet stationed on the Aegean island of Rhodes, a key hub with three airfields. Its strategic significance in this theatre of operations placed it in the line of fire from all sides: after Italy's surrender in 1943, Rhodes was attacked by both Allied and German forces during the Dodecanese campaign. Lamborghini spent several months as a prisoner of the Allies once hostilities ceased in 1945.

BELOW: Long before it adorned sportscars, the Lamborghini name featured on agricultural machinery.

BELOW: Ferruccio well understood the importance of getting the V12 engine right.

Freedom brought its own challenges. In common with the rest of his generation, Ferruccio came home to a country still suffering the privations of war – and, in Italy's case, the hangover from subjugation. Unemployment, poverty and starvation were rife in an economy that had fallen into inactivity after being repurposed for war: factories which had been converted to munitions manufacture lay idle, vehicles had been stripped or melted down to make engines of war. But here lay an opportunity for those with mechanical gifts and an entrepreneurial mindset.

Italy's bread basket needed to produce again. Ferruccio, according to the company's origin myth, built his parents a new tractor out of scavenged components and then, while on honeymoon, came across a British army detachment disposing

12 THE SIGN OF THE BULL

of Italian military equipment. Whether this is true or not, Lamborghini started his first business repurposing ex-military vehicles for agricultural use or raiding them for spare parts to maintain existing farm machinery. The work was tough, but profitable; and, once the available stock of army-surplus hardware began to run low, he established Lamborghini Tractori SpA to manufacture complete new vehicles – including engines. Success enabled Ferruccio to employ more staff and step back from the hands-on work, though he continued to modify road cars, souping up several 569cc Fiat Topolinos for himself and other acquaintances. With one, bored and stroked to 750cc, he entered the 1948 Mille Miglia road race; the records enshrine him as a plain DNF – Did Not Finish – but the story behind the acronym is typically flamboyant.

"I finished my Mille Miglia in an osteria [pub]," he said, *"which I entered by driving through the wall."*

Whether you believe it or not, this plausibly accounts for Lamborghini's future aversion to motor racing. He became a wealthy man in the 1950s as his tractor company prospered and he established a second business building and maintaining air-conditioning systems, a wildly popular growth industry that had sprung up in the USA. Like any new technology manufactured at scale it was inclined to be temperamental, and Lamborghini was careful to ensure his aftersales service was among the best in the field, encouraging repeat business.

When Lamborghini began to reward himself for his success by acquiring luxury cars, he was therefore on a collision course with the notoriously prickly Enzo Ferrari. If, once again, the myth is to be believed.

Ferruccio certainly delighted in repeating the legend often enough to establish it as fact, though certain details would often shift to suit the occasion. He said the following in a 1991 interview with *Thoroughbred & Classic Cars* magazine:

OPPOSITE: In 1968, for the third year in a row, Lamborghini turned heads on the motor show circuit – this time with the launch of the dramatic Espada.

"After I got my first Ferrari, my other six cars – Alfa Romeo, Lancia, Mercedes, Maserati, Jaguar – were always left in the garage. In 1958 I went to Maranello for the first time to buy a 250GT coupé, the two-seater by Pininfarina. After that I had one, maybe two, 250GT Berlinettas, the short-wheelbase car from Scaglietti. I did like that one very much. It was ahead of its time, had a perfect balance and a strong engine. Finally, I bought a 250GT 2+2, which was a four-seater by Pininfarina. That engine was very strong too and it went very well.

"All my Ferraris had clutch problems. When you drove normally, everything was fine. But when you were going hard, the clutch would slip under acceleration; it just wasn't up to the job. I went to Maranello regularly to have a clutch rebuilt or renewed, and every time, the car was taken away for several hours and I was not allowed to watch them repairing it. The problem with the clutch was never cured, so I decided to talk to Enzo Ferrari. I had to wait for him a very long time. 'Ferrari, your cars are rubbish!' I complained. Il Commendatore was furious. 'Lamborghini, you may be able to drive a tractor but you will never be able to handle a Ferrari properly.' This was the point when I finally decided to make a perfect car."

Subsequent accounts from Lamborghini's early employees have applied somewhat unwanted layers of reality to this story. Ubaldo Sgarzi, sales manager and the man who did so much to keep the company alive during the 1970s, would later say Ferruccio's 250 GT 2+2 merely had faulty spark plugs and poorly set up carburettors.

Both test driver/engineer Bob Wallace and his successor, Valentino Balboni, have suggested that comparing what Ferrari was charging for a new clutch with what Lamborghini billed customers for tractor clutches set Ferruccio to thinking what profit could be made from building grand touring cars. He was too astute to enter such a potentially risky start-up

BELOW: Local government concessions enabled Lamborghini to build an impressive new factory.

business based on a clash of egos alone, but he recognized the opportunity to turn a profit if the product hit the mark.

"In the past I have bought some of the most expensive Gran Turismo cars," he explained in a 1964 interview with *Sporting Motorist* magazine.

"And in each of these magnificent cars I have found some faults. Too hot. Or uncomfortable. Or not sufficiently fast. Or not perfectly finished. Now I want to make a GT car without faults. Not a technical bomb. Very normal. But a perfect car."

Ferruccio enjoyed telling interviewers how he and his mechanics improved his Ferrari themselves in the Lamborghini tractor workshop, fitting a larger aftermarket Borg & Beck clutch and adding new twin-camshaft cylinder heads and horizontally mounted carburettors. With equal relish he would describe waiting for Ferrari factory test drivers outside Modena and then racing them up the A1 autostrada.

Lamborghini would receive no pushback against his plans from local authorities. The state of the economy was such that the Communist party held the majority in regional government, signing off on his plans for a new factory and granting an interest-free loan to build it provided he employed local workers – and provided they were members of the sheet metal workers' union. While this limited Ferruccio's own financial risk, the deal for inexpensive labour left his young company vulnerable to union caprice for years to come.

In a corner of the tractor factory, the chassis of the first prototype came together through the energy of an ambitious team of young engineers: Giampaolo Dallara, who had joined Ferrari immediately after graduating from the Milan Technical Institute at the age of 24, became technical director, assisted by recent University of Bologna graduate Paolo Stanzani. Giotto Bizzarrini, one of the architects of the iconic Ferrari 250 GTO, took on a freelance engagement as a consultant. Design and production of the bodywork was to be outsourced, as was customary at the time in low-volume car manufacture: in the early days of Ferrari the company simply produced rolling chassis with engines and transmissions which were clothed in bespoke shells by traditional coachbuilders. Soulless production lines which stamped out homogenous tin boxes were for the likes of Ford.

The project was beset with difficulties from the outset. As we will explore in the following chapter, the headstrong, individualistic Bizzarrini was paid based on the final power output of the 3.5-litre V12 engine. The initial result was not to Ferruccio's liking. Nor would it fit in the prototype car Lamborghini unveiled to the public at the 1963 Turin motor show. Ferruccio had the front end ballasted with tiles and the bonnet locked; if any sales prospects asked to look inside, Lamborghini would gesture at one of his employees and say, "*See*

RIGHT: From the earliest models, such as the 350 GT pictured here, Lamborghini aimed for a luxurious interior feel with plenty of leather.

that idiot? He's lost the keys." The engine was displayed separately to the rest of the car.

The 350 GTV prototype's bodywork design was credited to Franco Scaglione, working to a tight brief from Ferruccio, and the show car was built by the newly established Carrozzeria Sargiotto. But Lamborghini's plans had already changed by the time the car made its public debut: he was dissatisfied with the dated styling, as well as the raciness of Bizzarrini's tube frame chassis and the indifferent build quality of the shell.

Dallara and Stanzani took over onward development as Bizzarrini moved on to other freelance projects. Their new chassis design, based on square sections, was more suited to scale production. Carrozzeria Touring of Milan, early Ferrari collaborators and inventors of the patented Superleggera (super-light) construction technique, reworked Scaglione's design into a simpler and more classically elegant shape. Dallara also revised the engine for a more relaxed power delivery.

Unveiled at the 1964 Geneva show, the 350 GT received favourable press but didn't really manage to engage with potential customers at all: Lamborghini took just 13 orders all year. Ferruccio, keen to offer a larger and more powerful car to compete with Ferrari's 275, abandoned plans to introduce a smaller-engined model and went the other way, asking Dallara to increase the swept volume of the V12 to four litres. He hired Wallace, an aspiring racing driver from New Zealand who had worked as a mechanic for the Scuderia Serenissima racing organization, to improve the driving dynamics of Lamborghini's cars.

BELOW: Although reviews of the 350 GT were positive, sales proved disappointing.

OVERLEAF: Restyled and boasting a larger engine, plus room for two (small) rear passengers, the 400 GT was a step up from the 350 GT.

ABOVE: The bold Marzal show car prefaced the arrival of the Espada.

Despite financial issues, Touring were able to handle production demands for the new 400 GT model, although Zagato pitched for business with a pair of concept cars based on that car's running gear. The definitive 400 GT 2+2 was launched in 1966, featuring a Lamborghini-made gearbox and differential in place of the off-the-shelf ZF components used in earlier cars, as well as a reshaped chassis to accommodate a pair of rear seats in place of the original – and curious – sideways-mounted single rear seat. When Touring went bust, production shifted

to Carrozzeria Marazzi, a new company whose workforce was boosted by the recruitment of ex-Touring personnel.

While accomplished enough in their own way, these first Lamborghinis were relaxed grand tourers – the kind of car Ferruccio and other middle-aged men of means would choose to reward themselves for their success. They sold steadily but not in exciting numbers. Realizing the range needed to be expanded, Ferruccio signed off on the attention-grabbing Marzal concept vehicle and Miura supercar, followed

BELOW: It may seem unfamiliar now, but the Espada was Lamborghini's biggest seller of the 1970s across three model generations.

OPPOSITE: Relaunched as the Islero with pop-up headlights and a new interior, the GT model still failed to excite buyers.

eventually by a first attempt at a higher volume model, named the Urraco.

In 1968 Mario Marazzi rebodied the 400 GT – reputedly, his pen very much guided by Ferruccio – with more interior space, a larger glasshouse and pop-up headlights. The 'new' car was badged as the Islero, named after a famous fighting bull, and it sold in modest quantities – 125 – until the updated Islero S model was released a year later. Although Ferruccio adopted one as his daily driver, the Islero was never as successful as the more adventurous Espada, which was launched alongside it at the 1968 Geneva motor show. Designed by Miura stylist Marcello Gandini and based on styling themes established on the Marzal, it would become Lamborghini's biggest-selling model in the first two decades of the company's existence. The bull was up and running.

*Paid by
the Horse*

Inside the Engine Room

"I'll make it bigger and more powerful…"

The genesis of Lamborghini's astoundingly long-lived V12 engine – with development it powered the company's flagship cars for nearly 40 years – is as wreathed in myth as the origin story of Lamborghini itself. Popular legend has it that freelance engineer Giotto Bizzarrini was paid per unit of horsepower, an incentive which drove him to deliver an unusably peaky engine which would only have been useful in a racing car.

The truth is somewhat more nuanced. Lamborghini employees at the time recall that Ferruccio had not decided – or at least had not made it clear – what character the V12 should have. Bizzarrini's version of events was that he showed Ferruccio drawings of a 1.5-litre quad-cam V12 Formula 1 engine he had designed and was told to build a 3-litre version that would match Ferrari's equivalent road unit for power. "*I'll make it bigger and more powerful*," Bizzarrini claimed he replied, agreeing to a fixed fee with a bonus for every unit of horsepower over 300 he could squeeze from it.

OPPOSITE: Everything about the Miura was dramatic, right down to the black 'eyelashes' framing the pop-up headlamps.

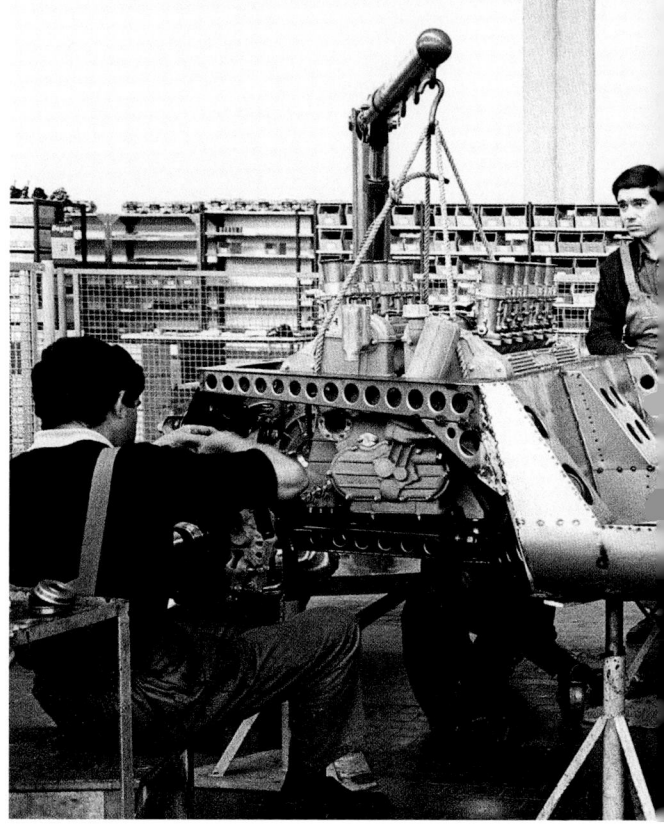

RIGHT: The Miura's chassis, with the V12 engine mounted transversely behind the cabin, was a rarity outside the world of motor racing.

Born in 1926, Bizzarrini graduated in mechanical engineering at the University of Pisa and spent four years in the mid-1950s working for Alfa Romeo on chassis development before joining Ferrari in 1957, initially as a test driver. At Maranello he quickly made a name for himself. Independent and iconoclastic, he led the work to cure the handling balance and aerodynamic issues plaguing Ferrari's new 250 GT SWB, a project eventually finished by Mauro Forghieri after Bizzarrini and a group of other senior staff quit *en masse* in November 1961.

The most outward nod to competition with the cars Ferrari was making was the presence of twin cams per cylinder bank rather than single ones, though the choice of alloy material for the crankcase was also rare in road cars. Initially displacing 3465cc, the 60-degree V12 was laden with race-inspired features including dry-sump lubrication and down-draught carburettors. Bizzarrini claimed 370bhp at 9,500rpm and insisted that with the right fuelling system it could be persuaded to reach 400bhp.

It ultimately fell to Dallara to make the engine less overtly racy, converting it from dry-sump to wet-sump lubrication and swapping out the vertical Weber carburettors for their less costly side-draught equivalents. A lower compression ratio and less edgy valve timing made it less peaky, although claimed maximum power was still reasonable: 270bhp at 6,500rpm in the first 350 GT models. The subsequent increase in displacement to 4 litres, achieved by increasing the cylinder bore from 77mm to 82mm, brought peak power to 320bhp at 6,500rpm while broadening the torque curve for a more relaxed delivery.

Another left-field theory about the Lamborghini V12's journey from draughtpaper to engine bay was put forward in the 1980s by motoring journalist L. J. K. Setright, a self-taught engineer. He claimed to have been told by a credible source that Bizzarrini's design was essentially discarded and a new V12 commissioned in secret from Honda. Described by no less an eminence than Bob Wallace as 'crap', the proposition has little evidence to support it bar some shared details between the Lamborghini engine and Honda's 1.5-litre V12, which raced in Formula 1 in 1965.

Dallara was also working on a pet project which would pave the way for the model that would truly put Lamborghini on the map. A persistent legend has it that the Miura was developed without Ferruccio's knowledge, and with the implicit aim of trying to steer him towards building a high-performance car rather than proceed with stately grand tourers. Certainly, according to the principals, the first brainstorming sessions took place outside office hours. But Dallara is on record as saying Ferruccio okayed the acquisition of a Mini to hack about into a rolling proof-of-concept chassis.

"I had nothing else to do on a Saturday or a Sunday anyway, and had a whole factory to play around with," wrote Dallara in

ABOVE: It might look unsophisticated to modern eyes but, at the 1965 Turin show, Lamborghini's mid-engined rolling chassis generated huge excitement.

his autobiography *It's A Beautiful Story*:

"*Let's build a lighter car to show it could be done. Have some sort of a mobile test bed for new ideas or trying something different, that sort of thing.*

"*He* [Ferruccio] *told me, 'You can do whatever the hell you want to do as long as it doesn't interfere with your daily job.' You get up and start testing at five in the morning, and drive and play around until three in the afternoon, and then go and play around trying to build something. Well, I didn't have anything better to do, and I've always enjoyed cars and still do. But as far as any serious effort to build a race car, no, that's something that writers and journalists and people in the past just sort of invented.*"

By the mid-1960s, mid-engined cars were common in motor racing – essential in Formula 1 and rapidly becoming so in other categories. When Lamborghini displayed a rolling chassis at the 1965 Turin show with the V12 mounted transversely behind the driver, the only road cars sharing this configuration were rareties: the De Tomaso Vallelunga, the ATS 2500GT and the René

BELOW: Bertone won the bid to design and build the bodywork for the Miura.

Bonnet Djet. On the racetrack, Ford's mid-engined GT40 was beginning to win the battle against Ferrari, a company which came to the concept only grudgingly (Enzo Ferrari famously opined that the horse should pull the cart rather than pushing it, and was resistant to changing that viewpoint). The show chassis, badged P400, clearly followed racing practice in that it was based around a central 'tub' with three longitudinal box-section members (drilled to reduce weight) connected by the floor and by bulkheads at each end. Further box sections extended fore and aft to act as engine and suspension mounting points.

As with the Mini dissected by Dallara for his proof of concept, the engine block was now cast in one piece with the transmission and differential, sharing the same oil sump, to achieve a compact form factor and sit ahead of the rear wheels. If Ferruccio had, as is said, agreed to exhibit the chassis merely

as a stunt to trumpet his company's engineering excellence, he came away from the show with a fistful of provisional orders for a car he had yet to build – and a queue of coachbuilders eager to provide a bodyshell design and final assembly service. The last one to bid, nervously, was Nuccio Bertone – on the last day of the show.

Since Carrozzeria Touring was lurching towards insolvency at this point, Lamborghini was open to alternatives and Bertone received the commission. New recruit Marcello Gandini worked closely with Dallara to create a new mid-engined vehicle which would define a new genre: the supercar. According to Paolo Stanzani's account, he and Dallara were very specific that it should be a race car for the road, citing the GT40 as the state of the mid-engined art. On Christmas Eve 1965 Stanzani and Dallara presented Gandini's styling proposal to Ferruccio, whose response (so they say) was: "*Make it.*"

BELOW: Despite a clamshell rear deck design, access to the engine was limited.

ABOVE: Later Miura SV models can be distinguished by the absence of eyelashes around the headlamps.

By the following March, a prototype bodyshell was ready to sit on the chassis for launch at the Geneva motor show, rendered even more eye-catching by the choice of colour: "*Poised somewhere between yellow and orange*" as Setright put it. Now officially christened the Miura P400 – after Eduardo Miura, the breeder whose fighting bulls inspired Lamborghini's logo – the new car caused a sensation. The GT40 had taken its name from its aggressively low stance, just 40 inches (1m) from ground level to roof panels, and the Miura was just 1.5 inches (3.8cm) taller. Shell-like one-piece nose and tail panels aimed to demonstrate the continued supremacy of Italian artisan construction. They also offered unusually easy access to the engine bay and luggage compartment, provided the owner or mechanic had the muscle to open them.

The interior was incomplete and would remain a work-in-progress throughout the Miura's life. Before the official unveiling, Ferruccio jotted down on paper how many he expected to sell that year, challenging the principals of the project to do the same. He wrote 20. Nuccio Bertone (perhaps with a view to how many bodyshells his company could realistically make) thought 5, chief salesman Ubaldo Sgarzi put down 50, while the ever-bullish Dallara imagined Lamborghini could build and sell 100.

It took until the end of the following year to hit Dallara's figure. Development and infrastructure snags delayed serial production until the second half of 1966, as the 300-strong staff at the new Sant'Agata factory got to grips with the process. Rather than building a rolling chassis which was then sent to the coachbuilder for finishing – the traditional model, as followed by Ferrari until the late 1960s – Lamborghini had Bertone send the painted shells to Sant'Agata for the final fit. Quality was initially sub-par and many early Miura owners had their interiors re-trimmed by other coachbuilders. The scattershot ergonomics

BELOW: Build quality was occasionally inexact – the large gaps between panels wouldn't be tolerated by modern supercar buyers.

ABOVE: Though shapely and beautiful, the Miura was aerodynamically poor and prone to front-end 'lift'.

were outside the influence of these seasoned professionals, though: only the speedometer and rev counter sat directly ahead of the driver, and were partly blocked by the steering wheel, while dials indicating parameters such as fuel level and oil pressure sat with no obvious hierarchy in a central panel. Deploying the headlights required the driver to operate two separate switches, one in the roof panel and one by the gearlever.

Externally, the production Miuras differed from the prototype only in details, such as the rear screen (changed from wraparound plexiglass to a black slatted arrangement) and headlamp 'eyelashes' (which popped up with the lights

on the show car). As with the general fit and finish, the driving dynamics of the first examples provided ample evidence of a product still in beta. "*Our customers were the test drivers,*" Dallara would later say, since Wallace was somewhat overstretched by having to combine general model development with quality assurance on the initial cars.

Some of the teething troubles, such as the overly heavy steering and the tendency of poorly set-up carburettors to cause flash fires, were straightforward to fix. Less so was the baked-in aerodynamic lift at high speeds caused by the long curve of the bonnet.

> *"Anyone who has achieved a true 170mph in a Miura can tell you that the effect experienced is that of a jet plane on a runway (complete with imminent take-off!),"* wrote marque enthusiast Joe Sackey in *The Lamborghini Miura Bible*, *"and the relationship between man, machine and God's green earth at that speed is a fragile one, compressed time-travel if you like, only to be undertaken by those brave souls who dare. You haven't lived until you've tried it… some say."*

While the bodyshell might have been aerodynamically sub-optimal, it was undoubtedly beautiful – and would become a source of controversy many years later as two of the twentieth century's most eminent automotive stylists tussled for credit over its authorship. Giorgetto Giugiaro, whose CV encompasses classics such as the Lotus Esprit, Volkswagen Golf, BMW M1, Maserati Ghibli and Alfa Romeo Giulia GT, worked at Bertone until 1965. In the mid-1990s he began to claim in a series of interviews that Gandini merely finished off the details of initial sketches he had left behind. Later on, Giugiaro engaged reverse gear on this claim.

In 1968 Lamborghini released the revised Miura P400S, with a stiffer chassis and revised transmission and rear suspension. While this did nothing for the aerodynamic lift issues, it improved mechanical refinement and sweetened the handling response. Larger intake manifolds and more aggressive camshaft profiles elevated the V12's claimed power to 370bhp.

At the Brussels motor show that year, the company demonstrated an open-top Miura. Resplendent in metallic powder blue with a white leather interior, this roadster model subtly defied convention: rather than simply decapitate the car and replace the metal with folding fabric, Lamborghini removed only the upper section of the roof. Here function dictated form, since the chassis had to be augmented for safety and to reduce flex caused by the loss of the roof panel. Gandini cleverly integrated the rollover bar into a flying buttress structure and removed the slatted black rear screen to expose the engine, making it a design feature.

The official company history claims that Ferruccio refused to build a production model. In truth Bertone insisted on a minimum of 50 orders before committing to production and, despite great interest at the show, Lamborghini did not pass this threshold. The show car then enjoyed an interesting second life as a promotional tool for the International Lead Zinc Research Organization, which stripped it and galvanised the bodyshell to demonstrate the corrosion-resistance of coated metals. While Lamborghini never offered a roadster model for sale to the public, a number of owners have subsequently committed the ultimate sacrilege of having their Miuras converted.

Dallara also took his leave that year, moving to De Tomaso to design a Formula 1 car. It is widely believed that Ferruccio's refusal to countenance a racing programme (*see* Chapter 5) played a part in his decision to move. Paolo Stanzani, who took

BELOW: The company's Polo Storico division now offers complete new body panels for restoration projects.

OVERLEAF: Conceptually the low, wide, mid-engined Miura had much in common with Ford's Le Mans-winning GT40.

ABOVE: Dynamically the Miura SV model was a great improvement over the original.

over as technical director, has claimed that Ferruccio wanted to step back and hand day-to-day management of the company to him rather than Dallara, prompting Giampaolo to quit in a temper. Dallara's account is that he saw the troubles which would result in the company's sale coming.

The eminent engineer might have required a crystal ball to reach this verdict. It was not until 1969 that Lamborghini encountered the first major bumps in the road, as industrial unrest rippled across Italy and a series of strikes called by the Communist-controlled unions brought work at Sant'Agata to a halt. To begin with this had little effect on car development, as Stanzani oversaw work on new models as well as the final iteration of the Miura, and Wallace quietly fettled his Miura race car outside office hours. And sales, at least of the flagship car, were going well: Frank Sinatra arrived unannounced one day, was given an impromptu tour of the factory by

Ubaldo Sgarzi, and left having placed an order for a P400S in metallic orange with boarskin leather trim and orange shagpile carpeting.

Launched at the Geneva show in 1971, the 400SV was the definitive Miura. Outwardly different only through the wider rear track and absence of 'eyelashes', the SV represented another significant step in performance and refinement. Revised suspension front and rear added further finesse to the Miura's dynamics, as did the limited-slip differential. New three-barrel carburettors and valve timing, as well as a different combustion chamber design, delivered a claimed 15bhp boost. Lamborghini also took the opportunity to split the oil reservoirs for the engine and gearbox, a measure which improved peace-of-mind rather than performance.

Was this to be the ultimate Lamborghini? No. 'Project 112' was already on the drawing board.

Countach!

An Icon is Born

"A high-speed, low-drag container for two lucky people."

Beautiful and beguiling as the Miura was, it was freighted with hardwired shortcomings – ones which Paolo Stanzani and assistant Massimo Parenti, along with test driver/engineer Bob Wallace, recognized that despite their best efforts could not be resolved without beginning again from a clean sheet. Ferruccio Lamborghini shared their concerns about the Miura's twitchy on-the-limit demeanour, recalcitrant gear change, the heat and noise of a V12's reciprocating parts just a few inches away from the driver's ears, and the front end's propensity to try to achieve take-off at high speed.

Ferruccio also had wider concerns about his model range. The De Tomaso Mangusta, Maserati Bora and Ferrari 365 GTB/4 had emerged as rivals to the Miura. And, while his supercar was achieving reasonable sales figures, Ferruccio's other offerings were failing to interest their respective demographics. His beloved grand tourers had fallen particularly flat; the 350GT begat the 400GT begat the Islero to widespread indifference, thanks in part to the outdated method of manufacture and hit-and-miss quality of

OPPOSITE: Cooling the engine was one of the biggest challenges as Lamborghini gradually expanded the V12's swept volume to 5.2 litres.

ABOVE: A largely complete Countach bodyshell arrives at the factory to be mated to the mechanicals.

Carrozzeria Materazzi's work. A final throw of the dice – the Jarama, named after a breed of fighting bulls rather than the dreary racetrack near Madrid – shared many mechanicals and some styling features with the more successful Espada, but still proved a flop. The Urraco, an attempt to colonize a market segment dominated by Porsche's 911 with Ferrari's Dino 246 GT as the challenger, received good reviews but was delayed by persistent problems with its transmission and new V8 engine. Permeating this scenario like a poisonous miasma, ongoing industrial unrest sapped both cash flow and Ferruccio's will, as production lagged and orders were cancelled.

'Project 112' began to come together in 1970, before the Urraco's first public appearance at the Turin motor show. At this point confidence was high that the new mid-market sportscar would be a success, and the Miura's replacement could therefore be more rarefied; Ferruccio even planned to offer it only to existing customers personally approved by himself. As such, money – both in terms of the development budget and the final asking price – could be less of an object. Project 112 would be neither a GT nor a race car. Stanzani could create his own genre – so long as the finished product hit its performance benchmarks.

Some might view the move to a spaceframe chassis as a retrograde step, but this was a logical response to the need for greater overall stiffness given that the engine was to be rotated and moved further forwards within the structure. A conventional north-south location for the engine opened the possibilities for better cooling architecture and improved exhaust routing, with potential power benefits. The key challenge was the inherent length of a V12: how to locate it far enough forwards to avoid the Miura's penchant for snap oversteer while still maintaining a polite distance from the driver? Stanzani addressed this by mounting the gearbox and clutch at the front of the engine with the differential at the rear, connected by a shaft running through a sealed tunnel within the sump. Although it added some weight, and raised the centre of gravity relative to a more conventional layout, it offset this by locating more mass within the wheelbase. It also offered a shorter and more direct linkage for the gear-selector mechanism, eliminating another Miura flaw.

The new layout, and the expansion of the engine to 5 litres by increasing both bore and stroke, led to Project 112 being renamed LP500 (LP for *Longitudinale Posteriore*, signifying the V12's alignment and location). Soon it would become *Countach*, a Piedmontese vernacular exclamation with no exact translation in English, usually uttered by young men appreciating the sight of an attractive woman. (These were the 1970s…). Quite who said it first when they witnessed Marcello Gandini's dynamic

OPPOSITE: Before it acquired the Countach name, the prototype appeared as the LP500 at the 1971 Geneva Show. It was later destroyed in crash testing, though Lamborghini's Polo Storico department recreated it for the 50th anniversary in 2021.

wedge-shaped design for the first time is impossible to say for certain. Differing accounts attribute it to Ferruccio Lamborghini and Nuccio Bertone, but plenty of others were moved to utter the word when covers came off the LP500 prototype at Geneva in 1971. This was not Gandini's first wedge – his Lancia Stratos Zero concept with a vast, hinged windscreen had wowed Turin show-goers six months earlier – but it still caused a stir. Gandini explained that his design began with a single sweeping line from nose to tail and every other aspect of the car's stance, proportions and detailing proceeded from there. To make the doors fulfil their function within the desired shapes, Gandini dictated that they hinge forwards and upwards like scissors.

Ultimately, some engineering features – such as the extensive use of magnesium in the suspension and steering, the aircraft-style yoke instead of a steering wheel, and the digital instruments – did not make it through to production. The spaceframe chassis design was also revised with additional tubing in place of sheet steel. Practicality also had to be accommodated, with a periscope-style rear viewing mirror arrangement on early models, and secondary windows which could actually open so the driver did not have to disembark to pay tolls on the Autostrada.

The LP500's journey to becoming the Countach would, like the Urraco's arrival on the market, suffer excruciating delays. If the Lamborghini stand at Geneva in 1971 – featuring the LP500, Jarama, new Series II Espada and Urraco – suggested a company continuing to grow aggressively, this was far from the case. A global energy crisis was brewing, threatening the marketability of high-performance cars, and the global economy was in slowdown, affecting this and Ferruccio's other businesses.

Also, it was a strategic mistake to flag up two new cars at the same time: customers were holding back from buying the established models. There was not enough money in the development pot to advance the Urraco and Countach to

production readiness quickly, even if Lamborghini had sufficient engineering resources to accomplish the task. The development team was stretched too thin.

The solution was to prioritize. The 5-litre version of the V12 persistently overheated so, since the Urraco's problematic V8 was already hogging resource, Stanzani reverted to the 4-litre. Once it was possible to drive the Countach prototype for more than a few miles without boiling the engine, the car proved to be far more skittish at the rear than expected as speeds built while travelling in a straight line. In an era before the widespread use of wind tunnels for research into road and race car aerodynamics, Wallace, Stanzani and Parenti glued wool tufts to the prototype's shell and fired off motor-drive shots of it at speed from a camera mounted to a chase car. This revealed the Countach was generating too much downforce at the front,

ABOVE: The Countach was also dramatic on the inside, if ergonomically challenging.

OPPOSITE: When cooling proved problematic, the first solution was to revert to the 4-litre version of the V12 and add NACA ducts and boxy scoops to the Countach's flanks.

hence the rear-end liveliness while pressing on, and not enough cooling air was reaching the radiators from the louvres on the car's shoulders.

Lamborghini's tractor business also faced headwinds. The company had made major investments to fufil a large order from Bolivia, but the country's socialist government was subsequently toppled in a coup d'etat. Another substantial order was cancelled.

Most companies would respond to these scenarios by, however grudgingly, reducing production and laying off staff. The Communist-controlled trade unions refused to accommodate such necessary big-picture thinking, forcing Ferruccio to dip into his own pockets to keep churning out tractors and cars destined to remain unsold. To ensure a comfortable retirement he held on to his air conditioning and pneumatic valve businesses, sold the tractor company to his main rival, and reached a deal with Swiss

ABOVE: Dramatic 'scissor' doors made it through to production. Tyre availability dictated a maximum 14-inch rear-wheel size on early models.

sportscar enthusiast Georges-Henri Rossetti to acquire a 51 per cent stake in the car manufacturer for a reported $600,000.

In May 1972 Stanzani and Wallace drove the Countach prototype to Sicily and back to watch the Targa Florio road race. It survived the journey and, upon its successful return to Sant-Agata, Ferruccio and Rossetti officially sanctioned production. It would be another two years before the LP400

Countach was ready for the market, by which time it had grown a pair of NACA ducts and boxy air intakes on each side for the sake of engine cooling. Of greater import was the fact that the company founder had retired to his Umbrian estate after selling his remaining 49 per cent stake to another Swiss, René Leimer, for $400,000. The decline in relative value of the stock was reflective of market conditions: conflict in the Middle East had

OPPOSITE: Giampaolo Dallara returned to Lamborghini as a consultant in 1976, overseeing important revisions that would result in the much-improved LP400 S model.

caused a spike in oil prices and sent already teetering economies worldwide into recession. Performance cars were out of fashion, and not just as a factor of increased costs at the pump; several countries, including Italy, imposed additional sales taxes on cars with engines displacing more than 2 litres.

As such the LP400 Countach was released into a very different atmosphere to the one which had greeted the LP500 three years earlier. What was once outlandishly alluring was now deemed borderline irrelevant. Contemporary road-testers were impressed by its performance, less so by its poise and roadholding. It had been developed on experimental Pirelli tyres which the company never put on sale, forcing Lamborghini to fit Michelin XWXs, then the largest tyres available in terms of width; but they were also high-profile, enforcing a maximum wheel size of 14 inches.

While Leimer and Rossetti were enthusiastic about cars, they had been born into wealth – Rossetti was the scion of a watchmaking dynasty – and lacked understanding of the ways of working folk. Neither was adequately equipped to handle febrile industrial relations or the effects of global recession on the sportscar market. The Urraco never achieved the originally anticipated sales volumes despite very favourable reviews in the motoring press; and the Countach proved too slow to make, since the spaceframe was outsourced and too many minor components had to be hand-crafted in-house. It is ironic that even in this climate Lamborghini proved unable to satisfy demand for its halo car, making just 23 in 1974. With the company in retrenchment, it was likely there would be no investment in development of new or existing cars, so both Stanzani and Wallace departed in 1975.

The arrival of new Europe-wide type-approval regulations in 1978, imposing tougher and more extensive crash-testing procedures, demanded action and signified the end for the Urraco and Espada models. Giampaolo Dallara returned on

BELOW: From the LP400 S model onwards the Countach gained a rear wing, wheel arch extensions and bigger tyres, as the engine expanded.

COUNTACH! 61

ABOVE: The original design was so futuristic that it remained iconic over a decade later, in the 1980s, an era when anything else from the 1970s was considered passé at best.

a consultancy basis in 1976, reworking the Urraco into what would become the Silhouette and overseeing an important redevelopment of the Countach. Pirelli's new low-profile P7 tyres enabled Dallara to completely rework the suspension geometry, fit 15-inch wheels at the rear, and install larger brake rotors, all of which contributed to a more confidence-inspiring drive. The LP400S was launched in 1978 – shortly before failed projects instigated by Leimer and Rossetti left Lamborghini bankrupt.

Thanks to a sympathetic administrator (*see* Chapter 4), production of the Countach continued during this period and onward through several of Lamborghini's subsequent custodians. The eminent engineer Giulio Alfieri, architect of many iconic road and racing Maseratis, produced the next iteration. In fitting a large rear wing to improve stability, along with the necessary bodywork extensions to accommodate the larger wheels and tyres, Dallara had exacerbated drag on a car that in reality was already less slippery than it looked to the naked eye. To improve performance, Alfieri and new recruit Luigi Marmiroli fell back on the expedient of enlarging the engine to 4.8 litres. Though offset slightly by a modest rise in roof height to improve interior space, the additional power was enough to yield a new top speed of 180mph (290km/h) in the new LP500S.

The Countach was so far ahead of its time that a car which was first exhibited in 1971 literally became a poster child for the conspicuous consumption of the 1980s. It continued to evolve, sprouting ever more outrageous aerodynamic addenda – necessary to keep the show on the road after Alfieri and Marmiroli increased the stroke in 1985 and fitted four-valve cylinder heads, enabling the 5175cc Quattrovalvole model to boast 470bhp.

BELOW: Despite updates, including better trim, the interior dated much more than the exterior.

BELOW: Horacio Pagani restyled the Countach for its 25th Anniversary model, substantially revising the cooling intakes and ducting.

Under Chrysler's ownership, the model bowed out with the 1988 Countach Anniversary, engineered by Horacio Pagani and featuring extensive use of carbonfibre. While marque purists consider this celebration of Lamborghini's 25th year the ugliest of the Countach family, some of the more flamboyant styling features served to distract from the larger bumpers required

by new US safety regulations. It was also the biggest-selling Countach: 650 examples left the factory, almost as many as the first three models combined and narrowly eclipsing the 610 achieved by the Quattrovalvole.

Of greater concern to Lamborghini aficionados was what the giant US corporation planned to do with its new acquisition.

The Show Must Go On

The Road to Ruin

> "I didn't buy Lamborghini because I want a company that produces 300 cars a year."

For all but 10 of its first 35 years in business, the Lamborghini car company was passed around between owners like a bargain box of chocolate brownies. Each proprietor brought particular ambitions and some were more invested in love for the brand than others. But all lacked the right combination of vision, willpower and resource to resolve the operation's deep-seated issues.

First to fall was the partnership of Georges-Henri Rossetti and René Leimer. As a general principle, human beings are fearful of change. Add to this the disposition of overly powerful trade unions to throw their weight around (an issue not confined to Italian industry in the 1970s) and the result was a vicious circle of stuttering production, indifferent build quality, slow sales and weak

OPPOSITE: When the limited-edition Diablo SE30 was launched to mark the company's 30th anniversary in 1993, Lamborghini was already on its fourth set of owners.

BELOW: Designed as an 'affordable' model, the Urraco failed to lure buyers away from the Porsche 911 and barely registered in the important US market.

cash flow. In Rossetti's general absence, Leimer and sales director Ubaldo Sgarzi shouldered the burden of administration, usually only accepting orders for Countachs after full payment in cash. Cleverly, to reduce transport costs, Sgarzi would often invite motoring journalists to test-drive newly built cars… all the way to their destination country. The customer received their car with 'delivery mileage' and Lamborghini received free publicity in the form of some of the decade's most evocative travel writing.

To comply with tougher US safety and emissions laws, and similarly tighter type-approval regulations in Europe, the owners had to invest. Hence, Giampaolo Dallara's return as a consultant after Lamborghini stalwarts Paolo Stanzani and Bob Wallace left in 1975. He had two main problems to resolve: the wayward road manners of early Countach models (*see* Chapter 3) and the forthcoming obsolescence of the Espada and slow-selling Urraco.

Stanzani had engineered the Urraco cleverly to bring it in at an affordable price point, using many standard parts bought in

ABOVE: The targa-roofed Silhouette was a clever repurposing of the Urraco, but it too failed to catch on.

from BMW, Mercedes and Fiat. Its stylish Gandini-designed body looked the part and the driving experience attracted positive reviews – but the car never recovered from the two-year hiatus between 'reveal' and production, during which many buyers cancelled their orders. The transverse mid-mounted V8's performance was also underwhelming until it was expanded to 3 litres in late 1974, by which time Ferrari's 308 had arrived and set the bar even higher. A specially adapted version for the US market, with larger bumpers and a detuned engine to comply with new rules there, proved barely worth tooling up for – just 21 were sold.

Following the popularity of targa-roofed 308 and Porsche 911 models, Lamborghini's bosses directed Bertone and Dallara to rework the Urraco into a similar car that might finally conquer America. Shown as a prototype at the 1976 Turin show, the Silhouette even recycled the Urraco's doors and windscreen to reduce tooling costs. Dallara and new chief engineer Franco Baraldini reworked the chassis for greater stiffness, adding a roll bar to compensate for the loss of the roof panel, and adopted new suspension geometry to maximize the potential of Pirelli's new P7 low-profile rubber. Another key area of concern was the interior, where the previously poor fit and finish had been a major turn-off for customers – especially in the USA.

Chasing opportunities elsewhere, Lamborghini entered two partnerships that offered extraordinary potential but ultimately plunged the company into financial turmoil. It reached a deal with BMW to manufacture the M1, a new Giugiaro-styled performance car, and committed to co-develop an off-road vehicle codenamed Cheetah with the US military contractor Mobility Technology International. The M1 might have been niche, but BMW had a deal to run a one-make race series for it on the Formula 1 support card, plus it needed to build 400 examples to homologate it for the World Sportscar

BELOW: Development issues and legal threats stymied the Cheetah project and worsened the company's financial position.

Championship; similarly, the continuing tensions in the Middle East had created demand for armoured rapid-attack vehicles.

These deals were enough to secure a $1.5 million grant from the Italian government, but both projects went south. Poor labour relations hit production of the M1 as well as the Silhouette and Countach, prompting BMW to shift production elsewhere. (One recipient of a contract was the UK racing organization Project 4, run by Ron Dennis; money from this project enabled him to employ visionary designer John Barnard to start on what would become the first composite-tub Formula 1 car, after Project 4's merger with McLaren in 1980.) The Cheetah, powered by a rear-mounted waterproofed 5.9-litre Chrysler V8 after Dallara abandoned a 7-litre version of the Lamborghini V12, was a hit at the 1977 Geneva show, but testing revealed it needed much more development. (In his autobiography, test driver Valentino Balboni recalled a truck coming the other way generating enough air pressure to pop all four doors out.) An intellectual property lawsuit from another putative military contractor over similarities with its own project hurried the Cheetah concept into extinction.

Scrambling for more cash, Leimer obtained a loan from US businessman and Countach owner Zoltan Reti, secured on the factory. Reti soon demanded his money back and had the company declared bankrupt. Fortunately for Lamborghini the receiver, Alessandro Artese, was a car aficionado who believed it *might* just be possible for the company to survive as a going concern and find a new buyer. Lamborghini also became the beneficiary of another Italian marque's woes: troubled Maserati had come under the control of Alejandro De Tomaso, who had cut half the workforce. Giulio Alfieri, an engineer who had a hand in the legendary 1950s Maserati 'Birdcage' as well as finessing the likes of the Merak and Bora, reputedly arrived for work one day to find the contents of his office in the car park. Artese wasted no time in appointing him managing director of Lamborghini. Alfieri prudently abandoned production of all Lamborghini models bar the Countach, which proceeded on a cash-upfront basis. This was not enough to save the company from ruin. It was a much, much humbler machine that came to the rescue.

The industrious Alfieri noticed that one of the many overseas-market derivatives of the Fiat 127 'supermini', the Brazilian Fiat 147, was sold with raised suspension and additional anti-rust measures to suit the country's often treacherously rutted roads outside urban spaces. He pitched Fiat on the idea of a 'ruggedized' 127 for the Italian market with faux off-road styling touches such as bull bars and chunky wheels. Fiat agreed and contracted Lamborghini to build 5,000 examples of what would be sold (in Italy only) as the 127 Rústica, handing the company a financial lifeline and enabling Alfieri to re-employ many workers left destitute by Lamborghini's insolvency.

Alfieri was also able to quietly work on a 'new' model, a cut-price revamp of the Silhouette. Though that model died after just 50 examples had found buyers, Alfieri remained confident that an affordable open-top Lamborghini should sell. Marc Deschamps, Marcello Gandini's successor at Bertone, had caught the eye with the Silhouette-based Athon concept car demonstrated on Bertone's stand at the 1980 Turin show. Alfieri commissioned the company to revise the Silhouette with the emphasis on integrating safety features (such as large bumpers) necessary for the US market. More extensive use of leather in the interior and an increase in engine capacity to 3485cc completed the transformation. Peak power remained at a claimed 255bhp, but the V8 achieved that output 500rpm earlier and enjoyed a fatter torque curve – the peak going from 130lb-ft to 232 – which made for a substantially different driving experience.

In badging this car the Jalpa, Lamborghini returned to the tradition of naming models after fighting bulls. Although a meagre 410 would be sold over 10 years in production, its mere existence at the time was significant. During the Jalpa's short development Lamborghini found new owners: African sugar barons Patrick and Jean-Claude Mimran, who arrived at the factory for the first time dressed in jeans and T-shirts.

In a complicated piece of financial engineering the assets of Automobili Lamborghini changed hands for $3 million in January 1981, transferring to a new legal entity, Nuova Automobili Ferruccio Lamborghini SpA, of which 24-year-old Patrick was the president. The transaction involved sacking the workforce and rehiring them the following day, a move which did much to bring the more febrile elements into line.

Just two months after the acquisition, Lamborghini emphasized its fresh start with a Geneva show line-up that included the new Jalpa and a second stab at the Cheetah concept, the LM001, produced in response to an expression of

BELOW: Working with minimal funds, Lamborghini revised the Silhouette and relaunched it as the Jalpa in 1981. Though sales ultimately proved disappointing, the Jalpa's mere existence was enough to impress the company's new owners.

ABOVE: Beloved of customers from royalty to drug lords, the LM002 was ugly and failed to interest its target market – but it caught a moment in the 1980s.

interest from Saudi Arabia. The rear-engined layout proved unsuitable for desert use – Balboni escaped a roll-over incident during testing near Jeddah – and the Mimrans pushed ahead with development of an all-new model. The resulting LMA002, shown a year later, now had the 4.8-litre V12 from the Countach LP500S sitting in the front of a spaceframe chassis which now had the room for ten occupants rather than four. Despite much-improved off-road performance, the car became a victim of timing as the key customers, Saudi Arabia and Kuwait, became distracted by the onset of the Iran–Iraq War.

Still the Mimrans persisted and the off-road concept would have its moment, though not with the clientele originally envisaged. As the inflationary, recession-speckled 1970s diminished in the rear-view mirror, the booming global economy triggered a new era of conspicuous consumption and displays of wealth. At the 1986 Brussels motor show Lamborghini revealed the LM002, still angular (enabling armour plating to be fitted) and rugged but more luxurious inside, and now powered by the latest 5.2-litre V12 from the Countach Quattrovalvole – albeit with a lower compression ratio to make it sympathetic to lower-octane fuel.

Rapidly nicknamed 'the Rambo Lambo' after the film character played by Sylvester Stallone, the LM002 attracted a constituency of people who liked to stand apart from commoners. Royalty, actors (including Stallone himself), rock stars, dictators and criminals flocked to sign on the dotted line. The Sultan of Brunei placed an order. Even Colombian drug lord Pablo Escobar kept one to patrol his private estate.

Even if market conditions had become favourable independently of Lamborghini's owners, the Mimrans had done well – and they cashed out to the tune of $33 million in May 1987, selling the company to Chrysler. Lido Anthony 'Lee' Iacocca, a self-styed titan of the automotive industry, was credited with turning the Chrysler corporation around after negotiating a government bailout in 1979. One of the pillars of this renaissance was a restructuring of the corporation's brands to use shared components and platforms, reducing costs at the expense of individuality. Fundamental to this was the front-engined K platform, introduced in 1981 and, by 1987, underpinning many Dodges, Plymouths and Chryslers. Iacocca's '87 shopping spree also included the struggling American Motor Corporation, whose brands were soon rolled into the mothership.

"I didn't buy Lamborghini because I want a company that produces 300 cars a year," Iacocca told his executive team. *"There's tremendous value in the brand. I want you guys to figure out what to do with it."*

The Mimrans had ceased 'unnecessary' spending in advance of the sale, leaving plans for successors to the Jalpa and Countach

78 THE SHOW MUST GO ON

in limbo. Iacocca's agenda did not necessarily include rescuing them from it, either.

The initial signs were good. Chrysler designer Kevin Verduyn had produced a concept model called the Navajo the previous year and reworked it into a full-size vehicle for display at the Frankfurt motor show in late 1987. Based on Jalpa mechanicals, including the engine, and built by Carrozzeria Coggiola of Turin, it featured a pair of opposed scissor doors on each side granting access to a full four-seater cabin. Was this a pointer to a future Lamborghini model? No, but it was an indicator that Detroit would be calling the shots on design.

It was also becoming horrifyingly clear to the 'car guys' on the executive floor that Iacocca's real plans for the Lamborghini name were tantamount to blasphemy: he saw the bull logo as just another piece of tinsel which could be added to a badge-engineered high-profit stock platform. As part of a deliberate programme of 'malicious obedience' which included back-door involvement in Formula 1 (*see* Chapter 5), design chief Tom Gale took one of the most ostentatious K-platform models – the Chrysler Imperial – and made it even more ghastly by adding Lamborghini wheels, painting the whole ensemble bright red, fitting pale leather upholstery and adding Lamborghini logos to more or less any flat surface.

This monstrosity helped persuade the board that devaluing the brand would cost more in the long term, so the Countach and Jalpa replacements exited their stasis as part of a new strategy to grow Lamborghini's volume quickly. The deadline for the new Countach – the Diablo – was set unrealistically early: 1988.

Marcello Gandini returned as designer and his proposal was suitably dramatic, with an exaggerated rear deck bearing large air scoops, and sweeping flat-topped rear wheel arches. Chrysler's board did not like it and, as part of a wider operational schism between Sant'Agata and Detroit, Gale's team began reshaping

OPPOSITE TOP: Development of what became the Diablo was 'frozen' before the Chrysler takeover – and nearly left in the deep freeze.

OPPOSITE BOTTOM: The Diablo's rear deck and wheel arches were more 'conventional' than originally proposed after Chrysler's stylists adapted Marcello Gandini's original designs.

OVERLEAF: To stimulate flagging sales in the recession of the early 1990s, Megatech launched the Diablo SV, stripped out but with a more powerful engine than the standard car – and less expensive too.

BELOW: To remain competitive the venerable Bizzarrini V12 had to grow to 5.7 litres.

OPPOSITE: Although dynamically the Diablo was an improvement on the Countach, the interior remained cramped and uncomfortable.

the car to smooth off the edges even as Balboni was starting to test a disguised prototype in Italy early in 1989. While the envelope of the Diablo remained unfixed, these tests did serve to demonstrate that it needed more power to beat newer competitors. Accordingly, the venerable V12 grew from 5.3 litres to 5.7.

While Gandini was irked by having the design taken out of his hands, enough to sell his original sketches to start-up supercar manufacturer Cizeta-Moroder (co-financed by music producer Giorgio Moroder), he deemed the final Diablo good enough to allow his signature to be appended to the flanks of production models. Not only was the Chryslerized Diablo less self-consciously edgy, it looked less bulky around the hips than the initial designs and features such as the coolant intakes were more neatly integrated. It was timeless enough to stay in production for over a decade before a minor facelift.

The Diablo was longer and taller than the Countach, and

ABOVE: The Diablo VT Roadster featured a removeable lightweight roof panel which could be fixed to the engine cover; an electric folding mechanism was shelved during development.

more lavishly upholstered. Heavier, too, since the underpinnings had to be strengthened to meet new crash regulations and handle the additional power. But it was substantially slipperier, having a drag coefficient of 0.31 compared with the late-model Countach's 0.42. Lamborghini claimed a top speed of 202mph (325km/h), while Balboni later admitted he had clocked that only after removing the mirrors and rear wing.

Deliveries began in September 1990. Once again Lamborghini suffered from poor market timing: the boom of the 1980s had turned to bust as Japan went into recession and tempers flared in the Middle East once again. When Iraq invaded neighbouring Kuwait, the price of oil doubled. Chrysler had taken on debt to fund Iacocca's acquisition spree and was now forced to unwind it, offloading Gulfstream Aerospace and instructing the investment bank J. P. Morgan to value

Lamborghini for sale. The mooted new Jalpa, codenamed P140, went into hiatus and Lamborghini struggled to fund the four-wheel-drive Diablo VT model. An open-top Diablo Roadster prototype designed by Gandini appeared at the 1992 Geneva show, but would not go into production while Chrysler's logo remained on the company notepaper.

In January 1994 Chrysler sold to a consortium of three Bermuda-based, Indonesian-owned companies (all ultimately owned by Hutomo 'Tommy' Mandala Putra, the son of Indonesian President Suharto) and the multimillionaire Setiawan Djody for a reported $40 million. Djody intended to use this as a platform to create a new car for the Indonesian market under the Megatech brand, though this would ultimately come to naught when Suharto was ousted in 1997 during the wider Asian economic crisis.

The Megatech era began optimistically enough for Giugiaro's ItalDesign company to make a styling pitch for the putative Jalpa replacement, exhibiting the Calà concept vehicle on its stand at the 1995 Geneva show. Nothing came of this – for now – and, indeed, not much eventuated from the Megatech era bar a number of Diablo special editions and the much-delayed Roadster model. Former Lotus and General Motors Executive Mike Kimberley came and went, frustrated as promises of investment in new models failed to materialize and Megatech chose retrenchment and cost-cutting instead.

Kimberley's replacement, former Fiat executive Vittorio Di Capua, dispatched chief engineer Maurizio Reggiani to the Volkswagen Audi Group with a view to using its 4.2-litre V8 engine and Quattro four-wheel drivetrain in a rebooted P140 project. Rather more would come of these tentative negotiations than that…

OPPOSITE: Unlike the Countach, the Diablo had one-piece retracting door windows. On the SE30 model, the electric mechanism was removed to save weight and the windows replaced by plexiglass with a sliding inset panel.

BELOW: ItalDesign's Calà was a fully functional prototype, but Lamborghini's owners lacked the funds or ambition to build it.

THE SHOW MUST GO ON 87

The Audi Renaissance

Bigger, Better, Faster, More

> "The Murciélago undisputedly still remains relevant, or as relevant as a 212mph 1.7-tonne two-seat lorry can be."

Lamborghini's approach during the Megatech era to the Volkswagen Group to use Audi's V8 engine and Quattro drivetrain in the long-gestating P140 project resulted in the opportunity for the financially troubled owners to divest. VW overlord Ferdinand Piëch, grandson of Ferdinand Porsche and chief engineer of the Le Mans-winning Porsche 917 racer, was in accumulation mode thanks to the group's expanding mainstream market share. He had already snapped up Bugatti and was negotiating to acquire Bentley, chiefly to keep it out of rival BMW's hands. News that Lamborghini's owners were wavering provided an irresistible opportunity to bring another potentially lucrative premium brand into the fold.

In June 1998, after protracted negotiations, Audi bought Lamborghini for a reported $110 million – rather less than the $790

OPPOSITE: To launch the Murciélago within three years of Audi buying Lamborghini meant the new car had to be based on the Diablo's chassis architecture.

million VW would ultimately pay to steer Bentley away from Munich. Within months a facelifted version of the Diablo was released, but the legwork on this – including the replacement of the pop-up lights with cheaper, simpler fixed units bought in from Nissan – had been done before the takeover. The wider automotive world would have to wait a little longer to work out what Piëch's people planned.

During the extensive due-diligence process, Audi calculated that Lamborghini would have to sell 1,500 units per year to balance the books – a figure hitherto unseen during the procession of different owners. Costs could be cut, yes, through that dread word 'synergies' – using as many existing parts as possible, preferably hidden, just as Paolo Stanzani had done with the Urraco but on a larger and more organized scale from within the wider VW empire. Given the direction of travel Lamborghini nearly took under Chrysler, marque aficionados were right to be concerned about what agenda the new owners might have. But it was never part of the plan to simply slap Lamborghini badges on humdrum saloons and sell them at a premium.

Obviously a new tentpole model would be required to replace the Diablo. But a more affordable one would also be required – along the lines of the Urraco, Jalpa, and so on, though this one would have to achieve more traction in the market.

Lamborghini had been tentatively working on a new Diablo, to be called the Canto. Carrozzeria Zagato, one of the last independent Italian coachbuilding houses, had provided a design for this as well as presenting the Raptor concept car. Marcello Gandini had also produced a proposal called the Acosta. Piëch ordered these scrapped in favour of an all-new concept to be generated by Belgian-born designer Luc Donckerwolke, who had styled the first new models to be built by Skoda, another of VW's acquisitions. Donckerwolke would become the first Lamborghini design chief of the Audi era.

Audi set an ambitious launch date of 2001 for the Diablo replacement, now to be called the Murciélago, after a fighting bull said to have been brought into the Miura line as a sire after surviving 90 sword strokes. While that figure was debatable, the resonance with Lamborghini's recent history was clear. In the meantime, Lamborghini fettled the Diablo with a final flurry of updates which would pave the way for its successor: not only was the engine brought out to 6 litres, the pedal box was redesigned to free up more space in the footwell and improve the driving experience.

Though timescales dictated extensive use of the existing Diablo chassis architecture, Donckerwolke's Murciélago

BELOW: The Murciélago cleverly and respectfully integrated design themes from the Countach and Diablo into a contemporary style.

ABOVE: Ergonomics and interior quality vastly improved under Audi's ownership.

design was a masterstroke, setting a clear direction for future Lamborghinis while incorporating enough familiar themes to demonstrate Audi's respect for the brand. It also avoided many of the potential pitfalls encountered by other designers in terms of accommodating the engineering requirements such as cooling. It was neat and modern but also unmistakably a Lamborghini – and the underpinnings, too, were unimpeachably the work of Sant'Agata, including a new six-speed gearbox transmitting power from the latest 6.2-litre version of the Bizzarrini/Dallara V12 through to Lamborghini's own four-wheel-drive transmission. Road-testers criticized the brakes on early models, and the cramped footwell remained a bugbear, but in 2002 alone 424 Murciélagos left the factory – well over a hundred more sales than the Diablo had accomplished annually.

Fast-tracking the new entry-level model to production entailed some compromises. In early 2000, Audi invited styling proposals from Donckerwolke's new in-house studio as well as Italdesign, Bertone and IDEA. To enable Lamborghini

Centro Stile to focus on the Murciélago, management selected Italdesign's pitch, essentially an updated version of the 1995 Calà show car. Its winning touch was that this concept had been a runner, with a spaceframe chassis and a Lamborghini-built V10 produced during the Chrysler era. Reduced in size and finessed by Donckerwolke to harmonize its look with the Murciélago, this would become the Gallardo – a mic drop to established competition including Ferrari's 360 and Porsche's venerable 911.

Audi declared the original V10 unsuitable, which left Lamborghini to design a new one based on the architecture of Audi's V8, mated to a new multivalve cylinder head created in partnership with Cosworth. Though early Gallardos attracted criticism for their standards of fit and finish, truculent 'e-gear' robotized manual gearbox and excessive clutch wear, there were compelling reasons for this: by the winter of 2002–03, just a few

BELOW: The Gallardo succeeded where the Urraco, Silhouette and Jalpa had failed, achieving record sales figures for the company.

months before deliveries were due to begin, the production line was still being installed, so many elements had to be outsourced. The aluminium spaceframes were fabricated in Germany by Krupp-Drauz and then painted at an Audi facility, the former NSU plant at Neckarsulm.

Despite its teething issues, the Gallardo was considered a threatening enough competitor for Ferrari to bring forward the launch of its 360 Modena replacement, the F430, by a whole 18 months. The F430 was 70kg (154lb) lighter than the Gallardo, chiefly by doing without all-wheel drive, and boasted a power output just 10bhp shy of the Lamborghini's 493bhp. The 360 Modena had made do with 394bhp.

As road-testers began to compare the Gallardo unfavourably with the more agile and responsive F430, Lamborghini hit back with revisions for the 2006 model year, plus a Superleggera model 100kg (220lb) lighter, before launching a second-generation model in 2008. Mildly facelifted, lightened and now featuring an all-new 5.2-litre V10, the latest Gallardo also incorporated Lamborghini's new designation format in its name – LP560-4, shorthand for the location and alignment of the engine, metric horsepower output and number of driven wheels. Spyder models broadened the car's appeal and, when the final Gallardo was built in November 2013, the company marked the occasion with a special ceremony for management and staff. Over a decade in production, 14,022 Gallardos had been built and sold, making this Lamborghini's most successful model until the Urus overtook it.

The Murciélago also kept Ferrari honest throughout its life. A Roadster model joined the line-up in 2004 and Lamborghini kept the refreshes coming – a necessary strategy, as the performance war with Maranello kicked off by the Gallardo meant theoretically lesser machinery began to hustle in its wheeltracks. A 2006 refresh included a 6.5-litre evolution of the V12, now peaking at 631bhp, but the limitations of the old-fashioned chassis construction were beginning to show.

"*The Murciélago undisputedly still remains relevant,*" said *Car* magazine's road test of the new LP640, "*or as relevant as a 212mph 1.7-tonne two-seat lorry can be.*"

Audi's response was two-pronged. For the long term it greenlit development of a successor model to be based around a composite structure rather than a steel spaceframe. It also signed off on the limited-edition Reventón, essentially a reskinned Murciélago with a mildly tweaked engine and composite body panels. The jet fighter-style design touches were as eye-grabbing as the colour, a grey which was both matt-finish and subtly metallic.

Anyone who thought this super-rarefied model, of which only 20 would be built, was a ridiculous fashion accessory for the super-rich was only half right. Megaprofits lay not in devaluing a brand by splashing its badge across humbler models, but by adopting a couture-style approach. The parallel business model that Lamborghini was about to adopt was hinted at in the VW Group's 2007 annual report:

"The idea behind this strictly limited edition of 20 vehicles was to create a model that would crown the success of the brand, that will serve as a four-wheeled ambassador for the uniqueness of Lamborghini – and that will also demonstrate the short development times of which the sports car manufacturer is now capable."

The world might have been in recession again in 2009 when Lamborghini unveiled the €1.1million Reventón Roadster at the Frankfurt show, but 12 of the 15 examples had already been sold to 'friends and collectors'. The company would return to this lucrative watering hole again and again over the coming decade and a half, spinning out bespoke one-offs and limited editions for high net worth individuals.

BELOW: The Reventón signalled Lamborghini's move to develop high-profit, limited-edition supercars based on existing models.

ABOVE: Everything about the Aventador was new, from its composite chassis to an engine which shared only its swept volume with the classic Bizzarrini V12.

The post-2008 global financial crisis did impinge on the buying habits of those slightly further down the income scale as Murciélago sales diminished towards the end of its life, although many buyers might simply have been waiting on its successor. Though just half of the planned 350 units were built and sold of the run-off LP670-4 SV model, during its nine-year lifetime 4,099 Murciélagos were made – over 1,000 more than the Diablo had achieved in 11 years.

To keep pace with competition, which now included F1 constructor McLaren, Lamborghini had to embrace a new construction format in the Aventador, launched in 2011 and named after a fighting bull which met its maker in a celebrated bout in 1993. Chasing the future also meant bidding farewell to a cherished element of the company's history, the Bizzarrini/Dallara V12. The new-generation V12 remained at 6.5 litres but was revvier and had more torque, thanks to wider bore dimensions and a shorter stroke. Peak power of 691bhp (a gain from its predecessor's 632) came higher up the rev range than before, amplifying the inherent aggression in the engine's character. A new seven-speed automated manual gearbox boasted shift times of just 50 milliseconds while weighing less than Volkswagen's 'seamless shift' twin-clutch DSG.

Filippo Perini, Donckerwolke's successor at Centro Stile, was responsible for styling that once again deliberately invoked the look and function of fighter jets. Beneath the extrovert bodywork lay a composite monocoque chassis with aluminium carriers for the suspension and engine, the better to ensure cost-effective repairability after minor accidents. Relocating the radiators to the sides of the car enabled Perini to integrate the aircraft-style air scoops into the flanks rather than having boxy projections at shoulder level. All in all the Aventador weighed

BELOW: Just as the exterior of contemporary Lamborghinis have taken inspiration from fighter jets, so too has the interior design.

ABOVE: To mark the company's 50th anniversary Lamborghini crossed an Aventador with a Le Mans-style race car. Just three were built, for sale at $4million.

OPPOSITE: Another 50th anniversary special was the jet-fighter-inspired Egoista, a one-off built (supposedly from anti-radar materials) to accommodate just one person.

90kg (198lb) less than the Murciélago. The Roadster model launched in 2013 incurred a 50kg (110lb) weight gain as a result of the additional bracing required, though this was less of an inconvenience than the dilemma of where to stow the carbonfibre roof panels – once inside the car, they took up all the luggage space.

"*What do we do with our luggage*," an American journalist asked CEO Stephan Winkelmann at the Aventador Roadster's launch. "*Send it by FedEx?*"

Winkelmann was able to brush off the question, safe in the knowledge that the 2000th Aventador had already left the production line. Lamborghini had only ever sold 2,042 Countachs. A mid-life refresh by new chief designer Mitja Borkert, along with continuous engineering revisions and a power boost to 730bhp, meant the Aventador retained its place among the state-of-the-art until it bowed out in 2022, by which time 3,196 Roadsters and 11,819 coupés had been delivered.

ABOVE: Replacing the Gallardo, the Huracán developed the stealth aircraft styling theme while featuring more synergies with high-end Audi products.

The Aventador also provided a handy donor vehicle for Lamborghini's side hustle of building super-limited editions such as the Centenario and Veneno, leading onto the bespoke tailoring service which produced the SC20 – a one-off which Borkert styled to a customer's order. Likewise the Gallardo donated running gear to rarities such as the Egoista show car (built to celebrate the company's 50th anniversary) and the carbonfibre showcase that was the $6.5million Sesto Elemento (believed to have sold no more than 10 of the planned 20).

In following up the Gallardo with the Huracán, Lamborghini collaborated with Audi engineers to develop the MSS (Modular

Sportscar System) platform which would underpin the next-generation R8, among others. Its spaceframe structure is part-steel, part composite, with panels made using Lamborghini's patented resin-transfer process. Despite Sant'Agata's involvement, Audi's R&D chief Dr Ulrich Hackenberg was a highly unwelcome presence at the Huracán launch, where he repeatedly sought to remind the audience how much Audi DNA was present in the car. Nevertheless the Huracán took just five years to reach the sales figures the Gallardo achieved in ten.

Enthusiasts cavil, but SUVs are now a vital element of any car manufacturer's model portfolio. In 2012 Lamborghini displayed

OVERLEAF: It took the flamboyant Huracán just five years to equal its predecessor's sales figures.

BELOW: The limited-edition off-road Huracán Sterrato attracted rave reviews and sold out so quickly that the production run was increased from 900 to 1499.

OPPOSITE: While many car enthusiasts profess to loathe SUVs, they are an essential part of any manufacturer's range. The Urus is Lamborghini's best-selling model ever.

the prototype Urus at the Beijing show. Supposedly powered by the Gallardo V10, the concept car was in fact a non-runner – and the final production vehicle was the result of a judicious raid on the VW parts bin by Maurizio Reggiani and his team. Tweaked only slightly by Borkert from Perini's original look, the Urus launched in December 2017 sat on the same VW MLB-evo platform as the Porsche Cayenne, VW Touraeg, Audi Q8 and Bentley Bentayga. In the engine bay sat a 4-litre twin-turbo Audi V8 reworked to produce 640bhp. Polarizing it may be, but the Urus sold over 15,000 units in its first four years.

In 2022, despite war in Ukraine and a chilly global economic climate, Lamborghini delivered 9,233 cars – six times the figure of a target once considered out of reach. But it now faced the same difficult choices as rival high-performance car builders: how to stay relevant as the world's supply of fossil fuels dwindled.

Electric Dreams

Facing the Future

> "A Lamborghini super-sports car is driven maybe
> 3,000 miles a year, not every day, so electrification
> has to offer an added intensity to justify its inclusion."

The inevitability that declining fossil fuel resources will make oil more expensive – and conspicuous consumption of it more problematic – is a challenge for the entire automotive industry and a bitterly divisive issue for its customers. An existential threat, too, for brands such as Lamborghini which are predicated upon an intoxicating combination of performance and spectacle. In this market space, noise is a powerful element of the desirability factor – or at least it has been until recently. And the customer base for big-beast V10 and V12 sports cars is not one for whom the cost of a tank of fuel is an issue (indeed, many hail from those parts of the world where black gold is still pumped from beneath the ground in large quantities).

OPPOSITE: Lamborghini showed the hybrid-boosted 900bhp Asterion in 2014 but abandoned production in favour of the Urus.

ELECTRIC DREAMS

ABOVE: All-electric and powered by supercapacitors rather than lithium ion batteries, the Terzo Millennio was theoretically capable of 186mph (299km/h).

All the more reason for Lamborghini to take small steps at first. The world got a first look at what a hybrid-powered Lamborghini might look like at the 2014 Paris motor show. It left largely unimpressed. Based on an Aventador monocoque, the Asterion had a two-door composite bodyshell and was powered by a Huracán-derived V10 augmented by three brushless electric motors. Though theoretical peak power was 898bhp, CO_2 emissions were nearly a quarter of the Aventador and Lamborghini described the Asterion as "*conceived more for comfortable luxury daily cruising than for ultimate track performance.*"

This sounds more like the preserve of the Urraco and sundry other vintage Lamborghinis which failed to find an audience, which may explain what happened next. CEO Stephan Winkelmann admitted that the lukewarm customer reaction prompted him to drop plans to put the Asterion into production and shift the budget towards the Urus instead.

> *"They told us that they were open to innovation, including hybrid technology, but only if it came with the benefit of added performance,"* he said.
>
> *"A Lamborghini super-sports car is driven maybe 3,000 miles a year, not every day, so electrification has to offer an added intensity to justify its inclusion."*

This was not quite a slamming of the door on electrified Lamborghinis, but it was obvious that Winkelmann and the board were struggling to see a future which did not involve V12s. Market shifts, along with governments worldwide taking an increasingly hostile position on the internal combustion engine, would force the company's hand. In particular, Elon Musk's electric-car challenger brand Tesla began to rake in sales among wealthier customers who liked to signal they were forward-thinking.

Lamborghini joined the rush of manufacturers showing EV hypercar concepts in 2017. The Terzo Millennio – 'third millennium' – fulfilled the company's long tradition of majoring on the wow factor. Its ostentatious shell, Mitja Borkert's first clean-sheet design since slipping his feet under the desk at Centro Stile, was just part of the drama. Underneath it used supercapacitors rather than traditional lithium ion batteries to power four electric motors which could, theoretically, propel the Terzo Millennio to 186mph (299km/h). Developed in conjunction with the Massachusetts Institute of Technology and publicly unveiled there, the car was the first product of an ongoing partnership researching future technologies such as self-healing body panels and the integration of the electrical power transfer into the structure of the car.

Supercapacitor technology also underpinned Lamborghini's next electrification project, the company's most powerful road car ever until that point. Based on Aventador SVJ donor elements, the Sián FKP37 (named after a Bolognese dialect word for a lightning bolt, together with Ferdinand Piéch's initials and

ABOVE: Dramatic as the Sián was, it was essentially an Aventador SVJ with a hybrid kick.

date of birth) could accelerate from 0 to 62mph in 2.8 seconds. And it was popular – every one of the 63 examples of this $3.3million speed machine was sold before the public unveiling at Frankfurt in 2019.

Many industry figures derided the Sián FKP37 as possibly Lamborghini's most cynical high-margin limited edition yet, so much did it have in common with the donor car. But Lamborghini was about to be yet more provocative, announcing a hybridized reboot of the Countach (just three years after Winkelmann had announced "*retro design is not what we are here for*"). Also based on the Aventador platform and running a Sián-based 800bhp four-wheel-drive powertrain, it was announced as a 112-car limited edition – a figure based on the original's

conceptual designation 'Project 112' – during Monterey Car Week in August 2021. Priced at $2.5million, substantially more for those who failed to exercise self-control while perusing the options list, the Countach LPI 800-4 also sold out before its launch – despite *Road & Track* magazine branding it "*a cynical cash grab aimed at ultra-wealthy collectors*".

Rather more of a hit with media and the customer base, the Revuelto – launched in 2023 as the Aventador replacement – signalled an end to Lamborghini's apparent policy of stamping its hooves in the face of electrification. The new-generation L545 V12 remains on the large side (6.5 litres) but weighs 17kg (37lb) more than that which propelled the Aventador. Three electric motors, two of which propel the front wheels

BELOW: The Revuelto features detailed lightweighting and a hybrid powertrain and is essentially Lamborghini's first 'proper' mainstream electrified vehicle.

(helping to save weight by eliminating 4WD running gear) are responsible for 187 of the total claimed 814bhp and help push the car from rest to 62mph in 2.5 seconds. While each motor is capable of providing 148bhp, in practice this is constrained by the use of small battery packs to save some weight.

Lamborghini's first all-electric vehicle is also on the horizon. Due in 2028, the Lanzador will be a 2+2 coupé presented in

modish SUV proportions, powered by two electric motors outputting the equivalent of 1,340bhp. A concept version presented in 2023 featured an off-the-shelf electric powertrain for dynamic photography purposes only; at the time of writing Lamborghini has not ruled out incorporating some form of augmented engine noise. It will not, however, offer a synthesis of the original V12. That one will have to live on in the memory only.

OVERLEAF: With the Revuelto, Lamborghini has faced up to electrification without compromising on drama.

Lamborghini at the Races

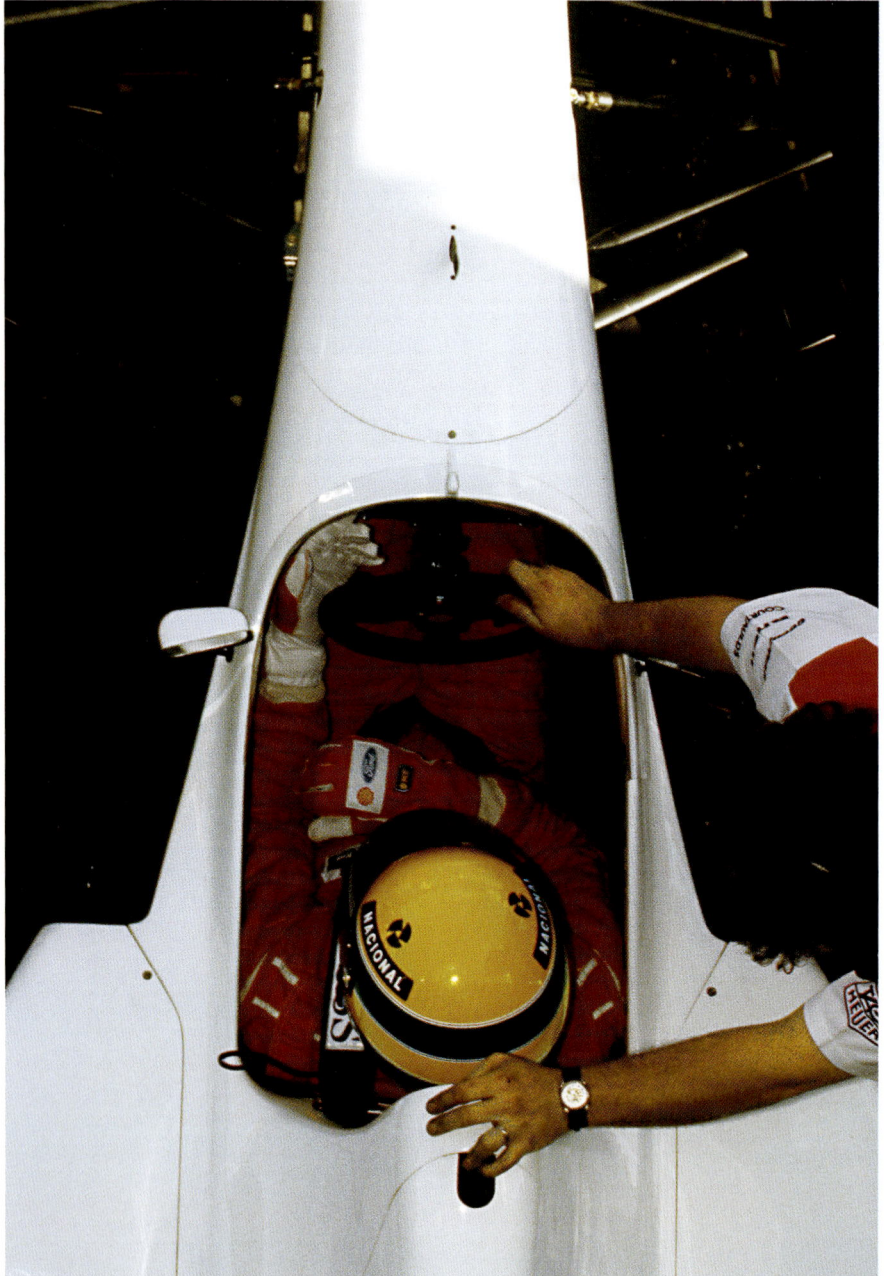

The Bull Enters the Ring

> "The fastest way to make a small fortune in motor racing is to start off with a large one."

Before the mobile phone there was the car phone, a piece of kit so costly to install and run in its heyday that it unequivocally signalled the owner as a person of means – a person of *business*. So, naturally, McLaren Formula 1 team boss Ron Dennis, a man whose entrepreneurial drive, punctilious attention to detail and sheer energy for breaking boundaries had done so much to establish F1 as the cutting edge of motorsport technology, had one of these executive tools close at hand in his chauffeur-driven limo.

On 23 September 1993 it buzzed with a call of singular importance. "*Ron, hi, it's Ayrton,*" said the voice at the other end of the line. The unmistakable Brazilian-accented timbre rendered the introduction superfluous. Of course it was Ayrton Senna, three-time world champion, arguably the greatest racing driver alive. And Ayrton had something to say: he was very, very excited by the Lamborghini-engined McLaren F1 car he had just tested.

OPPOSITE: Ayrton Senna tested a McLaren F1 car adapted to house Lamborghini's V12 – but the partnership never came to fruition.

McLaren and Lamborghini are one of Formula 1's great 'woulda couldas shoulda' and yet this test – indeed Lambo's entire foray into F1 – are now footnotes to history. It would never have happened in Ferruccio Lamborghini's day; one of the many traits which separated him from Enzo Ferrari was that while he was a keen driver (if not, according to those close to him, as skilled as he believed himself to be), he had little passion for or appetite to become involved in motorsport. This firm red line in his thinking was one of the factors which influenced the departure of Giampaolo Dallara and curtailed Lamborghini's relationship with Giotto Bizzarrini. A few miles away in Maranello, Enzo's company had always been racing first, road cars second – selling cars was just a means of funding the racing.

Ferruccio's coolness towards motorsport did not stop third parties – including some of his own staff – attempting to fettle his cars for racing purposes. After stepping up to the technical director role, Paolo Stanzani quietly allowed Bob Wallace to modify a standard Miura P400 by drilling out sections of the monocoque, replacing other steel elements of the chassis and bodywork for lightweight materials, redesigning the fuel system, adding race-spec suspension components and fettling the engine to deliver more power. Skirts and spoilers aimed to cure the Miura's chronic problem of aerodynamic lift generated by the bonnet profile. The resulting car – christened the Jota – remained the most powerful Miura built, its 440bhp output eclipsing even the later SV model.

However, it remained a one-off, apart from later conversions commissioned by customers; the original was crashed by an overenthusiastic driver, caught fire, and was damaged beyond repair. Though the Jota would likely have been competitive in sportscar racing, then a more lucrative arena than F1 in terms of prize money, the rules were in seemingly constant flux. Appendix J of the FIA regulations (popularly believed to have inspired the model's name) required manufacturers to build a minimum number – in the case of the grand touring class, 500, which was not a given in 1970. By the time production ceased in 1973, only 764 Miuras are believed to have been built.

Motorsport remained off-menu as Lamborghini's initial cycle of post-Ferruccio owners struggled to keep the marque afloat. In the mid-1980s David Jolliffe, a keen amateur racer and managing director of Lamborghini's UK importer, wanted to prepare a Countach LP5000S for competition in the Group B sportscar racing category but was thwarted by the minimum-build regulations. Merely inconvenienced by this obstacle, he set his sights on the more rarefied Group C and the world championship. Gordon Spice's eponymous engineering company created a bespoke chassis for what would become the Countach QVX – which looked nothing like the road car, though it was powered by a factory-modified version of its V12. North Yorkshire-based team CC Racing Developments, who had run Spice and Belgian privateer Teddy Pilette to victory in the 1978

BELOW: While the original Miura Jota was destroyed, the factory converted a handful of SV models to Jota spec – including this one for German Lamborghini importer Hubert Hahne.

ABOVE: Japanese racer Aguri Suzuki scored a career-best third place in his home grand prix in 1990. It would also be the best finish for a Lamborghini-powered car.

Spa 24 Hours, were tasked with race preparation, and sometime F1 drivers Mauro Baldi and Tiff Needell (who brought Unipart sponsorship) were engaged to drive. But money was always tight and the project fizzled out in early 1987 after contesting just one significant international event.

While this privateer sportscar programme evaporated, US car giant Chrysler was completing due diligence on its $25-million acquisition of Lamborghini, having already swallowed the American Motors Corporation. Executives, including design chief Tom Gale and head of global product development Bob Lutz, then set themselves the task of heading off Chrysler boss Lee Iacocca's plans to use the Lamborghini brand as a means of sprinkling gold dust on humdrum family cars.

Further impetus for the executive floor's programme of

'malicious obedience' to Iacocca came from François Castaing, the French engineer who had arrived at Chrysler via the AMC deal. Earlier in his career Castaing had been the architect of Renault's V6 turbo-powered Formula 1 entry and now he championed the cause of deploying Lamborghini's engineering potential as well as the value of the badge.

There would never be enough money in Castaing's engineering budget to support a Ferrari-style vertically integrated Formula 1 team, but he was able to divert funds towards an engine programme, with Lutz greasing the mechanism by selling Iacocca on it as a brand-bolstering exercise that would have particular value in Chrysler's planned return to Europe. The timing was right, since motorsport's governing body had signalled a direction of travel away from the turbo engines which

ABOVE: In 1991 Lamborghini unwittingly ended up as a Formula 1 entrant when a key sponsor ran off with the money

held sway in the 1980s, progressively limiting their potential via boost and fuel limits ahead of an outright ban in 1989.

The personnel were available too, since long-time Ferrari technical director Mauro Forghieri had quit after being sidelined in favour of the British engineer Harvey Postlethwaite. Working in a new company named Lamborghini Engineering, run by ex-Ferrari team manager Daniele Audetto, Forghieri set about creating an 80-degree, naturally aspirated 3.5-litre V12 with which to take on the nemesis from Maranello.

Limited financial resources hampered the F1 project at every step. The first iteration of the LE3512 engine was overweight and not reliable enough in comparison with competitors. Its deliberately low-key introduction in 1989 – an alliance with the midfield team run by ex-F1 driver Gerard Larrousse – netted little in the way of actual results. The Lola-designed chassis was only adequate, a description which also aptly suited the drivers: Philippe Alliot in one car and a rotating cast in the other.

1989 ended with just one points finish in the bag. Lamborghini's official history naturally blames Larrousse: "*The fault for these poor results lay above all with the French team, which did not have the money and organization required to compete at the highest levels.*" This rather overlooks the engine's tendency to blow up, as in the British Grand Prix, when Eric Bernard was running fifth before an almighty belch of smoke signalled that he would be returning to the pits on foot.

Despite the addition of the once-mighty Lotus team to the list of Lamborghini's F1 clients in 1990, the engine's best result came via Larrousse. Aguri Suzuki benefited from disarray at the head of the field to finish on the podium in front of his home crowd at Suzuka.

Forghieri had also been designing a Formula 1 car to accommodate the engine – not with money from Chrysler itself but on a promise from the Mexican GLAS (Gonzalez Luna Associates) consortium fronted by self-styled entrepreneur Fernando Gonzalez Luna. This entity raised a reputed $20 million from sponsors before Gonzalez Luna disappeared into the ether – along with the money – in the summer of 1990.

Thus Lamborghini faced a problem. Canning the project after a substantial sum had been spent would invite difficult questions from the US parent company. Proceeding was virtually out of the question, too, since Iacocca would never sanction the required investment. Keeping it in the wider family was an appropriately Italian solution: the financier and industrialist Carlo Petrucco was persuaded to open his wallet. And so, in 1991, the hitherto unheard-of Modena Team Lamborghini arrived on the Formula 1 entry list with a pair of metallic blue cars badged as Lamborghini 291s.

This was not an automatic ticket onto the grid, since the barriers to entry were not so high as they are in the twenty-first century. In 1991, the heady days before yet another global

OVERLEAF: Lamborghini's factory-supported team fizzled out through lack of investment. By the closing races of 1991 they were struggling to qualify for races – here Nicola Larini was five seconds slower than the pole position time for the Portuguese GP.

BELOW: Although the Lamborghini V12 was longer and heavier than Ford's V8, Senna lapped faster with it and was impressed.

recession, F1 was oversubscribed and the newcomers and also-rans faced a brutal knock-out prequalifying session at an unsociably early hour on the Friday of each grand prix weekend. Like most low-budget F1 cars of the era, the 291 was some way short of the cutting edge and it survived prequalifying only occasionally. Nicola Larini got through and finished seventh at Phoenix, just one position short of the points; more frustrating still was when teammate Eric van de Poele was running fifth in the wet at Imola when his fuel pump broke in the closing laps.

"*What can I do?*" he asked his race engineer over the radio.

"*All you can do, Eric, is cry*," came the response.

With no further financial support from Lamborghini in prospect, and in the absence of sufficient results to tempt sponsors, Modena Team faded from the scene and ceased operations at the end of the season. While the company's official history, naturally, blames Chrysler for this failure, what it does not report is that the parent company *did* take a greater interest

ABOVE: McLaren put a lot of effort into creating a 'mule car' to test the V12, but team boss Ron Dennis ultimately did a deal for Peugeot V10s.

in Lamborghini Engineering after this point, as Iacocca retired and handed over the reins to Bob Eaton. Forghieri was replaced by long-time company man (and Sports Car Club of America regional organizer) Michael Royce and, over the winter of 1992 into 1993, the V12 was significantly revised with input from US-based engineers and rebadged as the Chrysler-Lamborghini CL01.

It was this engine which so delighted Senna on that sunny autumn day in southern Portugal. To reach that point had taken three months of intensive work by McLaren and Lamborghini engineers to adapt an MP4/8 chassis to accommodate both the longer engine and the team's preference for in-house TAG Electronics control systems. But McLaren, left relying on second-string customer Ford V8s after Honda's withdrawal at the end of 1992, were desperate. The MP4/8 was one of the most competitive cars on the grid, good for grand prix wins in Senna's hands, even though down on power compared with rivals. Even in compromised form, hacked about with a longer, heavier engine shoehorned in, it lapped faster than when pushed

BELOW: With the Diablo SV-R, Lamborghini created a lucrative one-make race series for high net worth customers.

by Ford's V8 – though accounts vary as to by how much.

Senna filed a wish list of suggestions for improvements and it is claimed that Ron Dennis had gone as far as shaking hands with Lutz and Audetto at the Frankfurt motor show earlier in September… only to go cold on the putative alliance and sign up with Peugeot for 1994 instead. Some say the allure of receiving 'free' engines from a recent Le Mans 24 Hours winner trumped the option of having to pay for the Italian-built V12s; others say Dennis felt Chrysler and Lamborghini were not committed enough, a sense magnified by the fact that his test engines were not fresh but drawn from a pool already used by other F1 customers. A spectacular blow-up during a Silverstone

test, in which at least one connecting rod punched through the block, was the decider.

Perhaps Dennis's instincts were right: Lamborghini was already being hawked around for potential sale. The F1 programme would have been unlikely to survive the transition to new owners.

When MegaTech took over and installed ex-Lotus and GM man Mike Kimberley as president and managing director, one of Kimberley's initiatives was to spice up Lamborghini's sporting appeal at relatively low cost by reviving the SuperVeloce (SV) badge last seen on the hottest Miuras and applying it to the Diablo. More powerful and shorn of its all-wheel drive system,

ABOVE: Lamborghinis have also featured in the annual all-star Race of Champions event.

OPPOSITE: The Super Trofeo one-make series now has regional championships all over the world, pairing professional drivers with wealthy amateurs.

this was an altogether rawer driving experience – and it begat a stripped-out version, the SV-R, with which Lamborghini launched its one-make racing series, the Supertrophy. Ferrari had already used this tactic to 'sex up' the image of their initially underwhelming 348 model and make a profit at the same time: offering wealthy clients a turn-key racing experience in identical machinery. For £160,000 per year the company would supply, store, maintain and transport the cars to various circuits (initially in Europe), and all the owner-drivers had to do was present themselves in the right place at the appropriate weekends. From small beginnings the concept has evolved into the globe-straddling Super Trofeo Lamborghini runs (now with Huracáns) which continue to this day.

But it was not until the turn of the century, after Audi took over stewardship of the brand, that Lamborghini made a concerted assault on inter-marque competition – and once again at arm's length, this time with Reiter Engineering, the German tuner which prepared cars for the Supertrophy. Again it was a

ABOVE: Lamborghini is now taking on Ferrari in the top category of sportscar racing with the SC63 'hypercar'.

case of building from a relatively small scale with a GT1-class version of the Diablo, then the Murciélago, which matured into a race winner.

The catalyst for Lamborghini getting properly involved in racing was Reiter's success with the Gallardo, after the creation of the less rarefied GT3 class in 2006. Closer to the road cars than GT1s, these were more accessible for non-professional racers and more affordable – and sold in their tens and hundreds. In 2013 Lamborghini established an in-house racing division, Squadra Corse, to develop and build future GT3-class cars rather than selling parts to third parties. Over the past decade the Huracán, in various evolution models, has become one of the dominant forces in international racing, with customer teams the world over enjoying close support from the factory.

Now, after much political push-and-pull behind the scenes and a couple of false starts, the Lamborghini name will grace the top level of international sportscar racing in the World Endurance Championship's new hypercar class. The SC63, launched at the 2023 Goodwood Festival of Speed, features a hybrid powertrain in which a 3.8-litre V8 internal combustion engine is augmented by a 50kW electric motor driving the rear wheels. A complex balancing mechanism devised by the organizers aims to equalize the playing field between different cars while encouraging individual engineering touches.

Most significantly, as Lamborghini enters its seventh decade, this is the first time one of the company's cars will meet its Ferrari equivalent at the pinnacle of sportscar racing.

On the Big Screen

Stunt Casting

"Will you be wanting the Batpod, Sir?"
"It's the middle of the day Alfred – not very subtle."
"The Lamborghini, then. Much more subtle."

Cars carrying the bull insignia have become a distinct element in popular culture's visual grammar, signifying a brazen unsubtlety that (usually) falls just short of outright obnoxiousness. To cast a Lamborghini is to consciously send a very different set of messages to the audience than casting a Ferrari.

Those wishing to explore the brand's history on the big screen should perhaps not begin their journey with the highly romanticized 2022 biopic *Lamborghini: The Man Behind The Legend*. Originally set to star Antonio Banderas and Alec Baldwin, it arrived after several years 'in turnaround' (to use Hollywood parlance) and featured Frank Grillo as Ferruccio Lamborghini and – very curiously – Irish actor Gabriel Byrne playing Enzo Ferrari in an incongruous hairpiece. Audience and critical reception were tepid at best.

OPPOSITE: An official biography of Ferruccio Lamborghini, written by his son, was recently made into a film starring Frank Grillo.

ABOVE: Grillo arrived at the Rome Film Festival in a Miura.

The Lamborghini brand was still a young one in 1969 when it made a huge impact – literally – on the general population in the seminal crime caper film *The Italian Job*. For many people this will have been the first sight-and-sound experience of the Miura, hustling and bellowing through the foothills of the snow-capped Colle de Gran San Bernardo with heist mastermind Roger Beckerman at the wheel, a cigarette jauntily hanging out of his mouth. The sequence lasts almost precisely three minutes, the V12 chatter fading in the mix as Matt Munro croons 'On Days Like These' while the credits roll… and then the Miura skids and crashes in a tunnel, to be pulled out by a bulldozer that has been waiting along with a mafia 'welcoming' committee. The burned wreckage is pushed off a cliff edge. Romance and roguery rolled into one exquisitely shot and tightly edited reel.

Not only did this capture the imagination of the cinema-going public, it begat many myths. Enzo Moruzzi, then a junior salesman and demo driver and latterly Lamborghini's head of sales, not only drove the Miura to the location, he was also at the controls for every shot except the in-car footage of actor Rossano Brazzi. Moruzzi's orders were simply to bring the car back undamaged, especially the white leather upholstery (Moruzzi sensibly had the seats swapped out for black equivalents, leaving only the head restraints white). For half a century the precise identity of the Miura used in filming was a mystery and the focus of intense speculation among marque aficionados. It was not destroyed. A second car, already wrecked – accounts differ as to how and where – was used for the post-crash sequence and, it is claimed, had already been removed when the crew went to recover it the next morning.

Since the 'running' Miura was to be delivered to its customer as new, Lamborghini had disconnected the odometer and, once back at Sant'Agata, it was carefully refinished and sent on to a dealer in Rome without a hint of its starring role. Only in 2019 did the company tally up its own records with the research of previous owners, confirming chassis 3568 – currently in the

BELOW: The Miura's brief appearance in *The Italian Job* has ensured it a place in popular culture.

OPPOSITE: While the Countach and its occupants are mere footnotes to the plot, it took centre-stage in the poster for *The Cannonball Run.*

hands of celebrated Liechtenstein car collector Fritz Kaiser – as the star of the film.

'Lesser' Lamborghinis have also appeared on screen as generic Italian exotica. Roger Moore, in his last film before donning James Bond's tuxedo, drove one of only five right-hand-drive Isleros in *The Man Who Haunted Himself*. But for the most part, films and TV series featuring milder Lambos have been relatively obscure themselves, such as 1971's TV film *Mooch Goes To Hollywood* (Islero, 400 GT 2+2), the animated series *Archer* (350 GT), and the peculiar potboiler *Bloodline* (Silhouette) – Audrey Hepburn's only R-rated film, described as "*the worst film of 1979*" by critic Roger Ebert.

It was in the early 1980s that Lamborghini became the go-to brand for on-screen excess, a ruder and less elegant counterpoint to Ferrari in an era characterized by libertarian ostentation. In *The Cannonball Run*, a film whose reliance on lazy gender and racial stereotyping renders it niche viewing in the twenty-first century, spandex-clad Adrienne Barbeau and Tara Buckman race across America in a Countach LP400S, flashing cleavage to distract traffic police. More recently Kanye West based the lyrical hook of his 2012 hit 'Mercy' around the Murciélago; detail-minded R&B fans continue to be vexed by the fact that the car in the video is actually a Gallardo (apparently the only model available on the day of shooting).

As films aspiring to blockbuster status grew bigger, noisier and more expensive, naturally the Murciélago and its relatives were deployed as visual shorthand: a Centenario LP770-4 appears as both a car and an autobot in *Transformers: The Last Knight*, Benedict Cumberbatch's egomaniac *Doctor Strange* drives a Huracán, and Murciélagos and an Aventador have given the custom machinery a run for its money in Christopher Nolan's *Dark Knight* trilogy. There is an amusing exchange in *The Dark Knight* in which butler Alfred asks if Bruce Wayne will be using

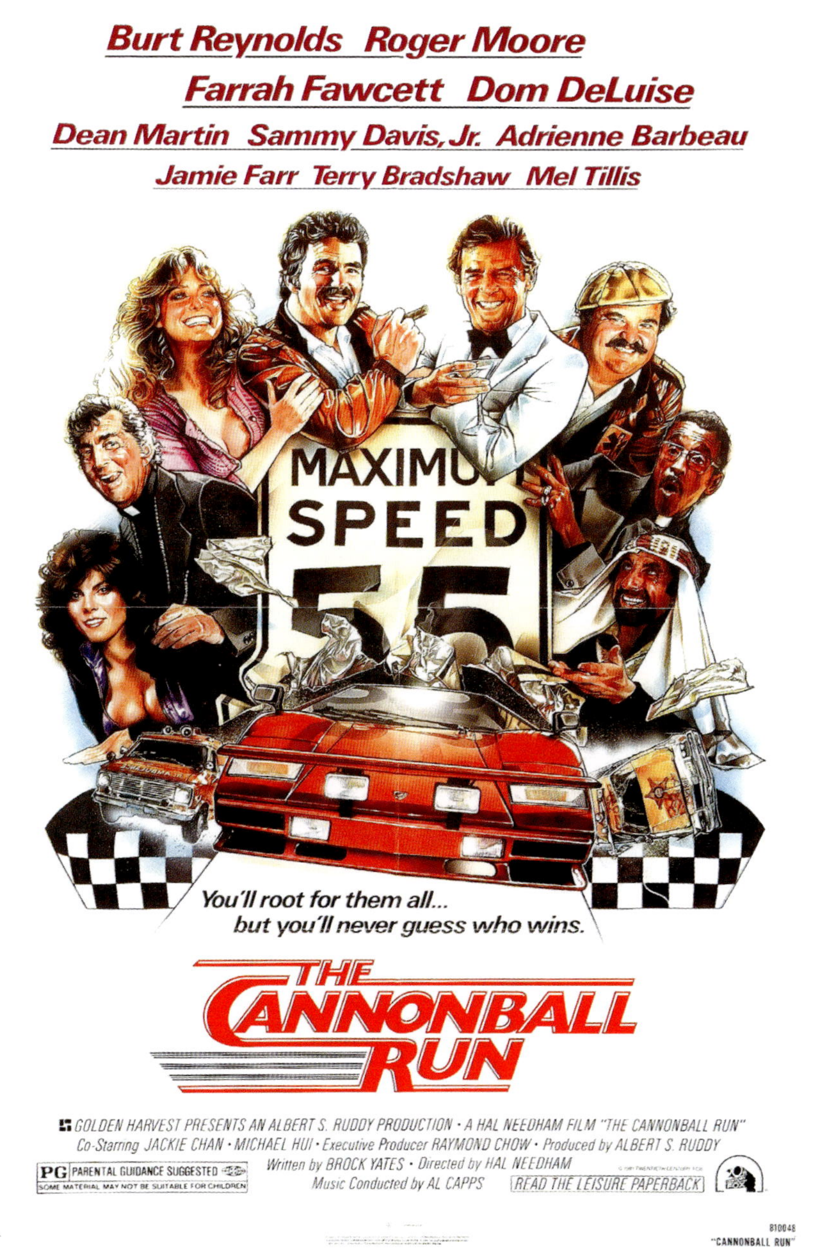

Burt Reynolds Roger Moore
Farrah Fawcett Dom DeLuise
Dean Martin Sammy Davis, Jr. Adrienne Barbeau
Jamie Farr Terry Bradshaw Mel Tillis
MAXIMUM
SPEED
55
You'll root for them all...
but you'll never guess who wins.
THE CANNONBALL RUN
GOLDEN HARVEST PRESENTS AN ALBERT S. RUDDY PRODUCTION • A HAL NEEDHAM FILM "THE CANNONBALL RUN"
Co-Starring JACKIE CHAN • MICHAEL HUI • Executive Producer RAYMOND CHOW • Produced by ALBERT S. RUDDY
PG PARENTAL GUIDANCE SUGGESTED
SOME MATERIAL MAY NOT BE SUITABLE FOR CHILDREN
Written by BROCK YATES • Directed by HAL NEEDHAM
Music Conducted by AL CAPPS
READ THE LEISURE PAPERBACK
810048
"CANNONBALL RUN"

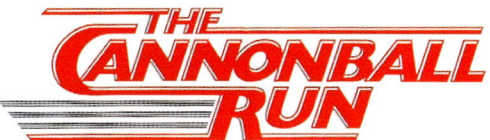

BELOW: Six Huracáns were used in filming *Doctor Strange*, and one was destroyed in the pivotal crash sequence.

ABOVE: One of only 40 Centenarios to be built stars as both car and autobot in *Transformers: The Last Knight*.

the Batpod for an urgent mission; when the response comes back negative he sighs, "*The Lamborghini then. Much more subtle.*"

Perhaps the ultimate alliance of the bull with absurd excess came in *The Wolf of Wall Street*, in which central character Jordan Belfort, the corrupt stockbroker played with gleeful relish by Leonardo Di Caprio, attempts to drive home from his country club in his Lamborghini Countach 25th Anniversary (white, naturally) after a quaalude binge. In his mind the journey unfolds without incident; a flashback sequence depicts the

violently chaotic reality. Cut to the car itself, wheels akimbo and no panel left straight.

Appropriately enough for Lamborghini, a fascinating myth developed around this sequence based on an anonymous trivia submission to the Internet Movie Database: director Martin Scorsese thought a substitute 'kit' car would look inauthentic… so he had the real Countach trashed. Would even this famously exacting film-maker order such a valuable asset to be virtually destroyed? Surely not.

BELOW: 'Lude conduct? Director Martin Scorsese had real 25th Anniversary Countach trashed while filming Jordan Belfort's quaalude binge in *The Wolf of Wall Street*.

In fact, it was. Two very rare US-spec Countachs were used in filming, one rented for second-unit purposes. The other was used for all the stunts and left with authentic damage after each impact. Then, deeming it not looking *quite* bent enough, Scorsese had a flatbed truck drive over it. It was the end of the road for that Countach, with just 11,300km (7,021 miles) on the clock. A decade after the film's release, it was offered for auction by Bonhams in a sale during the 2023 Abu

Dhabi Formula 1 Grand Prix weekend, with authenticating material and various merchandise including a director's chair and clapperboard signed by Scorsese. *"A time capsule of the era's elegant debauchery,"* claimed the catalogue. *"The very vehicle that had you contemplating quitting your day job for a Wall Street escapade!"*

Perhaps embodying the spirit of this age, the car was bid up to $1.35million but failed to meet its reserve of $1.5million.

INDEX

(Key: *italic* refers to photos/captions)

A

Abu Dhabi Grand Prix 154–5
Acosta 92
Aguri Suzuki *128*, 131
Alfa Romeo 14, 30, 40
Alfieri, Giulio 62–3, 73–4
Alliot, Philippe 130
American Motor Corporation (AMC) 77, 128–9
A1 autostrada 17, 52
Artese, Alessandro 73
Asterion *113*, 114–15
Athon 74
ATS 34
Audetto, Daniele 130, 136
Audi 87, 90–109, 138
Autocar 9
Automobiles René Bonnet, Djet 34
Aventador 100–4, *100*, *102*, 114, 116–18, *116*, *118*, 148

B

Balboni, Valentino 14, 73, 76, 84
Baldi, Mauro 128
bankruptcy 62, 70, *72*, 73
Baraldini, Franco 72
Barnard, John 73
Beckerman, Roger 146
Beijing Motor Show 108
Bentley 91, 92, 108
Berlinetta 14
Bernard, Eric 131
Bertone, *see* Gruppo Bertone
Bertone, Nuccio *34*, 35, 37, 52, 71
Bizzarrini, Giotto 17, 29–31, *82*, 94, 100, *100*, 126
BMW 40, 71, 72–3, 91
Bolivia 54
Borg & Beck 16
Borkert, Mitja 102, 104, 108, 115
Brazzi, Rossano 147
British Grand Prix 131
Brussels Motor Show 40, 76
Bugatti 91
bull logo 36, 79, 82
Byrne, Gabriel 145

C

Calà 87, *87*, 95
Car 97
Carrozzeria Coggiola 79
Carrozzeria Marazzi 23
Carrozzeria Materazzi 50
Carrozzeria Sargiotto 18
Carrozzeria Touring 18, 22–3, 35
Carrozzeria Zagato 92
Castaing, François 129
CC Racing Developments 127–9
Centenario 104, 148, *152*
Centro Stile 94, 101
Cheetah 72–3, *72*, 75
Chrysler 64, 73, 77–87, 92, 95, 128–9, 131, 134–5
Cizeta-Moroder 82
CL01 Chrysler/Lamborghini 135
Cosworth 95
Countach 50, 51–65, *52*, *54*, 70, 73–4, 76, 77, 79–84, *82*, *87*, *93*, 117, *148*
  Anniversary 64, *64*, 152–5, *154*
  QVX 127

D

Dallara, Giampaolo 17–19, 32–5, 37, 39, 44, *58*, 62–3, *63*, 94, 100, 126
De Tomaso 34, 41, 49
De Tomaso, Alejandro 73
Dennis, Ron 73, 125, *135*, 136–7
Deschamps, Marc 74
Detroit factory 79
Di Capua, Vittorio 87
Diablo *69*, 79–85, *87*, *79*, *82*, 87, *87*, *91*, 92–3, *93*, 100, *136*, 138, 141
Djody, Setiawan 85
Donckerwolke, Luc 92–5, 101

E

Eaton, Bob 135
Ebert, Roger 148
Egoista *102*, 104

Escobar, Pablo 77
Espada 14, 22, 24, 24, 50, 52, 62
European safety regulations 58, 70
EVs 112–22

F

Ferrari 9, 14, 16–19, 30–1, 34, 37, 49–50, 71, 95–6 129–30, 138, 140
Ferrari, Enzo 10, 13, 14, 34, 126, 145
FIA 126–7
Fiat 13, 71, 74, 87
50th anniversary 52, 102, 104
Ford 17, 34–5, 36, 41, 134, 135–6
Forghieri, Mauro 31, 130, 135
Formula 1 (F1) 29, 33, 41, 72, 73, 79, 100, 125–6, 125, 129–37, 130, 131, 155
Frankfurt Motor Show 79, 97, 116, 136
Fratelli Taddia 10

G

Gale, Tom 79, 128
Gallardo 95–6, 95, 104, 104, 105, 108, 141, 148
Gandini, Marcello 24, 35, 40–1, 51–2, 71, 74, 82, 85, 92
General Motors (GM) 87, 137
Geneva Motor Show 19, 36, 45, 52, 52, 73, 75, 85, 87
Giugiaro, Giorgetto 40, 72, 87
GLAS (Gonzalez Luna Associates) 131
Goodwood Festival of Speed 141
Gran Turismo 16
Grillo, Frank 145, 145, 146
Gruppo Bertone 40–1, 74, 94
Gulfstream Aerospace 84

H

Hackenberg, Dr Ulrich 105
Honda 32, 135
Hubert Hahne 127
Huracán 104–5, 104–5, 108, 114, 138, 141, 148, 150–1

I

Iacocca, Lido Anthony ('Lee') 77–9, 128–9, 131, 135
IDEA 94
Imola circuit 134
International Lead Zinc Research Organization 41
Islero 24, 24, 49, 148
ItalDesign 87, 87, 94–5

J

Jaguar 14
Jalpa 74–5, 75, 77, 79, 85–7, 92
Japanese Grand Prix 128, 131
Jarama 52
Jolliffe, David 127

K

K platform 77, 79
Kaiser, Fritz 148
Kimberley, Mike 87, 137
Krupp-Drauz 96

L

Lamborghini Engineering 130, 135
Lamborghini, Ferruccio 9, 10–13, 11, 12, 14–19, 14, 23–4, 29, 32–5, 37, 41, 49, 50, 52, 56, 126, 127, 145, 145
Lamborghini Polo Storico 41
Lamborghini: The Man Behind the Legend 145, 145, 146
Lamborghini, Tonino 145
Lamborghini Tractori SpA 13
Lancia 14, 52
Lanzador 119
Larini, Nicola 131, 134
Larrousse, Gerard 130–1
Le Mans 41, 91, 102, 136
Leimer, René 57–8, 62, 69–70
LE3512 engine 130
L545 117–18
LM001 75
LM002 ('Rambo Lambo') 76–7, 76
LMA002 76
Lotus 40, 87, 131, 137

INDEX 157

LP400 Countach
 57–8, *62*
LP400S Countach
 58, *60–1*, 62, *62*,
 63
LP500 Countach
 51–2, *52*, 56, 58
LP500S Countach
 63, 76
LP500S Countach
 127
LP560-4 96
LPI 800-4 Countach
 117
LP770-4 Centenario
 148
LP640 97
LP670-4 SV 100
Luna, Fernando
 Gonzalez 131
Lutz, Bob 128, 136

M

McLaren 73, 100,
 125–6, *125*, 135,
 135
malicious obedience
 79
Maranello 14, 30,
 96, 126, 130
Marazzi, Mario 24
Marmiroli, Luigi 63
Marzal show car
 22, 23
Maserati 14, 40, 49,
 62, 73
Megatech
 Corporation 79,
 85–7, 91, 137
Mercedes 14, 71
Mexico 131
Michelin XWX tyres
 58
Milan Technical
 Institute 17
Mille Miglia 13
Mimran, Patrick and
 Jean-Claude 75–7
Mini Dallara 32, 34
Miura 23–4, 28–45,
 49–51, 146–7,
 146, *147*
 Jota 126, *127*
 P400 34, 36–7,
 126
 P400S 40, 45
 P400SV *36*, *37*,
 44, 45, 126–7,
 127, 137
Mobility Technology
 International
 (MTI) 72
models of car *see
 under* Lamborghini
 models
Modena Team
 Lamborghini
 131–7, *131*
M1 72–3
Monterey Car
 Week 116
Moroder, Giorgio 82
Moruzzi, Enzo
 146–7
MP4/8 chassis 135
MSS (Modular
 Sportscar System)
 104–5
Murciélago *91*,
 93–102, *93*, 141,
 148
Musk, Elon 115

N

NACA *54*, 57
Navajo 79
Needell, Tiff 128
Nissan 92
Nolan, Christopher
 148
NSU 96
Nuova Automobili
 Ferruccio
 Lamborghini SpA
 75

P

Pagani, Horatio 64
Parenti, Massimo
 49, 53
Paris Motor Show
 114
Perini, Filippo 101,
 108
Petrucco, Carlo 131
Peugeot *135*, 136
Piëch, Ferdinand
 91–2, 116
Pilette, Teddy 127
Pininfarina 14
Pirelli P7 tyres 62, 72
Poele, Eric van de
 134
Polo Storico *52*
P140 85, 87
Porsche 50, *70*, 71,
 91, 95, 108
Porsche, Ferdinand
 91
Portuguese Grand
 Prix *131*, 135
Postlethwaite, Harvey
 130
Project 4 73
Project 112 45,
 50–1, 117
Putra, Hutomo
 Mandala
 ('Tommy') 85

Q

Quattrovalvole 63,
 65, 77

R

Race of Champions
 138
'Rambo Lambo', *see*
 LM002
Raptor 92

Reggiani, Maurizio 87, 108
R8 104–5
Renault 129
René Bonnet, *see* Automobiles René Bonnet
Reti, Zoltan 73
Reventón 97, *98–9*
Revuelto 117, *118*, *119*
Road & Track 117
Rome Film Festival *146*
Rosetti, Georges-Henri 56, 58, 62, 69–70
Royce, Michael 135

S

Sant'Agata factory 37, 44–5, 56, 79, 94, 105, 147
Saudi Arabia 76
Scaglietti 14
SC20 104
SC63 *140*, 141
'scissor' doors 52, *53*, *56*, 79
Scorsese, Martin 153–5, *154*
Scuderia Serenissima 19
Senna, Ayrton 125, *125*, *134*, 135–6
Sesto Elemento 104
Setright, L. J. K. 32, 36
Sgarzi, Ubaldo 14, 37, 45, 70
Sián, FKP37 116–17, *116*
Silhouette 62, 71, *71*, 73, 74, *75*, *95*, 148
Silverstone 137
Sinatra, Frank 44–5
Spa 24 Hours 128–9
Spice, Gordon 127
Sports Car Club of America 135
Squadra Corse 141
Stallone, Sylvester 77
Stanzani, Paolo 17–18, 35, 44, 49, 51, 53, 56, 58, 70, 92, 126
Stewart, James 10
Suharto, President 85
Sultan of Brunei 77
Super Trofeo 138–41, *138*
SuperVeloce (SV) 137
SUVs 105–8, *108*, 119
Suzuka circuit 131

T

TAG Electronics 135
Targa Florio 56
Terzo Millennio *114*, 115
Tesla 115
tractors *11*, 16
Turin Motor Show *9*, 17, *33*, 50, 71, 74
25th anniversary 64

U

Unipart 128
Urraco 50, 52–3, 58, 62, 70–2, *70*, *71*, 92, *95*, 114
Urraco volume model 24
Urus 108, *108*, 115
US safety/emission regulations 65, 70

V

Veneno 104
Verduyn, Kevin 79
Volkswagen (VW) 40, 87, 91–2, 97, 101, 108, 138–41

W

Wallace, Bob 14, 19, 32, 39, 44, 49, 53, 58, 70, 126
Weber 32
Winkelmann, Stephan 102, 114–15, 116
World Endurance Championship (WEC) 141
World Sportscar Championship (WSC) 72

Z

Zagato *22*
ZF Friedrichshafen 22

CREDITS

The publishers would like to thank the following sources for their kind permission to reproduce the pictures in this book:

ALAMY: Dave Adams 36, 37; Album 154-155; Ian Bottle 20-21; Mariusz Burcz 98-99, 109, 114, 118-119; Ivan Caravona 45; Joshua Claro 72; P Cox 102; culture-images GmbH 127; Grzegorz Czapski 101; Mark Fagelson 95; Goddard Archive 64-65, 108; Heritage Image Partnership Ltd 34, 38-39, 70, 84-85; John Heseltine 50; The History Collection 11; Imageplotter News and Sports 147; KL_Neo 106-107; Gennaro Leonardi 146; PictureLux/The Hollywood Archive 149; Sam Rollinson 152-153; TCD/Prod.DB 144, 150-151; WENN Rights Ltd 103; Tom Wood 18; Zuma Press 71

GETTY IMAGES: Simon Dawson/Bloomberg 112; Klemantaski Collection 30-31

MOTORSPORT IMAGES: 15, 25, 28, 53, 54, 55, 56-57, 62, 63, 68, 75, 76, 78T, 78B, 82, 83, 86, 87, 93, 138; Ercole Colombo 128-129; JEP 140; LAT Photographic 8; David Phipps 33; Jamey Price 139; Rainer Schlegelmilch 22-23, 130; Sutton 124, 132-133, 134, 135, 136-137

SHUTTERSTOCK: Lucille Cottin 41; FernandoV 24; Sergey Kohl 19, 48; Magic Car Pics 12; Jarlat Maletych 120-121; MarshyPhotography 80-81; Nolichuckyjake 35; Olycom Spa 16; Paul Pollock 60-61; Scott Sim 59; Jack Skeens 42-43; Sport car hub 4, 100, 104-105; Krivosheev Vitaly 116-117; Brandon Woyshnis 90, 94

Every effort has been made to acknowledge correctly and contact the source and/or copyright holder of each picture. Any unintentional errors or omissions will be corrected in future editions of this book.

THE STORY OF
Maserati

A TRIBUTE TO AUTOMOTIVE EXCELLENCE

STUART CODLING

Contents

HOUSE OF THE TRIDENT 6

MOVE TO MODENA 24

GRAND PRIX 42

WHEN LIFE GIVES YOU LE MANS 70

THE FRENCH CORRECTION 84

CHANGING HANDS 100

JOINING THE NEIGHBOURS 116

TO THE SECOND CENTURY 136

INDEX 156

CREDITS 160

House of the Trident

Seven Brothers

> An age-old maxim has it that you can choose your friends but you cannot choose your family. In over 100 years the Maserati company has passed through several different ownerships but it owes its stature, if not its continued existence, to the shared engineering passion of brothers for whom a delight in all things mechanical far outweighed any nagging sibling rivalries.

The first son born to Rodolfo Maserati and Carolina Losi arrived in 1881, a febrile time in Italian history. The country as we know it today was just 20 years old, following a consolidation of various states – some previously occupied by Austrian forces – into one kingdom ruled by Victor Emmanuel II. This energetic young nation was already making and breaking friendships with its neighbours as it eyed foreign expansion. Already it had captured more territory in further armed conflict with Austria, annexed the Papal States and ended the temporal power of the Holy See – and begun quarrelling with France, previously a key ally against the enemy to the north-east.

OPPOSITE: Isotta Fraschini entered Alfieri Maserati in the 1908 Grand Prix des Voiturettes in Dieppe.

OPPOSITE: Ernesto became the driving force of the Maserati company after Alfieri's untimely death.

Unification also drove the expansion of Italy's railways, a vitally important travel and communications network in this era before the invention of the motor car. Rodolfo worked on the railways – accounts differ as to whether he was a driver or a station master – and, shortly after his marriage to Carolina, moved from his native Piacenza to Voghera, an important junction between the Alessandria–Piacenza line and a recently completed line from Milan, the industrial and commercial engine of the north. His sons were captivated by the spectacle and noise of the mighty steam locomotives as they powered Italy towards its future.

Only six of the seven children born to Rodolfo and Carolina would live to adulthood. Carlo, the first, was joined by Bindo in 1883. Two years later a third son was supposedly to have been christened Alfiero, but a mistake on the registrar's part enshrined him in the records as Alfieri. This child lived a little over a year and the cause of his death remains unknown, such was the inexact nature of record-keeping at the time; when a fourth son came along, in September 1887, he was given the same name. Mario, the only son not to pursue a career in engineering, was born in 1890, followed by Ettore and Ernesto in 1894 and 1898.

Carlo was the ball of energy who gave his siblings leadership. As a pre-teen he began to build models of steam-powered cars. By the time Ernesto was born, Carlo was working in a bicycle factory – and had secured funding from a wealthy nobleman, the Marquis Carcano di Anzano del Parco, to develop and productionise a one-cylinder engine which could power a bicycle.

Between the births of the first and last of the Maserati brothers, Italy lurched into domestic ferment. Well-intentioned grain tariffs introduced to protect native farmers drove up food prices and provoked unrest, as did sundry political and

ABOVE: Alfieri Maserati at the wheel of a Diatto 4DC during the 1922 Italian Grand Prix weekend. Just three cars finished the arduous race on Monza's combined road course and oval.

financial corruption scandals and failures of the country's colonial ventures. Strikes and land occupations brought military intervention and, for a brief period, prime minister Francesco Crispi attempted to govern without parliament. In response, citizens gravitated towards Marxist demagogues. Railway workers were among those to form anarcho-syndicalist trade unions and agitate, often violently, for better pay and conditions.

Such were the conditions in which the brothers grew up. Despite Italy's delicate economic state, Carlo raced his bicycles successfully enough to catch the eye of his contemporary, Vincenzo Lancia, formerly a book-keeper for a bicycle importer but now making his name as a racing driver for Fiat, where he also worked as a tester. Like Carlo, Lancia was a self-taught engineer with a passion for speed. After three years working as a test driver with Lancia at Fiat's works in Turin, Carlo joined the Milanese luxury car manufacturer Isotta Fraschini as a mechanic and test driver, securing employment there for younger brother Alfieri too.

Carlo had a restless temperament and soon moved on to the car and motorbike manufacturer Bianchi, where he would have an opportunity to race, while Alfieri elected to stay at Isotta Fraschini. But as a racing driver Carlo was less successful than he had been on two wheels, finishing the 1907 Coppa Florio a distant ninth, 38 minutes behind the Isotta Fraschini of winner Ferdinando Minoia. Alfieri would enjoy a better result as a riding mechanic in the following year's event, partnering Vincenzo Trucco to second place. Shortly afterwards Carlo joined the recently merged Junior Automobiles/OTAV as general director and, while the company was on a downward trajectory, ceasing production by 1910, Carlo recruited brothers Bindo and Ettore and the three of them successfully designed a small aircraft.

Tragedy struck in 1910 as Carlo, having left to set up his own engineering consultancy with 15-year-old Ettore, succumbed to tuberculosis, the highly infectious lung condition which was the scourge of the urban working class. He was just 29 years old.

The brothers had lost their north star but, in Carlo's absence, Alfieri became the alpha male of the siblings. In common with his big brother he had an extrovert nature and a penchant for motor racing, though he was less impulsive. In staying at Isotta Fraschini while Carlo jumped from one employ to another, Alfieri had picked up a broader base of skills, becoming Cesare Isotta's mechanic and test driver, then assisting in sales and marketing as well as participating in the company's racing activities. In moving up the ranks – to the extent that he was trusted with overseas sales missions which took him as far as the Americas – Alfieri developed an understanding of the complete business.

Returning to Italy in 1913, Alfieri was tasked with opening a new sales and service centre in Bologna. While there an idea took root: opening his own business in partnership with his brothers. In December the following year they made it happen. While Bindo elected to remain with Isotta Fraschini, Ernesto and Ettore joined Alfieri in opening a garage on the Via de Pepoli, a tiny alley off the Piazza Santo Stefano. Paperwork lodged with the local chamber of commerce enshrined this enterprise as the *Società Anonima Officine Alfieri Maserati*, describing the purpose of the business as "the repair of cars".

Within months of opening up, the brothers had to put the business on pause, as Italy became embroiled in what would be known (until the next pan-European conflict) as The Great War. Ernesto was the last to be called up – in 1916, when he turned 18. But while the war destroyed a whole generation of young people across Europe, Alfieri, Ettore and Ernesto escaped unscathed – indeed, Alfieri and Ettore's mechanical skills ensured they never saw action on the front line.

Alfieri was dispatched to Milan, where the Nagliati company built Hispano-Suiza 8Aa aircraft engines under licence. As a side enterprise after his military service he developed a new type of spark plug with more durable mica-based insulation, which he patented and went into business manufacturing in partnership with his old Isotta Fraschini colleague, Vincenzo Trucco. Ettore worked for Franco Tosi Meccanica, a diesel engine manufacturer which had been turned over to aircraft engine production for the war.

As well as destruction, armed conflict also acts as a spur to innovation. Come peacetime, the brothers were eager to exploit new business opportunities and soon moved out of the cramped Via de Pepoli garage, relocating to a former glass-blowing factory outside Bologna on the old Roman road connecting Milan with Rimini. Within months of taking out the lease in April 1919, Alfieri had consolidated the spark plug manufacturing operation into the new facility and moved his (now retired) parents into an apartment upstairs.

Still it would be some time before the Maserati brothers graduated from fixing and tuning cars to building them. The slow-burn journey arguably began with Alfieri's decision to return to racing in the spring of 1920 with a second-hand 3-litre car built before the war by SCAT, a company later absorbed into Fiat. Among his rivals was a young Enzo Ferrari. The car was not competitive enough for Alfieri's liking and, after a disappointing and brief dalliance with a second-hand Nesselsdorf, he built his own 'Tipo Speciale' based on an

BELOW: Alfieri Maserati and riding mechanic Guerino Bertocchi claimed the company's first class victory, eighth overall, in the 1926 Targa Florio road race.

ABOVE: Celebrated racer Achille Varzi (centre) joined Alfieri Maserati (third from left) from Alfa Romeo, winning the Coppa Acerbo.

Isotta Fraschini chassis with an Hispano-Suiza engine and the SCAT's gearbox.

Although the Tipo Speciale was fast enough for Alfieri and Ernesto (acting as riding mechanic) to win the Susa-Moncenisio hillclimb, in road races it was still outgunned and for the 1922 racing season the Maseratis acquired an Isotta Fraschini which they extensively modified in-house. Further wins attracted the attention of Turin's Autocostruzioni Diatto, the second-biggest car manufacturer in Italy, who offered Alfieri and Ernesto positions as engineering consultants as well as the opportunity to race.

While the deal was irresistible it was also short-lived, and an object lesson in the perils of post-war Italy's seesawing economy. The 4.5-litre Diatto 20S was often beaten by smaller, lighter rivals and Alfieri was rewarded for reverting to his Tipo Speciale with a third consecutive victory at Susa-Moncenisio in 1923. The following season he was handed a five-year ban from racing after it was discovered that his car for a hillclimb in Spain, entered as a 2-litre, had undergone an engine swap to a 3-litre the night before the event. Diatto's official history claims the company was innocent and Alfieri was the culprit, while Maserati chronicles say the opposite; whatever the truth of the matter, the ban was rescinded after a year and Diatto continued to employ the brothers.

When motor racing's governing body announced a manufacturers' world championship for grands prix in 1925, Diatto wanted to get involved – and commissioned the Maseratis to develop and build a new supercharged 2-litre, 8-cylinder engine. Development work dragged on, stymied by the death of illustrious test driver Onesimo Marchiso in an accident, and the car was only ready for the final race of the season at Monza in September. It broke down after 39 of the 80 laps with Emilio Materassi at the wheel. It became clear the company's ambition exceeded their finances – they blamed the government for being slow to pay monies owed from wartime – and Diatto grudgingly withdrew from motor racing.

Such was the Maserati brothers' reputation on the domestic and international racing scene by this point that one of Diatto's customers, the Marquis Diego de Sterlich Aliprandi, an Abruzzo aristocrat with a huge personal fortune, offered to buy the company's remaining racing inventory and transfer it to the Maseratis. The Marchese Volante, as he was known to the racing public, would become a pivotal figure in the Maserati company's transition from tuning shop to car manufacturer.

ABOVE: Maserati's first car was the Tipo 26, based on inventory acquired from the moribund Diatto marque with funding from Marquis Diego de Sterlich.

The ten ex-Diatto chassis and engines formed the basis of the first cars to carry the Maserati name and badge. For this, brother Mario – by then an established and successful artist – took the trident motif from the renaissance fountain of Neptune in the centre of Bologna.

For 1926 the world championship was expanded to five races and engine displacement capped at 1.5 litres – regular fiddling with the rules was one of the reasons the races were poorly supported by manufacturers – and the Maserati brothers adapted the ex-Diatto design to take advantage of this, downsizing the engine from two litres. Alfieri gave the first Maserati-badged car, the Tipo 26, its public race debut

in the Targa Florio road race around Sicily in April 1926. As a non-championship event it was open to larger-engined cars and Alfieri and his riding mechanic, Guerino Bertocchi, finished eighth overall but top of the 1500cc class. Two months later Ernesto took overall victory in the Chilometro Lanciato (Flying Kilometre) race along the old Roman road in Bologna, reaching nearly 104mph, and the order books began to fill. In all, Maserati would build over 40 Tipo 26s to various specifications for gentlemen racers.

Major challenges lay ahead, though. As a small business, Maserati lacked economies of scale and it was difficult to turn a profit. Time and again Alfieri would have to lean on the

ABOVE: The trident badge, designed by brother Mario, first appeared on the Tipo 26 in 1926.

generosity of Diego de Sterlich to keep his company afloat, and his health became a problem after he lost a kidney in an accident on the Coppa di Messina in 1927. The following year, racing's governing body of national automobile clubs gave up on the 1.5-litre formula – and, owing to continued lack of big-manufacturer interest, the world championship itself. That idea would lie fallow until 1950.

Maserati responded to the challenges of the racetrack and developed bigger engines despite lack of funds. Ingenuity would have to trump spend – Maserati's next grand prix car was powered by a four-litre V16 engine made by joining two of the existing two-litre straight-eights via a common crankcase. The company acquired such a reputation on track that no less an eminence than Tazio Nuvolari, the Flying Mantuan, turned to Maserati when he flounced out of Scuderia Ferrari in 1933.

Still the company was in crisis mode. Alfieri, for so long the driving force of Maserati, died in March 1933 after surgery to save his remaining kidney failed. The city of Bologna went into public mourning and businesses closed down for the day as his funeral cortege passed through. Nuvolari and Enzo Ferrari were among the well-known racers paying their respects.

Bindo Maserati left Isotta Fraschini to join his brothers, assuming the business reins while Ernesto took over technical direction. But despite further success on track, the company's income from sales and prizes barely matched its outgoings. Production slowed to a crawl as suppliers declined to provide raw materials for which they might not be paid. The Maseratis turned to Italy's national motoring club for loans and offered Piedmontese industrialist Gino Revere the presidency of the company in exchange for further investment.

Ultimately, though, commercial salvation would come from closer to home.

BELOW: Tension at the start of the 1934 Nice Grand Prix as Tazio Nuvolari (2) lines up his Maserati 8CM alongside Achille Varzi's Alfa Romeo P3 (28) and the Bugatti of René Dreyfus (20).

HOUSE OF THE TRIDENT 21

BELOW: The second Maserati V4 was rebodied as a roadster by Zagato after racing in the 1934 Grand Prix season.

Move to Modena

Exit The Brothers

Shorn of Alfieri's entrepreneurial drive, the Maserati brothers struggled against financial and competitive headwinds through the 1930s. The Great Depression touched businesses all over the world and, arguably, played a role in igniting the populist tinderbox in Germany, where the newly elected fascist government saw motor racing as an important propaganda and national prestige tool.

Unable to compete on equal terms with state-backed enterprises on track (*see* Chapter 3), Maserati built just nine cars in 1936 despite the backing of wealthy benefactors such as industrialist and amateur racer Gino Rovere, one of the co-investors in the Scuderia Subalpina team which acted as Maserati's 'works' team in grands prix.

Salvation arrived via the Bolognese-based sports newspaper *Littoriale*. To describe the remarkably well-connected Corrado Filippini as a 'reporter' is to undersell the significance of an individual who would later act as the company's formal entrant in the Indianapolis 500 and broker the sale of many historically significant Maserati race cars to the US after World War II.

OPPOSITE: Wilbur Shaw won two consecutive Indianapolis 500s in a Maserati 8CTF.

ABOVE: Adolfo Orsi poses with a new Quattroporte in 1963. Commercial necessity had driven him to begin expanding the road car range in the 1950s.

Aware of Maserati's predicament, Filippini brokered a meeting between the brothers and self-made Modenese businessman Adolfo Orsi, another of his acquaintances.

Born in March 1888, Orsi was one of nine siblings. His father was a rag-and-bone man and, after leaving school at the age of 11, Adolfo became a butcher's apprentice. This entailed early starts and a lunchtime finish; in the afternoon he would pull a cart around the areas not covered by his father, selling fruit and collecting rags. When his father died two years later the young Adolfo in effect took over the family business, acquiring more horses and carts and pressing his siblings into service as sorters of the scavenged items. Soon he was sending wagonloads of scrap metal to local foundries and eyeing up the possibility of going into the metal foundry business himself. By the mid-1930s the Orsi Group owned dozens of foundries and was expanding into other fields such as railways, agricultural machinery and automobile sales.

Although Orsi's lack of interest in motor racing rendered him an outlier among putative Maserati investors, Filippini sold him on the potential promotional value of racing to his existing businesses, plus the untapped potential of the spark plug business which had been drifting since Alfieri's death. On the weekend of 20–21 September 1936, the brothers made the short trip from Bologna for the non-championship Circuito de Modena races, where Ferdinando Barbieri was racing a 6C 34 against stronger Alfa Romeo machinery in a thin field of grand prix cars but Maseratis formed the majority of the field in a separate event for 'voiturettes'. In that, early Scuderia Ferrari investor Count Carlo Felice Trossi beat former motorcycle racer Clemente Biondetti (nicknamed 'The Wolf of Tuscany') in a battle of the 6CMs.

BELOW: The 6CM was competitive in the 'Voiturette' racing class and production accelerated after Adolfo Orsi bought Maserati in 1937.

BELOW: Luigi Villoresi qualified on pole position for the 1949 British Grand Prix at Silverstone in a Maserati 4CLT.

In an Orsi-owned property adjoining the mechanical scrutineering area, the parties met – and quickly found common ground. On 1 May 1937 the obligatory paperwork was signed enshrining Orsi as owner of Officine Alfieri Maserati and Fabbrica Candele Maserati. The brothers' surname remained above the door, but they were now theoretically free agents. Ernesto, Ettore and Bindo agreed ten-year contracts as employees; Orsi assumed the commercial reins and installed his son, Omar, as managing director while the brothers focused on design, engineering and racing. Orsi also arranged for a new factory to be built at Modena to house the Maserati businesses, though it would not be ready until 1939.

In the interim, production accelerated immediately to 14 cars in 1937. And, though the company remained outgunned on the Grand Prix scene by the German government-backed

Mercedes and Auto Union, and challenged in the voiturette class by the new British ERA organization, a new opportunity beckoned.

In 1930 the organizers of the Indy 500, enticed by Maserati's burgeoning reputation on the European racing scene, had reached a tentative hand across the Atlantic. Then less than 20 years old, the event was still building towards its reputation as "the greatest spectacle in racing". European marques had made the journey and come away with victory several times in its first decade but had drifted away in the 1920s. That decade had been regarded as a golden era of competition at the 'Brickyard' but this did not prevent the new owners of the Indianapolis Motor Speedway, led by World War I fighter pilot Eddie Rickenbacker, from successfully lobbying the American Automobile Association to change its rules to accommodate "less expensive, less specialized" cars and broaden the scope of entries. They also substantially reduced the previously lucrative prize purse.

Derided as a "junk formula" to this day, the 1930–1937 Indy 500 technical package was interpreted as closing the door to European Grand Prix-type cars. The chief obstacles were the insistence on each car having a riding mechanic as well as a driver – a thoroughly outdated practice – and a ban on superchargers in four-stroke engines. Alfieri Maserati was interested enough to send one of his new 16-cylinder V4s to be driven by regular V4 racer Baconin Borzacchini, with Ernesto Maserati as riding mechanic. Textile magnate and amateur racer Letterio Cucinotta then filed an entry for his Maserati 26B. Running without superchargers, neither car was competitive in the race; Borzacchini, no doubt to the delight of the radio commentators struggling to wrap their tongues around his name, was forced out on lap seven with electrical problems. Cucinotta was still circulating an hour after eventual winner Billy Arnold had taken the chequered flag. After this low-key debut, Maserati would not return to the Brickyard for several years.

When the V8RIs proved unsuccessful in grand prix racing all four examples were sold into American hands. Steel magnate Henry Topping Jr – later famous for proposing to movie star Lana Turner by dropping a diamond ring into her martini – had his modified to accommodate a second seat and entered it in the 1937 Indy 500 as the 'Topping Special'. Despite the best efforts of experienced track racer Egbert 'Babe' Stapp, it scraped onto the grid 31st out of 33 and retired with clutch failure. But still there was a surge of interest among European marques for the Indy 500 and, more specifically, the financially lucrative Vanderbilt Cup. Further rule changes in the US (including the removal of the riding mechanic) and in European grand prix racing proved the spur to develop new cars and, by 1939, Maserati's new 8CTF was coming into its own, if still not a match for the German cars.

After the first two chassis demonstrated the 8CTF's potential on track in 1938, Maserati built a third and put out feelers to the USA. The buyer was a fascinating individual whose shady past and Chicago mob associations have caused him to be partially erased from motor racing history. Michael Boyle, known as 'Umbrella Mike' on account of his habit of collecting cash bribes in his umbrella, managed the International Brotherhood of Electrical Workers, Chicago's most powerful union. He also had a passion for the Indy 500 but, by 1939, his first win as a team owner was a receding memory and he had grown frustrated with the process of trying to wring more speed out of his existing cars. The 8CTF seemed like a perfect opportunity and his well-drilled crew prepared it beautifully, carefully tuning it to run on the methanol fuel used at Indy. With Wilbur Shaw at the wheel, the 'Boyle

ABOVE: With two wins, two third places and a fourth, the 'Boyle Special' Maserati 8CTF remains the most successful car to have raced in the Indianapolis 500.

Special' Maserati dominated the Indy 500 in 1939 and 1940, and would likely have won again in 1941 but for a wheel failure which put Shaw in the wall.

By this point Europe was in the grip of war again and the Maserati factories, along with other Orsi facilities, had been turned over to the maintenance of military vehicles and manufacture of electric wagons. The race cars were spirited away to avoid being melted down for munitions. As the US became enveloped in the conflict Rickenbacker closed Indianapolis Motor Speedway at the end of that year, cancelled the 1942 Indy 500, and announced there would be no more racing until after the war was over. By 1945 the predominantly wooden grandstands and pit buildings were rotting and the golf course Rickenbacker had installed on the infield was virtually a jungle. Local businessman Tony Hulman bought

ABOVE: The 1936 Imperial Trophy at Crystal Palace was notable not only for Luigi Villoresi's entry in a 6CM, but also for being the first motor race to be televised live.

the facility for $750,000 and installed Shaw as president and general manager. Ted Horn finished third in the Boyle Maserati in the first post-war Indy 500 of 1946, was third again the following year, then fourth in 1948. The car's swansong came in 1950, when future winner Bill Vukovich completed his rookie orientation in it.

Despite this success in the US, and decent showings by Maserati customers in European postwar races, as the brothers came to the end of their ten-year contracts with Orsi in 1947 they began to weigh their futures. Ettore, Ernesto and Bindo continued to live in Bologna and commuted by train or bicycle to Modena. They had no problem with Orsi, though it is also widely claimed that they had felt undermined by the appointment in 1940 of Alberto Massimino as technical director. Massimino, a longtime employee of Fiat and Alfa Romeo, was among the engineers who had 'left' Alfa along with Enzo Ferrari during the corporate bloodletting of 1937, and worked with Enzo on the 'secret' Auto Avio Costruzione 815 racer which preceded the birth of the Ferrari car company. If Massimino's recruitment was a problem, it did not prevent Ernesto from collaborating with him on a clandestine road car project kept secret from the Italian and German regimes.

Based on the 6CM race car, the A6 ('A' for Alfieri Maserati, six being the number of cylinders in the engine) was a neat sports-coupé designed by Battista 'Pinin' Farina, founder of the famous coachworking company, powered by a 1.5-litre inline six-cylinder engine producing 65bhp. Some elements of the prototype shown at the Geneva Motor Show in March 1947, including the retractable headlamps, were removed, and production cars featured more window area. The coveted Grand Prix d'Elegance prize at Monte Carlo followed, as did a steady parade of potential customers. Maserati was now a manufacturer of road as well as race cars.

BELOW: Shortly before leaving, Ernesto Maserati co-developed the A6, Maserati's first road car. Early versions had a radiator grille shaped like a race car's; the 'Extra Lusso' models featured a wider one.

ABOVE: Despite tough financial circumstances, Maserati launched the 3500 GT in 1957, and it was an instant hit. Customers included crowned heads such as Prince Rainier of Monaco as well as Hollywood royalty such as Elizabeth Taylor and Rock Hudson.

Nevertheless the brothers decided to strike out on their own, setting up shop in Bologna in May 1947 as OSCA (Officine Specializzate Costruzione Automobili). The connection between the Maserati companies and the brothers who had founded them was terminated.

Adolfo Orsi had a sound commercial brain and knew how to run a business but his operations would be sorely tested by political and social unrest in the years to come. Tensions which had been building in Italy during wartime between those who supported the now-deposed fascist regime and those who covertly fought it erupted into ugly bouts of score-settling. As one who had been seen to have profited from the conflict, Orsi was in the firing line as Communists became increasingly influential in the politics of the region. While Maserati was less affected than some of his other businesses by industrial unrest, the general election of April 1948 created a flash point.

Within a year, relations between Orsi and various trade unions had declined to the point where he closed his car and spark plug factories for three months. While this brought some unions back to the negotiating table, the rancour metastasized to Orsi's iron and steel foundries, which he also closed down after a series of wildcat strikes. His refusal to re-hire known Communist agitators precipitated a borderline riot outside one foundry on 9 January 1950. Police opened fire, killing six people and injuring dozens more.

Orsi also faced internal divisions within his own family as his siblings took advantage of his diminished stature. Forced to split the empire up among his sisters and brother in 1953, Adolfo elected to keep the Maserati factory and the machine tool operation. In an initial burst of investment he employed the renowned race car designer Gioacchino Colombo, racer-engineer Vittorio Bellentani, and the promising young

BELOW: The trendsetting Mistral, a fastback coupé, was the first Maserati to be named after a wind.

ABOVE: Styled by Pietro Frua, the 1963 Quattroporte's discreet appearance belied the power (260bhp) of the race-based V8 under its bonnet.

Innocenti engineer Giulio Alfieri. In terms of quality of engineering, what followed is widely held to be a golden period for the company as the 250F racing car contributed to two world championships for Juan Manuel Fangio, the Tipo 60/61 'Birdcage' showcased clever lightweighting techniques in sportscar racing, and the Quattroporte and 3500 GT road cars entranced buyers as rarefied as the Shah of Persia.

And yet financial troubles always lurked in the margins. A lucrative machine tool contract with the Argentinian state went south when President Juan Perón was deposed in 1955, leaving Orsi at the mercy of the banks who had funded the raw-material purchases. Despite selling the machine-tool operation to a Swiss company and closing Maserati's in-house racing team, Orsi was unable to stave off his creditors and in 1958 Credito Italiano demanded the company be put into administration.

The road to solvency required the company to focus on road cars through the 1960s, but even Maserati's end of this industry was changing. To build and sell enough cars at a sufficiently accessible price to turn a consistent profit, it would be necessary to step back from the artisan-construction approach. Come the end of the decade, even Ferrari would capitulate to the realities of mass production.

In 1968, with an offer on the table from Argentinian entrepreneur Alejandro de Tomaso, Adolfo Orsi – perhaps mindful of how his dealings with that country had brought near-ruin a decade earlier – accepted an alternative proposal from French car marker Citroën. The deal would leave him with 40 per cent of the company, a clear voice in its future direction, and jobs in the Modenese factory safe. Or so he thought.

BELOW: In the late 1950s Omar Orsi asked for a more dynamic version of the 3500 GT and prolific stylist Giovanni Michelotti – then working for Vignale – obliged with the Sebring. The Series II model is distinguished by its side vents and chromed headlight surrounds.

Grand Prix

Born on Track

> Like Ferrari, the Maserati legend was forged in the heat of competition. And while Alfieri and Ernesto Maserati, like Enzo Ferrari, were successful racing drivers in their own right, the brothers were competing in cars they had actually built themselves...

Long before 'the auto-car' supplanted the horse and cart as the essential mode of long-distance transport for the masses, people began to race this new invention. Alfieri Maserati was born just over a year after Carl Benz demonstrated his Patent Motorwagen on the streets of Mannheim; just before Alfieri's seventh birthday in 1894 the first competitive event for this genre of vehicle was held, the Paris to Rouen Horseless Carriages contest. But this was hardly the kind of wheel-to-wheel spectacle you might expect: since the nascent motor industry had the common agenda of proving the reliability and usefulness of its products, these early races tended to be point-to-point trials of durability rather than performance.

Grand Prix ('great prize'), already a familiar term in horse racing, definitively entered the motorsport lexicon with the 1906 Grand Prix de l'ACF (Automobile Club de

OPPOSITE: Maserati's A6GCM Formula 2 car was based on the 4CLT 'Voiturette'.

BELOW: Henken Widengren contested the 1931 Ards TT in this Maserati with a supercharged 1100cc engine. Heavily modified by subsequent owner John Appleton and raced as the 'Appleton Special', it has been restored to 26M spec by the Mazjub family.

France). While the format was familiar – a time trial held on a triangular course of public roads, with two sessions on separate days – the winning prize of FF45,000 was unprecedented. National car clubs were taking the first steps down the road to promoting harmonious international competition by forming the *Association Internationale des Automobile Clubs Reconnus* (AIACR, later to become the FIA). By the 1920s the racing scene had matured to a point where the AIACR's sporting committee was framing a uniform technical formula that would enable it to run a world championship.

While this first attempt would founder after three years, a change to allow 1.5-litre supercharged cars facilitated Maserati's Grand Prix debut in 1926 with the Diatto-based Tipo 26. While the brothers continued to build larger-engined

variants for road-racing competions such as the Targa Florio, and smaller-engined cars for customers in less rarefied national events, the allure of racing for the biggest prize purses of all was irresistible. But the key challenge was a rulebook seemingly in constant flux; having abandoned the world championship concept after 1927 and embraced a laissez-faire approach at Grand Prix level, the AIACR realized that the so-called Formula Libre ('free formula') muddied the waters of what top-level racing should be.

An open rulebook also threatened to hand the competitive edge to the richest competitors, but Maserati's low-budget, high-ingenuity response showed how it was possible to do more with less. The V4 might have been hobbled by rule changes at Indianapolis, and come up short against the likes of Alfa Romeo in Europe, but the sheer audacity of mating two inline-eights to create a four-litre V16 deserves respect – even more so because it worked. This despite a plethora of vulnerable moving parts and friction surfaces: 32 valves, two crankshafts, four camshafts, two water pumps, four oil pumps and two superchargers.

The V4's significance in motor racing history goes beyond its modest success at Grand Prix level. On 28 September 1929, Baconin Borzacchini gunned the prototype V4 along the old state highway outside Cremona at an average of 152.93mph over two timed runs, a new ten-mile world speed record. Later the Bolognese automobile club held a gala dinner for Borzacchini and the Maserati brothers to celebrate this magnificent achievement. Also in attendance was Enzo Ferrari, working the room for potential clients for the racing team he had in mind: he encountered Alfredo Caniato and Mario Tadini, amateur racers and heirs to successful textile businesses. A month later Scuderia Ferrari was incorporated, with them as key investors.

ABOVE: Bought by Count Erno Fesetics in 1937, this 8CM spent 70 years in Hungary, surviving German and Soviet occupation, before being acquired by its current Swiss owner and returning to competition in historic events.

In 1929 the AIACR had tried to curb increasing car speeds by introducing a fuel consumption formula. Combined with the financial crash of later that year, this had the effect of driving away competitors rather than encouraging them. But, amid a hotch-potch of cancelled races and occasionally thin fields, a fascinating battle of the Italian greats played out: Tazio Nuvolari in a Scuderia Ferrari-run Alfa Romeo P2 vs Achille Varzi, predominantly in Maserati's new 8C 26M. Bugatti Type 35s did most of the winning at Grand Prix level but it was the contest between the flamboyant Nuvolari (credited by Ferrari as inventing the four-wheel drift method of cornering) and the clinical, calculating Varzi which captured the imagination of racing fans at home and abroad. Sadly, having captured Maserati's first Grand Prix victory, in Spain in October, Varzi

then decided Bugatti would offer him a better opportunity for 1931; later in the decade his career would come unravelled as he developed an addiction to morphine.

The AIACR tinkered further with the rules as it tried to reboot the championship idea as a European competition, announcing a new formula coming in 1934 based around a maximum car weight of 750kg. Alfieri's last projects before he died were the V5 – a five-litre version of the V4 – and a new 8C model based around an inline-eight enlarged to three litres and, with an eye on cutting a cleaner path through the air, mounted in a noticeably narrower chassis than rivals. Making its debut at the 1933 Tunis Grand Prix, the definitive 8CM-3000 single-seater flexed so much that it alarmed spectators as well as drivers. In this era chassis structure continued to

BELOW: Based on the 26M chassis but with a larger version of the six-cylinder engine, the 8C 2800 of 1931 was an interim step as Alfieri Maserati worked towards a three-litre engine.

follow the ancient practice of twin horizontal beams with cross-bracing and a body fixed on top; in the 8CM-3000's case the gap of just 50cm between the beams exacerbated a natural tendency to flex.

Nevertheless Maserati was well placed to succeed against Alfa Romeo, which was in the grip of financial crisis in 1933 and withdrew its new P2s from competition, leaving Scuderia Ferrari to field lesser models until later in the year, when Alfa was rescued by the fascist government's *Istituto per la Ricostruzione Industriale* investment programme. One consequence of this was Nuvolari temporarily severing his ties with Enzo Ferrari after a series of mechanical failures had eliminated him from race-winning positions. Matters came to a head shortly before the Belgian Grand Prix, when news emerged that Nuvolari would try a Maserati as well as his regular Ferrari-prepared Alfa Romeo.

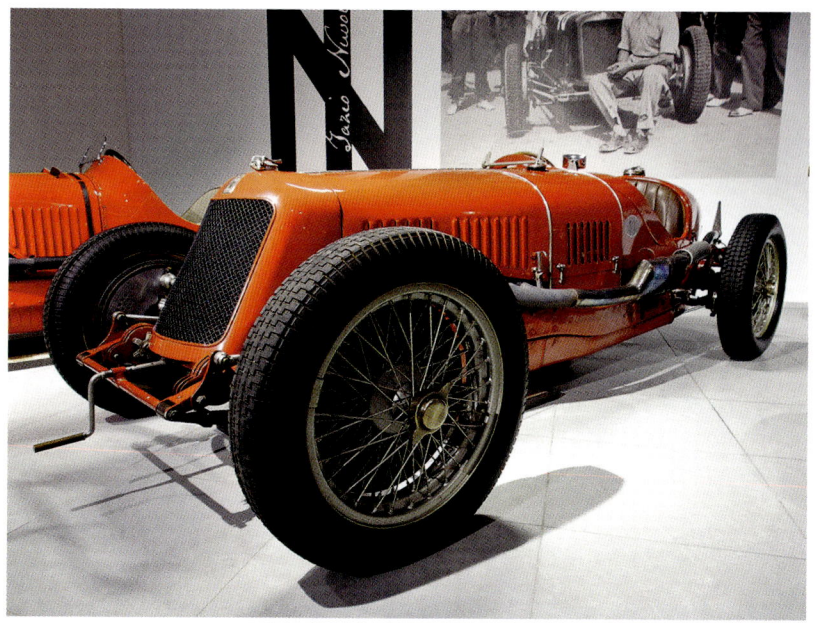

ABOVE: The 8C 3000, Maserati's last two-seater Grand Prix car, won at Montlhéry in 1933 in the hands of Giuseppe Campari.

As it happened, there was an 8CM-3000 available: the first customer chassis, returned to the factory by Raymond Sommer after a disappointing Monaco Grand Prix. Despite Sommer's misgivings, Giuseppe Campari – a burly 41-year-old who planned to retire from racing and become a full-time opera singer at the end of the season – had demonstrated Maserati's competitiveness by winning the French Grand Prix in an 8C 26M before sustaining an eye injury at Reims. The morning after that race, Enzo Ferrari grudgingly reached an arrangement with Ernesto Maserati for the ex-Sommer 8CM-3000 to be entered by Scuderia Ferrari for Nuvolari in Belgium.

Even in the 21st century, Spa-Francorchamps is a stern test of skill and bravery. In 1933 its layout was over double

ABOVE: Tazio Nuvolari's win for Maserati in Nice in August 1933, following victories in Spa and Livorno, prompted Alfa Romeo to make its Tipo B cars available to Scuderia Ferrari again.

the length and consisted entirely of public roads. Practice convinced Nuvolari that the Maserati's bigger engine would be an advantage if he could cure its alarming handling. Accompanied by two mechanics, he took it to the Imperia car factory in Nessonvaux, just outside Liège, and modified the steering as well as the longitudinal chassis members. Qualifying, decided in those days by a lottery system – the 1933 Monaco Grand Prix was the first to rank the starters by practice times – placed Nuvolari on the back row of the grid. Ahead sat five Bugattis and five Alfa Romeos. By the end of the first lap – 9.3 miles – Nuvolari had seized the lead and went on to win the gruelling four-hour race by nearly four minutes. This notable scalp, plus two other victories for Nuvolari that season, bolstered Maserati's reputation at a crucial time for the company.

Widened to meet the minimum-width regulations brought in with the 750kg formula, the 8CM-3000 remained competitive in lesser events into 1934 as Maserati prepared its new 3.7-litre inline-six engine, which promised to be 13kg lighter than the eight. But the new Grand Prix car, marketed as the 6C-34, arrived late in the year and was outgunned by competitors from Alfa Romeo, Mercedes and Auto Union. A development with a 4.2-litre V8, named the V8 RI – *Ruote Indipendenti*, signifying its independent suspension – won just one non-championship Grand Prix in which the German cars and Scuderia Ferrari were absent, though it found success in the USA (*see* Chapter 2).

The state-backed German cars brought new technologies and ideas (such as locating the engine behind the driver for better balance), lighter materials, sleeker aerodynamics, and horsepower-boosting fuel additives. Italy's competitors had no way of keeping up, not least the increasingly cash-poor Maserati. Nuvolari's fastest lap of Spa in an 8CM-3000 in 1933 had been 6m01s; four years later Hermann Lang went round in 5m04s in a Mercedes-Benz W125. Spooked by the sharp increase in speeds, the AIACR changed the rules again to cap engine sizes – but this did not change the picture of German domination. Once rescued by Adolfo Orsi, Maserati produced the 3-litre inline-eight 8CTF, which found success in the Indy 500 although unreliability blighted the car in Grands Prix – but in the absence of great European interest in its large-engined offerings, the company retreated to the 1.5-litre supercharged 'voiturette' class.

Maserati had been offering its 4CM ('Corsa Monoposto') model with both single-seat and sportscar bodies, and with supercharged inline-four engines from 1.1 litres to 2.5 litres, since 1931. Increased competition in the 'voiturette' class had rendered the 4CM obsolete, so in 1936 the brothers had

OVERLEAF: Franco Cortese battles with rivals in the 'voiturette' class aboard his 6CM in the 1937 German Grand Prix at the Nürburgring. Maserati did not have the resources to compete with Mercedes and Auto Union GP cars financed by the Nazi government.

BELOW: Almost 30 examples of the 6CM were built and it won the Targa Florio road race three times between 1937 and 1939.

unveiled the 6CM at the Milan Motor Show, based on the same chassis concept but with a supercharged 1.5-litre inline-six engine and independent front suspension. Production was stymied by the company's financial problems but, with Orsi's investment and the move to Modena, and impressive results on track, more customers began to beat a path to Maserati's door, including 1931 Le Mans 24 Hours winner and British Racing Drivers' Club co-founder Earl Howe. By the outbreak of war in 1939, 27 examples had been sold and Maserati's success in the class had even tempted Enzo Ferrari to follow suit: the Alfa Romeo 158, designed by Gioacchino Colombo, made its race debut in 1938. But while Maserati's successes in voiturette racing bolstered the brand's prestige, Alfa Romeo's apparent

ABOVE: When racing began again after World War II it relied on pre-war cars and drivers to make up competitive grids. Here Louis Chiron, a month short of his 48th birthday, is pictured racing to second place in the 1947 Jersey Road Race aboard an eight-year-old 4CL.

capitulation in the top class caused political ructions and led to Ferrari's departure from the company's racing operations.

Despite developments to the engine which brought power from 155bhp to 175bhp, a lowering of the chassis rails, and aerodynamic fairings around the suspension, the relative competitiveness of the 6CM began to decline and Ernesto returned to the four-cylinder concept for its replacement. Introduced in 1939, the 4CL ('L' for 'linguette', meaning 'inline') was based on essentially the same chassis concept, but with a wider track and a lower stance. The new 1.5-litre engine featured an identical cylinder bore and stroke of 78cm, a higher compression ratio and a multi-valve head, blown by a more potent supercharger. All this, together with lower frictional

ABOVE: Countess Howe, second wife of British Racing Drivers' Club president Earl Howe, presents a garland of flowers to Luigi Villoresi, winner of the 1948 British Grand Prix at Silverstone. Villoresi had started from the back of the field after the Maserati team was delayed in transit.

losses through having fewer moving parts, brought power to over 200bhp.

Initially, though, the new engine was unreliable. Humiliated on track by their German allies, the Italians in 1939 decided that all Grands Prix they organized would be for voiturettes only. On the 4CL's competitive debut, the Tripoli Grand Prix, Luigi Villoresi claimed pole position in one of three 4CLs entered – but all succumbed to engine issues as Hermann Lang and Rudolf Caracciola finished 1-2 in a pair of Mercedes W165 voiturettes which had been designed and built for this race in just eight months. The first race winner in a 4CL was a customer, the British privateer John Wakefield.

At the onset of World War II, Maserati spirited away 12 4CLs into the care of Arialdo Ruggeri, another amateur racer from a family made wealthy by its textile interests. Concealed

ABOVE: Seven Maseratis contested the 1950 Monaco Grand Prix, including this 4CLT/48 driven by Toulo de Graffenried.

in Milan, these cars would form the core of Maserati's racing activities when competition got underway again – remarkably quickly – after hostilities ceased. The first peacetime motor race, the Coupes de Paris, was held in the French capital on 9 September 1945. Scarcity of materials and the damaged economies of Europe dictated that motor racing was the preserve of those cars which had been successfully hidden from looters, conquerors, and those who would have melted them down for munitions and army vehicles. Ruggeri's Scuderia Milano team, founded in 1946, became a key ally to the factory in the post-war racing scene, even fielding a new 8CL for Luigi Villoresi and a 4CL for Duke Nalon in the Indy 500.

Equipped with a 4CL, Villoresi won what is believed to be the first post-war Grand Prix, on a street circuit in Nice in April 1946; across the Atlantic, the first post-war street race

BELOW: 4CLT chassis 1600, originally bought by Argentina's national car club with financial support from President Juan Pérón and raced by Juan Manuel Fangio, still competes in historic events today.

took place in the village of Watkins Glen in upstate New York in 1948. George Weaver led the first two laps in his recently acquired Maserati V8RI, nicknamed 'Poison Lil'. Between these historically significant events, a Maserati 8CTF won the Pikes Peak hillclimb twice in the hands of Louis Unser. 6CMs and 4CLs formed the bulk of the grids in many post-war races, which were mostly run to Formula Libre rules to attract as many entrants as possible. Later in the decade, racing's governing body essentially inked in the voiturette as the car of choice when it codified Formula A, later known as Formula 1, based around cars with up to 1.5-litre supercharged or up to 4.5-litre naturally aspirated engines. The intention was to build towards a world championship for drivers, beginning in 1950.

Alfa Romeo had also successfully concealed its 158s and

to contend with these Ernesto Maserati evaluated several modifications to the 4CL, chiefly to combat chassis flex. The fruit of this was the 4CLT, which featured tubular rather than box-section chassis rails, forged rather than cast suspension uprights, and a new crankshaft bearing design for the engine as well as twin superchargers. Alberto Ascari won on the car's first appearance, the 1948 San Remo Grand Prix, and it went on to win many more prestigious races including the two British Grands Prix held at Silverstone before that circuit hosted the inaugural world championship race in 1950.

By then the Maserati brothers had departed the company they founded, but there was sufficient strength in depth in the organization to keep the 4CLT competitively quick through engine developments and lightweighting. But it was not quite

ABOVE: In 1957 Maserati evaluated a V12 engine in the 250F.

OPPOSITE: Scarcity of Formula 1 cars meant the world championship races of 1952–53 were open to F2 cars only. The A6GCM, seen here at the 1952 French GP in the hands of Philippe Étancelin, only challenged the dominant Ferraris after engine and chassis revisions.

quick enough as Alfa Romeo unlocked more performance in the 158 through more aggressive supercharging and Enzo Ferrari reappeared under his own name with new V12-powered machinery. Louis Chiron's third place in the 1950 Monaco Grand Prix was as good as it got at world championship level.

Alberto Massimino and Ernesto Maserati had developed a sportscar racing cousin of the A6 road car, the A6GCS ('Corsa Sport'), which had proved successful enough for 15 examples to have been built and sold. In the post-brothers era Massimino worked with new recruit Vittorio Bellentani to develop the A6GCM single-seater for competition in the Formula 2 class, based on the standard ladder-frame chassis concept of the 4CLT and powered by a naturally aspirated two-litre DOHC inline-six engine producing 160bhp. The first two were sold straight into private hands in 1951. To produce more power Maserati revised the bore/stroke ratio of the engine in later cars,

ABOVE: Gioacchino Colombo (right) with fellow engineer Aurelio Lampredi in the Ferrari workshop in 1949. After leaving for Maserati he transformed the A6GCM and designed the company's first 2.5-litre F1 car, the 250F.

unleashing a further 20bhp, but the greatest progress came with the arrival of Gioacchino Colombo in 1952. Following his input the engine's cylinder bore was increased and the stroke shortened, the cooling fins on the brake drums were enlarged, the rear suspension completely revised and the twin-spar chassis setup replaced by a stronger yet lighter network of triangulated tubes.

Not only did this transform the A6GCM into a race winner, it pointed the way to the company's next Formula 1 car. The world championship was adopting a 2.5-litre unsupercharged engine format for 1954 which would in theory offer competitors a clean slate with more modern cars. Enlarging the A6 engine architecture and carrying over the already proven chassis philosophy made the new project quick and straightforward. Maserati's offering would become one of the seminal Grand Prix cars of the 1950s.

The 250F was so closely based on the A6GCM that several examples of the F2 chassis had to be repurposed as F1 cars when demand outstripped supply at the beginning of 1954. It was known that Mercedes and Lancia were also working on bespoke cars for the new formula but these would not be ready until later in the year. Though Maserati had hoped for the 250F to be purely a customer car, the situation regarding supply required the factory to provide a great deal of operational support, albeit underwritten by outside finance.

Juan Manuel Fangio was contracted to Mercedes but, in order to score points, was 'loaned' to Maserati for the first two F1 Grands Prix of 1954 – which he won. Thereafter the 250F would claim just six more world championship wins but this was chiefly a factor of Mercedes' dominance for two seasons and Ferrari taking on the technically advanced D50 project for 1956 when Lancia, like Mercedes, withdrew from racing.

BELOW: Having won the first round of 1957 on home ground in Argentina, Fangio built towards a fourth consecutive world title with an imperious victory aboard his 250F in Monaco.

The 250F's historic significance goes beyond its modest record of victories. Perhaps most importantly, its presence in good numbers ensured healthy grids at a time when the world championship was on shaky ground, having had to adopt F2 cars from 1952–53 owing to the lack of competitive F1 entries. It was affordable and drivers loved its sweet handling balance. It offered great talents such as Stirling Moss a platform upon which to prove themselves. The first woman to race in F1, Maria Teresa de Filippis, did so in a 250F.

It was also the car in which Fangio clinched the last of his five world championships and his final Grand Prix win, one considered to be among the finest race drives of all time. When a long pitstop at the Nürburging in 1957 dropped him far away from the lead, Fangio broke the lap record of the 14-mile circuit nine times in 10 laps to catch and pass the Ferraris of Peter Collins and Mike Hawthorn.

The 250F's longevity is also a testament to the skill of Giulio Alfieri, who took over development after Colombo's departure and who designed a 2.5-litre V12 which was evaluated during 1957 before Maserati was forced to close its racing department. Ongoing financial difficulties militated against further involvement at the top level, although Alfieri designed a diminutive transverse-mounted V12 when F1 became a 1.5-litre naturally aspirated formula in 1961. While this never saw action, for the 'return to power' from 1966 onwards Alfieri cost-effectively enlarged the decade-old V12 design to three litres, powering John Surtees and Pedro Rodríguez to wins in Cooper cars.

OPPOSITE: Maria Teresa de Filippis was the first woman to race in Formula 1, starting three Grands Prix in 1958 in a 250F.

OVERLEAF: Fangio's victory in the 1957 German Grand Prix, where he broke the lap record nine times in ten laps while fighting back from a slow pitstop, is still considered one of the greatest drives of all time.

When Life Gives You Le Mans

Enter The Birdcage

Maserati's Grand Prix racing heritage in the pre-World War II era and post-war decade is such that it is easy to overlook the success the company enjoyed in sportscars and road racing at the time. Perhaps it is also because modern audiences view Formula 1 as the richest and most technologically advanced form of motorsport – whereas, up until the 1960s, sportscar racing was often more financially lucrative for drivers and manufacturers even if the cars were slightly less rarefied. It is also an unfortunate fact that, while Maserati has won Grands Prix and powered some of the most celebrated drivers of the 'golden era', success at the Le Mans 24 Hours has eluded the company.

When the French city of Le Mans hosted the first Grand Prix de l'ACF in 1906, the 24-hour endurance race which would become a celebrated annual event was 17 years away. A month before the Grand Prix de l'ACF, Sicilian wine magnate Vincenzo Florio organized a race intended to be the sternest test of all: three laps of a 96-mile circuit around the Madonie mountains in northern Sicily, a perilous combination

OPPOSITE: The Tipo 61 cleverly subverted new windscreen height regulations.

of gradients, poor surfaces and free-roaming wildlife. The Targa Florio became infamous and would provide the stage for Maserati's first victory, Alfieri Maserati's class win in 1926 in a Tipo 26. The company also helped save the race when Alfa Romeo's dominance in the early 1930s chased away the majority of the other competitors and threatened to make the Targa Florio financially unviable. In 1937 the organizers were forced to relocate to the smaller 3.5-mile Parco della Favorita in Palermo and open the race to voiturettes; Francesco Severi won in a 6CM, kicking off four consecutive years of Maserati victories. Luigi Villoresi's win in May 1940 in a 4CL brought down the curtain on competitive motor racing in a Europe already embroiled in war.

The A6GCS provided Maserati with a presence in the world sportscar championship in the early 1950s, but it was not until Vittorio Bellentani reworked the engine and chassis of the 250F Grand Prix car into a two-seat sports-racer that the works team and its customers began to record significant results. American racer Bill Spear claimed a first podium for the 300S in the 1955 Sebring 12 Hours behind Mike Hawthorn in a Jaguar D-type and Phil Hill in a Ferrari 750 Monza, although the question of who actually finished first was not settled until a fortnight later owing to a protest by the Ferrari team. But while Maserati fielded a works team in 1956 with driving talent including Stirling Moss, Jean Behra and Carlos Menditiguy, and won 1000km races in Buenos Aires and at the Nürburging, it ultimately finished second in the championship to Ferrari. Furthermore, the Le Mans 24 Hours was off the calendar since its organizers had excluded sports-racers with engines larger than 2.5 litres in response to the catastrophic 1955 accident in which a driver and over 80 spectators had been killed.

For 1957 Maserati returned with Juan Manuel Fangio

now on the driver roster and a larger range of cars. As well as the 300S it had the 350S, with a strengthened chassis and a larger 3.5-litre straight six modified for competition from the 3500GT road car. Just three examples were built since this was viewed as a stopgap for the 450S, a big-engined sports-prototype the company had initially shelved after the 1955 Le Mans disaster. The impetus for rebooting this concept had come from a wealthy customer, US amateur

BELOW: One 450S was rebodied by Zagato in a coupé shell and raced at the 1957 Le Mans 24 Hours.

ABOVE: Maserati took on the might of Jaguar at Le Mans in 1957. This is the cockpit of the 450S shared by Grand Prix drivers Jean Behra and André Simon.

racer Tony Parravano, who had commissioned Maserati to build a 4.2-litre V8 for his Indycar. Expanding it to 4.5 litres and installing it in a modified 350S chassis revealed prodigious power – which would require much better braking and handling.

Fangio and Moss led the opening round of the 1957 season, the Buenos Aires 1000km, in the definitive 450S until its clutch failed. Fangio and Behra then won at Sebring but Maserati's championship was derailed by a series of different mechanical failures. At Le Mans – now back on the calendar after the organizers realigned themselves with the championship's rules – Maserati entered both a 'standard' 450S and one with a special streamlined bodyshell designed by Frank Costin, but both cars had retired by nightfall. Then, in the championship decider in Venezuela, catastrophe: Masten Gregory flipped the 450S entered by US racer Temple Buell on the second lap; Stirling Moss crashed into a wandering backmarker in one of the works 450Ss; and the other works 450S briefly caught fire in the pits before crashing out when the third factory Maserati, a 300S, suffered a tyre blow-out in front of it. The ruinous expense of the damage was a major contributor to Adolfo Orsi having to close the factory racing programme.

As Orsi tried to pry back control of the company from the administrators, in 1958 Alfieri drew up plans for a customer racing car using as much existing running gear as possible

BELOW: The company's financial difficulties prevented the 450S from fulfilling its potential, but its engine would enjoy a long life in Maserati's road car range.

and requiring few raw materials. Here the racing demands for light weight aligned perfectly with Maserati's tight budget. The new sports-racer, designated Tipo 60, was based on an extremely light structure of 200 small-gauge steel tubes welded together into a spaceframe. It was this which led to the Tipo 60 and its successors being nicknamed 'Birdcage'. With the 200bhp, 2-litre inline-four from the 200S installed the complete car weighed around 570kg, yielding a power-to-weight ratio of 350bhp per tonne. Canting the engine over at a 45-degree angle enabled it to be mounted lower, for better handling, and facilitated a distinctive and aerodynamically slippery body shape. The possibilities were extraordinary and Moss demonstrated the Tipo 60's potency by winning its first race, a sportscar event run on the Rouen Formula 2 Grand Prix weekend in August 1959.

In response to demand from US customers, Maserati subsequently produced the Tipo 61, powered by a 2.9-litre

version of the engine. 22 Tipo 60 and 61s were built, of which three went to American racer Lloyd 'Lucky' Casner's Camoradi team. Alfieri subsequently relocated the engine to behind the driver in the Tipo 63, 64 and 65 models, whose customers raced them in a variety of body shapes created by celebrated coachbuilders including Scaglione and Fantuzzi, and with V8 and V12 engines up to five litres.

But it is the Tipo 60 and 61s which are considered the seminal Maserati sports-racers of the 1960s even though, like the 250F single-seater, their roster of victories at the top level is less than extensive. Camoradi's Tipo 61s had the pace to win at Le Mans in 1960, Alfieri having interpreted new windscreen regulations more cleverly than Ferrari, but electrical issues cost them – Masten Gregory had a four-minute lead after a mighty opening stint, only for his car to be stuck in the pits for over an hour when it failed to restart. Another US customer, Briggs Cunningham, entered a Tipo

LEFT: The Tipo 60 (pictured) and larger-engined 61 models were based on the spaceframe-chassis concept of the 250F model, a network of around 200 small-diameter tubes – hence the 'Birdcage' nickname.

60 for himself and a pair of Tipo 63s the following year but once again time lost in the pits proved costly, and the highest-placed Maserati was a Tipo 63 co-driven by brewery heir Augie Pabst in fourth, behind three Ferraris.

As sportscar racing plunged into an expensive arms race during the 1960s, Maserati embarked on a toe-in-the-water exercise in the new closed-top category largely dominated by Ferrari's 250 GTO. Since the larger engines in latter Birdcages had challenged the ability of the small-gauge spaceframe to put down all that power, Alfieri returned to the traditional spaceframe concept for the Tipo 151, which located the four-litre quad-cam V8 ahead of the driver in a striking Kamm-tailed coupé bodyshell. Again the lack of development budget showed as the three cars failed to make the finish at Le Mans in 1962. Returning in 1963 with a five-litre engine installed in the Tipo 151, French racer André Simon had a mishap at the start when the hot sun made his door stick shut. Not only did he lose ground on his rivals, but in finally wrenching the door open, he struck himself in the face. Still bleeding from the nose, Simon seized the lead on the opening lap, only for the car to stick in gear later on with Casner at the wheel. The same chassis competed at Le Mans in 1964 and '65 in a new 'streamliner' bodyshell created by Carrozzeria Drogo, clocking a then-record top speed of 192mph. But the impetus for the project fizzled out when Casner flipped, with fatal consequences, during testing for the 1965 race.

Le Mans, then, remains unfinished business for the trident marque.

OPPOSITE: Just one of the three original Tipo 151s survives and fetched nearly £2m when last auctioned in 2006. At least one 'recreation' has been built.

OVERLEAF: All three Tipo 151s were entered for the 1962 Le Mans 24 Hours. Number 2, driven by Bruce McLaren and Walt Hansgen, lasted the longest, succumbing to diff failure in the 13th hour while running in fifth place.

MASERATI ②

The French Correction

A Convenient Marriage

In 1969 Maserati's near-neighbour, Ferrari, became part of the Fiat empire in a deal which left Enzo Ferrari in control of his beloved racing activities but ultimately answerable to Fiat's suits in all other aspects of the business. It was an acknowledgement that the realities of car manufacture, even at the high end, were shifting towards mass production: faster, more consistent, and rigorously cost-controlled. The curtain was coming down on the era of hand-built sportscars of which no two examples were quite the same. Businesses that specialized in the bespoke were going to have to learn to stamp their basic products out of a mould.

Maserati had already begun its journey down that road but with a somewhat more unusual companion. The French car manufacturer Citroën had acquired a reputation for innovative engineering through its mould-breaking Traction Avant, the first mass-produced front-wheel-drive car, the 2CV – among the definitive post-war economy vehicles – and the DS, a sleek saloon which rode on sophisticated hydropneumatic suspension. Launched in 1955, the DS still looked futuristic

OPPOSITE: Citroën's SM featured a Maserati-built V6 engine.

BELOW: Giulio Alfieri – pictured here with Stirling Moss at the 1954 Italian Grand Prix – remained a key figure in Maserati's car and engine development through the Citroën era.

a decade later. And Citroën's intention was to capitalize on the bold spirit of the 1960s by offering a performance variant of it: the inline-four engine under the bonnet of the DS could trace its ancestry back to the 1930s, a putative flat-six engine having been abandoned late in the day.

Under the codename 'Project S' the company had been evaluating a series of prototypes since the beginning of the decade but had yet to alight on a suitable engine concept. Walter Becchia, designer of the 2CV's flat-twin, was working on a six-cylinder engine while Citroën also formed what would be an abortive partnership with German manufacturer NSU to create a triple-rotor Wankel rotary unit. Amid uncertainty over the production viability of these engines, in January 1968 Citroën approached Maserati to design and build a 2.7-litre V6. By the end of the year these negotiations had bloomed

ABOVE: The SM's mechanical complexity – note the green pressurized spheres for the hydropneumatic suspension crowding the engine – put off many potential owners.

into a full-scale acquisition in which Citroën bought 60 per cent of Maserati, leaving Adolfo Orsi with 40 per cent and a position as honorary chairman. Omar Orsi stayed on the board of directors.

Giulio Alfieri was given six months to design the new engine but accomplished it in three weeks. The initial brief was for the new V6 to be light and compact, no larger physically than the existing inline-four, and (to accommodate French taxation boundaries) displacing no more than 2.7 litres. Alfieri based the prototype on the 4.2-litre version of his classic V8 he had developed for the new Maserati Indy road car, which was replacing the ageing Quattroporte and Sebring models. Removing two cylinders, narrowing the bore slightly and reducing the stroke yielded a 2.7-litre V6 capable of far more than the 150bhp laid down in the brief, though the final production unit shared only its 90-degree cylinder angle and

BELOW: With a drag coefficient of 0.34 the Citroën's sleek, futuristic bodyshell was remarkably aerodynamic.

the cam followers with the prototype. The definitive engine layout was expandable (through a longer stroke) to three litres for overseas markets, primarily the US, and it would also later be downsized to two when the Italian government brought in a new tax regime punishing larger-engined cars. Fitting the five-speed Citroën gearbox at the front enabled the engine to be mounted behind the front wheels, improving car balance.

Two design decisions would prove problematic, though. V6s have a less even firing order than V8s and generally have a narrower included angle to mitigate the vibrations that result. Retaining the 90-degree angle required counterweights on the crankshaft which added inertia, dampening throttle response. More critically the primary tensioners for the chains driving

the four overhead camshafts would prove insufficiently durable despite extensive testing. Maserati historians generally place the blame for this on Citroën engineers disregarding advice to use a stronger component on the grounds that these had seen service in the DS since the 1950s without issue.

Project S became one of the most significant new launches at the 1970 Geneva Motor Show. While the suspension was an uprated version of the system used on the DS – which remained years ahead of the steel springs and oil dampers employed by other car manufacturers – every other aspect of the SM was a step up which befitted its more elevated position in the model range. Brakes were now discs all round and the self-centring, speed-sensitive power steering was a fast two

turns from lock to lock. It also swivelled two of the six Cibie halogen headlights mounted in the fully glazed nose. Robert Opron's sleek bodyshell, tapering behind a long nose to flush rear wheels, had a remarkably low drag coefficient of 0.34 and remains starkly modern to this day, over five decades later. Not only did the SM offer a driving experience like no other, with its supple ride, rapid steering and brakes, and offbeat V6 growl, it inked in Citroën's status as a visionary car maker.

While the work of historian Marc Sonnery has done much to correct the long-held belief among Maserati purists that Citroën micromanaged its Italian outpost to the company's detriment, the response to early failures of the V6 demonstrates the flaws of Citroën's more bureaucratic approach. As customers returned SMs whose valves had enjoyed rather too close society with the pistons after the chain tensioners failed, the diktat came down from Paris to mend or replace broken engines rather than adopt a stronger component on the production line. As a result the SM acquired a reputation for unreliability and sales plummeted after strong early interest.

By 1971 the Orsis had come to the realization that their role was essentially ceremonial and Adolfo sold his 40 per cent stake to Citroën. Under French ownership Maserati was busily using the fresh investment to revise a model range which had begun to grow long in the tooth. The Mexico, named to commemorate John Surtees' 1966 Mexican Grand Prix victory in a Maserati-engined Cooper F1 car, found favour with celebrities including actor-turned-politician Ronald Reagan but was rather staid to drive; and the Ghibli, despite the attractions of its svelte styling (the early work of celebrated designer Giorgetto Giugiaro), suffered from a primitive rigid-propshaft arrangement which transmitted much drivetrain harshness through the suspension and into the body. Performance was never lacking but the perception of outdatedness was leading

ABOVE: It may have seemed an unlikely competition car but the Citroën SM won the Rallye Maroc in 1971, though it missed out on repeating the feat in 1972 (pictured).

Maserati to be viewed as a poor man's Ferrari, if such a thing could actually exist.

Named – like the Ghibli – after a wind, the Bora, launched at the 1971 Geneva Motor Show, was a timely course correction and the first new Maserati developed under Citroën's custodianship. Guy Mallaret, installed as Maserati's general manager by Citroën, had an eye on broader developments in the racing scene and in 1969 pitched Giulio Alfieri the idea of a two seater-mid-engined sportscar. At Le Mans Ford's mid-engined GT40 had humbled Ferrari, and Lamborghini's Miura, powered by a V12 mounted transversely behind the cockpit, was the most exciting and quick road car of the

BELOW: Low-slung seats and a dashboard with instruments built into the centre of a spokeless steering wheel completed the futuristic feel of the Boomerang concept.

era. Enzo Ferrari, though, was so averse to the engine being anywhere but ahead of the driver that his company's 1967 mid-engined coupé had been marketed under the Dino sub-brand, without a Ferrari logo on it.

Alfieri needed no further prompting. Having been stymied by lack of development funds for the Tipo 63, 64 and 65 racing cars, he was determined to make use of the opportunity.

Giugiaro was engaged to design a bodyshell, which bore a familial resemblance to the Ghibli, while work proceeded on a unitary bodyshell which would feature fully independent suspension for the first time in a Maserati road car. The final shape shared a number of features with the Ghibli, including the nose and pop-up headlamps, but naturally differed in stance and proportions owing to the engine's new location.

ABOVE: As evidence of Maserati's creative energy, and new investment under Citroën ownership, the Giugiaro-designed Boomerang showcar wowed visitors to the 1972 Geneva Show just months after the launch of the mid-engined Bora.

Brushed stainless steel on the window trims and A-pillars contrasted with the painted bodyshell and black belt line in a tasteful embrace of the wedge shape which was becoming fashionable at the time.

Development was marred by clashes between Alfieri and Guerrino Bertocchi, the engineer who also acted as Maserati's chief test driver. Though gifted behind the wheel – he was fond of telling interviewers he had been as fast as Maserati's Grand Prix drivers – Bertocchi was set in his ways, having been at the company since 1926. He disliked the notion of a mid-engined, GT car, fought against it, and was happy to share his opinions with anyone prepared to listen – indeed, he was eventually fired after being caught advising customers to buy De Tomaso's Pantera instead.

Although the longitudinally mounted 4.7-litre V8 was carried over from the Ghibli, the five-speed gearbox was bought in from ZF, while the braking system came from the Citroën parts catalogue. The engine and gearbox were located within a separate subframe mounted to the body via rubber bushes to reduce noise and vibrations; an access panel at the back of the cockpit was concealed under thick carpet to reduce the impact

ABOVE: The Bora had a familial resemblance to the Ghibli in its details but the shorter bonnet gave away the fact that the engine was mounted behind the passenger compartment.

of drivetrain din on the occupants. Later Maserati would add a 4.9-litre engine option, primarily for the US market.

Given the conceptual differences between the Ghibli and Bora, the newer car was offered alongside the existing model rather than replacing it. But sales of both – and the Citroën SM – were hit by the spike in oil prices in 1973 following the outbreak of hostilities in the Middle East. When oil-producing nations placed an embargo on countries which had supported Israel during the Yom Kippur war, the sudden contraction in supply sent further shocks through economies already affected by weakening stock markets.

Maserati had only just introduced another post-Citroën model, the Merak, also styled by Giugiaro but with a smaller engine – a three-litre version of the SM's V6 – enabling the cockpit to accommodate two smaller 'occasional' seats behind

ABOVE: Citroën's influence was clear to see in the Merak's interior, where the steering wheel and instrument panel were identical to the SM's.

the driver and passenger. Although the Merak was named after a star in the constellation of Ursa Minor, rather than a wind, it was identical to the Bora from nose to doors. As well as the braking system many interior elements, including the entire instrument panel, came from Citroën.

The timing of the oil crisis coincided inauspiciously with the launch of another new Maserati at the 1973 Paris Salon, a conceptual replacement for the Ghibli, also named after a desert wind: the Khamsin. Designed by Marcello Gandini at Bertone, the Khamsin is now regarded as something of a forgotten gem in the designer's canon – perhaps because his seminal Lamborghini Countach, a product of the same era, has taken all the oxygen. It is somewhat conservative in comparison but that is because the Khamsin was conceived as an elegant and subtle grand tourer rather than an eye-catching supercar.

BELOW: First shown at Geneva as a working prototype in 1974, the Marcello Gandini-designed Quattroporte sequel fell victim to the oil crisis and Maserati's change of ownership in 1975.

In five-litre form the V8 delivered plenty of acceleration with a suitably effortless torque curve, despite a proliferation of Citroën-derived hydraulic systems drawing power for the brakes and steering.

Maserati was also working on a successor to the Quattroporte and had got as far as building a prototype – Gandini styling on top of a Citroën SM floorpan, with a new front-mounted four-litre V8 engine based on the architecture of the SM's V6 – when the walls caved in. Citroën was facing a financial crisis of its own and could no longer afford to sustain an Italian subsidiary building cars for a denuded market. In June 1974 Michelin, Citroën's parent company, announced a 'merger' with French rival Peugeot; in fact it was more akin to a sale. Within months Peugeot's accountants were

ABOVE: Styled by Giugiaro, the Medici II pointed the way to the definitive Series III Quattroporte. The working prototype was sold to the Shah of Persia.

drawing red lines through various expensive projects including the SM, which was duly axed and many spare parts destroyed, and Maserati, which was put into liquidation in May 1975.

Alejandro de Tomaso, who had tried to acquire Maserati the previous decade, would get his prize after all. With financial support from the Italian government – which could ill-afford so many employers going bust – De Tomaso had been picking up distressed assets all over the country, including the coachbuilders Vignale and Ghia, and motorcycle manufacturers Moto Guzzi and Benelli. In August 1975 he added Maserati to his portfolio.

It is said that Giulio Alfieri played a key role in steering Adolfo Orsi towards Citroën rather than De Tomaso in 1968, and that this was the motivation for what happened next. Shortly after the takeover he arrived for work to find the contents of his office in the car park. His replacement was Aurelio Bertocchi, the son of his old sparring partner Guerrino…

Changing Hands

A Decade of Decline

Alejandro de Tomaso remains a polarizing figure for Maserati aficionados. Neverthless his intervention came at a time when Peugeot–Citroën had made the workforce redundant, and the workers had responded by blockading the factory: not an epoch in which any cars were likely to be built.

De Tomaso's modus operandi while snapping up distressed Italian businesses in the mid-1970s was to reduce the financial risk to himself by maintaining a minority shareholding via a holding company, while the majority of shares were owned by *Società per le Gestioni e Partecipazioni Industriali* (GEPI), a state-owned entity. Nevertheless he was granted full control of the businesses despite the lop-sided ownership structure; as a one-time racing driver and owner of his own eponymous marque, he was better placed to direct Maserati than some faceless technocrat with no interest in or knowledge of cars.

The new proprietor had the right instincts in terms of Maserati's direction but the execution was wanting. Ruthlessness was a De Tomaso trademark: this was a man who had left a failed political career in his native Argentina at the

OPPOSITE: Alejandro de Tomaso had tried to buy Maserati in the late 1960s.

OPPOSITE: In the recession of the late 1970s and early 1980s, Maserati marketing focused on low pricing.

age of 26, also abandoning his wife and children in the process, to set himself up as a racing driver and entrepreneur in Italy, where he had remarried into money. Apart from culling half of the workforce, his early moves included a purge of all Citroën-derived components in the model range simply because he didn't like the marque. While most of this would have escaped the notice of owners, it did extend to a complete revamp of the Merak's interior to something more in keeping with the brand.

De Tomaso also wanted to underline the fact this was the start of a new era by launching a new model. Given the scarcity of resources, including time, ahead of the 1976 show season, the 'new' car would actually be a reskinned version of a De Tomaso car which had already been in production for four years. Based around a somewhat primitive ladder chassis (albeit one designed by Gianpaolo Dallara, one of the 'fathers' of the Lamborghini Miura) and a Ford-sourced V8 engine, the Longchamp had been styled by Ghia's Tom Tjaarda, designer of the Ferrari 330 GT2+2 and 365 California. It wore its Ford sources in plain sight, including the headlamps, which were sourced from the Granada saloon. In executing a mild nose-and-tail job to transform the donor vehicle into the Maserati Kyalami – named after the circuit where Pedro Rodríguez won the 1967 South African Grand Prix in a Cooper Maserati – veteran stylist and coachbuilder Pietro Frua dispensed with these incongruous relics from the Ford parts bin. Frua had also designed the original Maserati Quattroporte and Mistral.

Naturally the Longchamp's Ford engine made way for a Maserati V8 – a 4.2-litre version of the extant eight-cylinder rather than the new one developed for the Quattroporte II, which De Tomaso axed. The car was not a massive sales success, reaching 200 customers in seven years of production – but neither was the Longchamp a hit, selling 410 in its 17-year life. Still, these figures dwarf those of the car that is perhaps

We've put the cat amongst the pigeons.

Now you can own one of the world's classic cars for less than you think.

Less, in fact, than most of the other exhilarating modes of transport you may be considering.

Ferrari 308 GTB	£20,100
Mercedes 380 SLC	£21,530
Porsche 928	£21,827
Maserati Merak	£18,987

And Maserati prices are down across the whole magnificent range.

A range of motor cars that is still very much in a class of its own.

Breathtaking performance.

The race bred handling. And the unsurpassed luxury and refinement. That's the beauty of owning and driving one of the world's great cars.

Cars like the exquisite mid-engined Merak SS. The executive 5-seater Kyalami with engine and transmission options. And the ultimate in high performance cars — the incredible 169 mph Khamsin powered by a 4.9 litre V8 with manual gearbox.

Maserati prices start at only £18,987 including air conditioning.

Talk Maserati. And watch the feathers fly. *Maserati*

SALES, SERVICE AND PARTS ENQUIRIES:-
INTERNATIONAL MOTORS LIMITED RYDER STREET, GREAT BRIDGE, WEST BROMWICH, WEST MIDLANDS B70 0EJ. TELEPHONE: 021 557 9951
PRICE COMPARISONS BASED ON MANUFACTURERS' LIST PRICES (INC. VAT AND CAR TAX) CORRECT AT THE TIME OF GOING TO PRESS.

BELOW: In 1977 the Khamsin was facelifted, gaining three slots in the nose and losing a lot of the Citroën-derived components.

the most niche production Maserati of all: built to order for territories which did not require European Type Approval, the Quattroporte II – powered by the three-litre ex-SM V6 – found 12 customers between 1976 and '78.

Fuel prices continued to be an issue for the performance car market, as did – albeit more locally – the Italian government's fiscal manoeuvrings. In 1977 the IVA purchase tax was doubled to 38 per cent for cars with engines displacing over two litres. Maserati, like Ferrari, responded by introducing variants specifically for the Italian market. The two-litre Merak could reach nearly 140mph given a flat and long enough stretch of road.

Another pillar of De Tomaso's new-model strategy would be a successor to that perennial 1960s favourite of the rich and famous, the Quattroporte. The original had sold in respectable numbers to a rarefied clientele. In the interregnum between the

end of production in 1969 and the attempt to develop a front-wheel-drive model under Citroën's ownership, Pietro Frua had designed and built two examples based on the Maserati Indy chassis; one was commissioned by the Aga Khan, the other was said to have gone to the King of Spain. While the definitive third-generation Quattroporte was shown in prototype form at the Turin Motor Show in 1976, part of De Tomaso's rush to put new models on display, it did not reach production until 1979.

The Quattroporte III's chassis was essentially another hand-me-down from De Tomaso, originally designed for the Deauville before being shortened for the Longchamp and Maserati Kyalami. If the Giugiaro-styled body also seemed vaguely familiar, that's because his ItalDesign company had already built Maserati Indy-based show cars badged as the Medici I and II as design studies for a putative four-door

BELOW: The more powerful Merak SS model arrived in 1975, later joined by a two-litre model aimed at the Italian market.

ABOVE: Opulence and conservativism defined the interior of the third-gen Quattroporte.

hatchback. For the third-generation Quattroporte Giugiaro repurposed a number of design features, particularly at the front end, to produce a sober but purposeful and elegant four-door saloon bodyshell with four square headlamps flanking the trident logo up front. The interior also featured the bar and fridge which were signature touches of the Medici II, later sold to the Shah of Persia shortly before his deposition in the Iranian revolution. At four metres long and weighing two tonnes, this was a car in which one made stately progress regardless of whether the 4.2 or 4.9-litre V8 had been specified. It was a favourite of Italian President Alessandro Pertini and opera singer Luciano Pavarotti, whose enthusiastic patronage led to over 2,100 examples being sold.

If the natural buyers of the Quattroporte were royalty, the political elite and celebrities – and therefore largely recession-proof – Maserati also needed a means of tapping into a broader market which was still affected by the decade's economic shocks. It was becoming increasingly difficult to get into the US, owing to emissions regulations and the imposition of disfiguring crash-protection measures such as large rubber bumpers. De Tomaso believed the answer lay in a car which could be produced in large volumes and considerably undercut opposition from the likes of Porsche and Ferrari on price.

Stylistically the 1981 Biturbo owed a debt to BMW's front-engine, rear-drive 3-Series. Designed in-house by Pierangelo Andreani, it straddled the worlds of the sports saloon and coupé: a two-door saloon bodyshell with a well-proportioned glasshouse and features derived from existing models in the lineup, particularly the nose and tail of the Quattroporte. It was a very different beast from the Khamsin and the Bora, which were being quietly dropped from the range. If its sobriety seems peculiar to modern eyes, it was entirely in keeping with an era of social unrest in which ostentatious displays of wealth were off the menu for buyers who did not travel with a security detail. Using the two-litre version of the V6 enabled Maserati to circumvent Italy's punitive IVA; a pair of small IHI turbochargers, one for each cylinder bank, brought power to 180bhp without incurring the 'lag' in delivery suffered by larger turbo impellers.

Maserati's official history includes the caveat "first-generation versions challenged the factory's production capacity". This is the company being considerably economical with the *actualité*, although the Biturbo does not really deserve its place in the countless lazily written 'listicles' of the world's worst cars which populate the internet. Certainly the rapid scaling-up of production to meet the enthusiastic initial

BELOW: Just over 1800 Meraks were built between 1972 and 1983 – modest numbers but more than double those of the rival Lamborghini Urraco.

demand – using the Innocenti car factory to manufacture various elements – brought quality-control problems, but the rushed development phase also baked in certain undesirable characteristics. Figures within Maserati at the time blame De Tomaso for targeting an unrealistically low price point, such that corners had to be cut – there was no budget for a cover for the spare wheel which hung below the boot, where it was a permanent eyesore.

Cheap materials meant the interior palpably looked built down to a price when new, and wore poorly. Inferior-quality steel – in fairness, an inherent problem for the Italian car

industry at the time – led to issues with rust. The engines were prone to overheating which required expensive rebuilds, and the electrics needed little prompting to go into meltdown. Reputational damage dented sales but Maserati continued to develop the Biturbo, adding the S model in 1983 with a much needed intercooler along with a higher compression ratio, bringing power to 205bhp. A 2.5-litre model was added for the export market in the same year.

De Tomaso was determined to milk the Biturbo format for all it was worth. Through the 1980s new variants appeared almost by the week, including the Biturbo 425, a four-door

version with a wheelbase extended by 86mm. Alongside this Maserati introduced a new model to replace the moribund Kyalami: wider, longer and taller than the Biturbo and based on a lengthened version of that car's chassis, the two-door 228 model aimed to bridge the gap in the range between the Biturbo and the Quattroporte. Mechanically similar to the Biturbo as well as bearing a strong family resemblance – they were chiefly distinguishable by the bigger car having a broader-rimmed chrome grille – the 228 had a larger 2.8-litre version of the twin-turbo V6 producing 250bhp, enough to propel the car from 0–60mph in six seconds. The interior was also more opulently trimmed, as befitted a more premium price point. But by the time the 228 reached the market in 1986, the Biturbo's early quality issues had tarnished Maserati's reputation to the point that it barely registered a blip in the sales charts – particularly in the US market at which it was so clearly aimed.

Still, the company had done enough to attract the interest of Lee Iacocca, head of US giant Chrysler and self-defined 'car guy'. In the 1980s he was on an acquisition trail that would lead to Lamborghini entering US ownership, but his company's relationship with Maserati would be a fleeting one – thankfully. Iacocca believed it was possible and indeed desirable to spread premium glitter on humdrum machinery by adding a well-known badge. The result was the Chrysler TC by Maserati, a badge-engineered horror based on a shortened version of the K platform which had spawned the Chrysler LeBaron and Dodge Daytona. Initially powered by the Daytona's 2.2-litre turbocharged inline-four, driving through a three-speed automatic gearbox, it lumbered from 0-60mph in an unimpressive 11 seconds. The model lasted three years from launch in 1986, cycling through three different engine variants (latterly a Mistubishi V6) to diminishing interest. Little wonder, since it cost twice as much as a LeBaron and had little to show for it except for the Maserati trident within the Chrysler logo on the nose.

Maserati kept the Biturbo alive through a Zagato-engineered convertible variant in 1984, followed by a Marcello Gandini restyle of the tin-top model in 1987 and the introduction of the Kharif coupé in 1988. Dropping the Biturbo name in favour of number-based nomenclature put some distance between the

BELOW: Zagato designed and engineered a convertible version of the Biturbo in 1984.

SOLE UNITED KINGDOM CONCESSIONAIRES

MERIDIEN
Maserati

77 HIGH STREET, LYNDHURST
HAMPSHIRE, SO43 7PB
FOR SALES, SERVICE & PARTS
TELEPHONE: 0703 283404
FAX: 0703 282791

326 Horses.

Almost an unfair advantage.

OPPOSITE: The Shamal two-door coupé carried over a great deal of the Biturbo, including the doors – and the architecture of the new V8 engine was based on the Biturbo's V6, too.

car and its troubled early years, but not enough for Maserati to escape niche manufacturer status: when the Gandini-designed, twin-turbo V8 Shamal was launched in 1989, among the more obvious evidence of Maserati's tight financial circumstances were the carry-over doors and interior from the Biturbo. Such budget as existed had been spent on developing the all-new engine, a definitive break from a family line which had begun with the 450S in 1956.

Faced with continued operating losses, De Tomaso had to seek outside investment to buy out GEPI's interest in the company. In 1990 Fiat took a 49 per cent shareholding in Maserati; Innocenti was split off from the company and its factory in Lambrate closed two years later.

After another Gandini restyle in 1990, the Biturbo gave way to the Ghibli II in 1992. Development budgets dictated little change to the bodyshell and interior, though the engine range received a mild performance uplift. There were plans to introduce a mid-engined sportscar to be called the Chubasco but it was deemed too expensive to build so the concept was recycled into the Barchetta, a two-seater racing car with a backbone chassis based on the De Tomaso Guara; with this Maserati aimed to stage a potentially lucrative one-make racing series for high-net-worth customers.

This idea fell by the wayside after Alejandro de Tomaso suffered a stroke in 1993. Although he subsequently recovered, declining health prompted him to remove himself from public life, place his son in charge of his eponymous car company, and sell the remainder of his shares in Maserati to Gianni Agnelli's Fiat empire. Rivals for so long, Maserati and Ferrari would now have to find a way to coexist.

Joining the Neighbours

The Trident and the Prancing Horse

> For the best part of four years Maserati existed in a sort of limbo, the proverbial elephant in the room for an industrial empire which also included Ferrari, at one time Maserati's bitter rival on track. Such were the entrenched cultural divisions between the two marques that aficionados of each – particularly in the Modena area – preferred not to speak the name of the other.

As the cliché goes, the squeakiest hinges get the most oil. And in the early 1990s Ferrari, for so long the Fiat group's halo brand, was almost permanently in crisis. Infighting after Enzo Ferrari's death in 1988 had rendered the Formula 1 team almost a national embarrassment – it went winless for three seasons between 1991 and '93 – and the 348, its 'volume' road model, was well outclassed by rivals. Fiat's suits patently failed to understand the performance car business and it was not until Fiat magnate Gianni Agnelli drafted in Luca di Montezemolo, Ferrari's F1 team manager in the glory days of the mid-1970s and more recently an architect of the successful Italia '90 football World Cup, that the company entered turnaround.

OPPOSITE: New ownership restored the value of the brand.

BELOW: While the fourth Quattroporte's style broke little new ground, a lighter bodyshell conferred greater agility.

Amid the corporate firefighting up the road at Maranello, Maserati quietly got on with a policy of 'more of the same' in product terms. At the 1994 Geneva Motor Show the company unveiled a mildly restyled Ghibli II with a refreshed interior, larger wheels, electronically adjustable suspension and anti-lock brakes, the latter elements simply keeping up with modern performance car trends. A month later, in Turin, Maserati revealed its first post-De Tomaso product: the fourth-generation Quattroporte, based on a stretched version of the Biturbo chassis and powered by the twin-turbo V6 2.8-litre V6 as used in the Ghibli II (the two-litre was also offered for the Italian market). Again, Marcello Gandini was responsible for

the exterior, essentially a modernized take on what had gone before; the most obvious points of difference were the interior, which was more richly trimmed, and the driving experience, which was more sprightly since the car was up to 300kg lighter depending on engine choice. Eighteen months later another variant joined the range, featuring the new all-aluminium V8 as used in the Shamal.

Otherwise, Maserati existed in a quiet backwater of the Fiat empire – until a major scandal erupted in 1996. As part of the official transfer of assets between entities old and new during Fiat's acquisition, Alejandro de Tomaso had in effect retained ownership of 19 historic Maseratis on display in the company

museum. Besides examples of the first-generation Quattroporte it included race cars with cherished history, including a V12-engined 250F, the Drogo-bodied Tipo 61 'Birdcage' in which Masten Gregory and Lloyd Casner won the 1961 Nürburgring 1000kms, and the one-off 420M/58 raced by Stirling Moss in the 1958 'Monzanapolis' Race of Two Worlds with sponsorship from the Eldorado ice cream company – one of the earliest examples of on-car sponsor branding in European motor racing. In July 1996 De Tomaso had the cars removed and sent to England, where they were subsequently advertised for sale by auction.

This news caused sensation and outrage in Modena. But the cars had already gone – it was claimed by some sources that they had been offered to Fiat, but the company was not interested in buying. Local anger reached the seat of national government; even the minister for culture got involved. But there would be no rescue from the taxpayer this time. Private capital was required – and it arrived in the form of Umberto Panini, brother of football trading card magnate Giuseppe Panini. The auction house removed the cars from sale and they were returned to Italy, where Umberto accommodated them in a new museum on his farm.

Fiat may or may not have been offered the historic machinery but it now identified Maserati as a problem which needed to be solved. Under Montezemolo, Ferrari's F1 team was returning to competitiveness and its road car range was improving in performance, modernity and quality. It seemed logical to Agnelli to expand Montezemolo's remit to incorporate Maserati – and, courtesy of some financial engineering within the Fiat Group, Maserati became a 50 per cent subsidiary of Ferrari in 1997. Montezemolo would later describe the scene when he first visited the Maserati works at the Viale Ciro Menotti as "a peaceful home for stray cats".

OPPOSITE: Having turned Ferrari around in the early 1990s, Luca di Montezemolo mapped out a similar plan for Maserati.

ABOVE: Maserati's first all-new model under Fiat ownership, the 3200 GT was a vital step in the company's evolution.

A clean break was required, both in terms of the model range and the means of production. As Ferrari drew up plans for a new facility to replace the existing factory in Modena (ultimately only some external walls would remain), it pushed through development of a new model to replace the Shamal and begin the process of repositioning Maserati as a slightly softer and more luxurious brand. Initially the intention was to continue the tradition of naming Maseratis after winds, but the chosen name – Mistral – had already been registered by the Volkswagen Group, so instead the company looked further back in history to its first production grand tourer, the 3500 GT. Since the new car was to be powered by an evolution of the Shamal's twin-turbo 3.2-litre V8, it was named the 3200 GT.

Giorgetto Giugiaro was responsible for styling the bodyshell, neatly accomplishing the feat of incorporating some recognizable flourishes from previous Maseratis without veering into pastiche. And Giugiaro himself was present, alongside Stirling Moss, when Montezemolo presented the 3200 GT to the world's press in September 1998, just before the Paris Motor Show. By then Maserati was in dire need of the car. Despite the unveiling earlier that year of the Quattroporte Evoluzione, a refreshed model claiming to have 50 per cent new parts, Maserati managed to sell a little over 500 cars worldwide in 1998.

From this nadir the recovery was rapid. In 2000, as the new buildings on Viale Ciro Menotti approached completion, Maserati moved four times as many units as it had two years earlier. The 3200 GT proved transformative, even though

BELOW: The Spyder signalled Maserati's imminent re-entry into the important US market.

when pushed to the limits of adhesion it began to show some of the truculent manners of the company's previous proprietor. These traits were accentuated slightly in the automatic model, introduced in 1999: circumstances dictated that the four-speed gearbox was bought in rather than developed in-house, and it occasionally struggled to transmit the V8's prodigious torque to the road in a decorous fashion. Not that this dissuaded buyers, and the 3200 GT's success moved Montezemolo to persuade Fiat to grant Ferrari 100 per cent control of the company.

Maserati's future was now clear: along with better quality, there would be more engineering synergies with Ferrari, a return to the track – and, most significantly, a return to the lucrative US market Maserati had been absent from since 1990. Employees would just have to become accustomed to being part of the Ferrari family, a process which had begun when production briefly transferred to Maranello during the factory reconstruction. Among Ferrari's plans was a new, cutting-edge paint shop on its Maranello site which would set new

ABOVE: Pininfarina styled the fifth-generation Quattroporte, establishing a new design language for future Maserati models.

OVERLEAF: Improving build quality and material feel were key targets as the company moved upmarket.

standards in finish for both its own cars and future Maseratis. Additionally, and somewhat controversially for purists, all engines would be designed and built by Ferrari in Maranello.

To some it was heresy but the results justified the means as sales volumes continued to expand. The 3200 GT was quickly replaced by a new model, although the open-top Spyder variant was launched first, at the Frankfurt show in 2001. The Coupé, signifying Maserati's ambitions, was launched on US soil – Detroit – the following year. Though stylistically similar to the 3200 GT it had been completely re-engineered with an emphasis on build quality, and was now powered by a dry-sumped 4.2-litre Ferrari V8 also used in the hugely popular 360 Modena.

Half a century after the last Pininfarina-bodied Maserati, the famous coachbuilder – historically associated with Ferrari – was brought in to design the bodyshell for the fifth-generation Quattroporte. Again the intention was to signal a break with the past, the fourth-generation model having sputtered out sales-wise in 2001. ItalDesign had pitched a radical idea for

BELOW: Five metres long and two metres high, ItalDesign's Buran concept envisaged the future of limousines in MPV form.

a successor that mixed limousine and SUV elements but its concept car, the Buran – named after a Siberian wind – was considered a step too far, even with the American market in mind.

Based on the new M139 platform, powered by the same Ferrari-sourced V8 as the Coupé, and riding on adaptive suspension, the latest Quattroporte was a remarkable departure from the conservatism of previous models – and the rest of its sector. Pininfarina chief designer Ken Okuyama cleverly integrated existing design cues into a shape with a genuinely imposing presence, while introducing new ideas such as the large-format grille which would define Maseratis for years to come. Shortly after its public debut at Frankfurt in September 2003 it was shown to the high-net-worth US audience at the Pebble Beach Concours d'Elegance, a confident statement of intent by the company. Its sheer size was a clear pitch to the US market: while the fourth-generation model had been criticized

ABOVE: Based on the Ferrari Enzo and bristling with advanced technology, the MC12 race car sparked outrage among racing rivals.

for having too small a cabin, this latest one boasted similar dimensions to the Mercedes S-Class.

All this took place against a background of disarray in the wider Fiat Group following the death of Gianni Agnelli from prostate cancer in January 2003. Fiat Auto's losses were contaminating the financial health of the wider organization, and would trigger a period of tumult as corporate predators circled while the Agnelli dynasty wrestled with the matter of succession. Ultimately his chosen heir, grandson John Elkann, would win out, making the key hire of lawyer and corporate turnaround specialist Sergio Marchionne, who became Fiat Group's CEO in 2004.

For a brief period Maserati would remain largely untouched by the chaos elsewhere in the empire and continued its plans to re-enter the racing scene. Giorgio Ascanelli, race engineer to Ayrton Senna and Gerhard Berger at McLaren in Formula 1 at the turn of the 1990s, led development of what would become the MC12, based on the carbonfibre monocoque underpinnings

JOINING THE NEIGHBOURS

BELOW: Fifty road-going examples of the 217mph MC12 were built to satisfy FIA homologation requirements, half of them 150mm shorter owing to a rule change.

ABOVE: The Coupé replaced the 3200 GT in 2001.

of the Ferrari Enzo supercar and using its gearbox and a dry-sumped version of its V12 engine. Only the windscreen was shared with the donor car; the MC12 received a longer and wider bodyshell which was among the first works at Ferrari–Maserati of new design director Frank Stephenson, acclaimed designer of the new Mini. Although the first sketch was produced by Fabrizio Giugiaro, son of Giorgetto, and subject to aerodynamic work by Dialma Zinelli at Dallara, Stephenson was responsible for one of the most important elements of its final evolution: making it road-legal. Among the chief requirements of the programme was the ability to produce 25 road-going equivalents to satisfy the homologation requirements of its target series, the FIA GT Championship.

Nevertheless, the MC12 had a troubled journey through the homologation process as other competitors lobbied against the FIA permitting such a technically advanced car to compete. The debate continued even as the first MC12s were finally allowed to compete in the final rounds of the 2004 FIA GT season. Thereafter it became one of the most competitive cars in the series, despite being subject to various balance-of-performance handicaps to furnish a more level playing field.

At the MC12's first 'shakedown' run at Ferrari's Fiorano test track in early 2004, the nearby factory practically emptied as staff rushed to see the new car in action: F1 team boss Jean Todt and world champion Michael Schumacher watched as Andrea Bertolini conducted its first lap. It then spent three hours in the garage while a broken driveshaft was fixed, but this was probably a positive in terms of Maranello productivity.

The operational intimacy between Ferrari and Maserati, unthinkable in the earlier years of the two companies, had set the trident marque on the road back to greatness – but a fork in that road was now approaching. As the Fiat Group restructured under Sergio Marchionne, with a view to ultimately splitting Ferrari off and floating it on the stock exchange, Maserati – still making a paper loss – had to be removed from Maranello's balance sheet. The companies were separated in April 2005 and Maserati became part of the Fiat Group once again.

"I believe very much in Maserati," said Marchionne at the time, "but Maserati must believe in itself."

To the Second Century

Sharing and Electrifying

When Sergio Marchionne, already CEO of the Fiat Group, replaced Herbert Demel as CEO of Fiat Auto in February 2005 it signified a major shift in direction for the troubled car maker – and the other manufacturers in the empire. Demel, the first non-Italian to head up Fiat, had been brought in just 18 months earlier with a mandate to repair relations with General Motors; a 'strategic partnership' between the two entities had soured when Fiat's previous leadership had sought to resolve their financial problems by triggering a contractual clause which would have forced GM to expand its 20 per cent shareholding in Fiat.

Regime change can be brutal. Within two months Marchionne had transferred Maserati from Ferrari's ownership, removed the recently appointed Martin Leach as head of Maserati and added the Modenese subsidiary to the remit of Alfa Romeo CEO Karl-Heinz Kalbfell – another newcomer to the Fiat conglomerate. After several years of intimate connection with one old track rival, Maserati would now be tied to another. The commercial realities of

OPPOSITE: Millennial Maserati cockpits were clearly Ferrari-based.

OPPOSITE: Sergio Marchionne rescued the Fiat Group but his ascent to power brought political turbulence in its wake, including a rotating cast of Maserati CEOs.

car manufacture in the twenty-first century dictated more use of common parts, including entire platforms; Maserati's adoption of Ferrari powertrains (and, in the case of the MC12, much of the underlying chassis and mechanical platform) represented the first steps into this new world. How would the marque retain its identity as its centenary approached?

Although Maserati was still booking an operating loss, owing to the recent and very necessary investment in its manufacturing facilities, sales were surging. It was Alfa Romeo which was the sick man of the Fiat Group. Decades of national ownership before it fell into Fiat's orbit had virtually killed the brand, as lackadaisical build quality and poor materials undid the appeal of quirky designs. Marchionne's vision was to relaunch it as an upmarket sporting brand, albeit at a price point some way south of Maserati.

On paper, Kalbfell was the ideal figure to oversee this brand transformation while continuing to nurture Maserati's return to health. A BMW man since 1977, he combined engineering savvy with a clear idea of product: Kalbfell had been instrumental in BMW's return to Formula 1 and superintended the rebirth of the Mini and Rolls-Royce brands under BMW ownership. But as a hire of the previous regime – headhunted by Demel – he would likely be on borrowed time in a period of corporate bloodletting under a new overall boss. It came to pass with startling rapidity. Just months after laying out his vision for Maserati – "Its relationship with Ferrari will continue, and it'll continue to build beautiful, individual, exclusive Italian cars" he told the *Telegraph* newspaper – he was effectively demoted, remaining CEO of Maserati alone as Antonio Baravalle was put in charge of Alfa Romeo. Life in the boardroom of Italy's biggest industrial group must have resembled an episode of *Game of Thrones*.

BELOW: Despite its short gestation period, the GranTurismo was a remarkably complete sportscar – and a commercial hit.

When Kalbfell arrived, development of a replacement for the 4200 Coupé and its Spyder variant was well underway. But the new sales target of 10,000 units per year (almost double what Maserati actually sold in 2005) prompted a change in priorities, as it became clear the new model would be more expensive to manufacture. Ferrari gratefully took on the project – it eventually became the F149 California – and Maserati pivoted to a new concept. Given the chosen launch date of the 2007 Geneva Show, the clock was ticking. Maserati had less than a year to design, develop and tool up for production – hence the decision to base the Coupé's replacement on a shortened version of the M139 platform which underpinned the Quattroporte.

At the time, industry insiders speculated that the cost-cutting measures would extend to Maserati dropping the V8 engine in favour of a 3.2-litre Alfa Romeo V6 originally developed by General Motors. Brand loyalists were therefore delighted when the new car, named the GranTurismo, was unveiled – not only did the muscular, purposeful shell (styled by one of Pininfarina's new stars, Jason Castriota) feature a grille which harked back to the A6GCS, under the bonnet the 4.2-litre V8 remained in place. Castriota had been involved in Pininfarina's Birdcage 75th, an MC12-based concept shown at Geneva in 2005 to mark the coachbuilder's 75th anniversary, and the lines of that car – which itself aped the Birdcage

ABOVE: In retaining the interior layout of the GranTurismo, the GranCabrio became Maserati's first cabriolet to offer proper seating for four people.

Maseratis of the 1960s – were reflected in the flowing lines of the GranTurismo's front wings.

Response in the media was mixed, since the GranTurismo's close relationship with the Quattroporte made it heavier and less agile than some rival cars. Writing in *Car* magazine, the comic actor and sportscar aficionado Rowan Atkinson summed up the GranTurismo's ethos: "If you were expecting a hardcore driver's coupé, this isn't it. But it was always Maserati's intention to make this car biased more towards luxury than performance: 40 per cent are US-bound, after all. And enthusiasts at least have the comfort of knowing that more focused versions will come later."

Maserati had signalled the arrival of a more performance-oriented option and that hit the market a year later, packing a 4.9-litre V8 with a six-speed Graziano automated manual gearbox. A racing version, the MC, followed in 2009 with a specific mandate for competition in the FIA GT4 series.

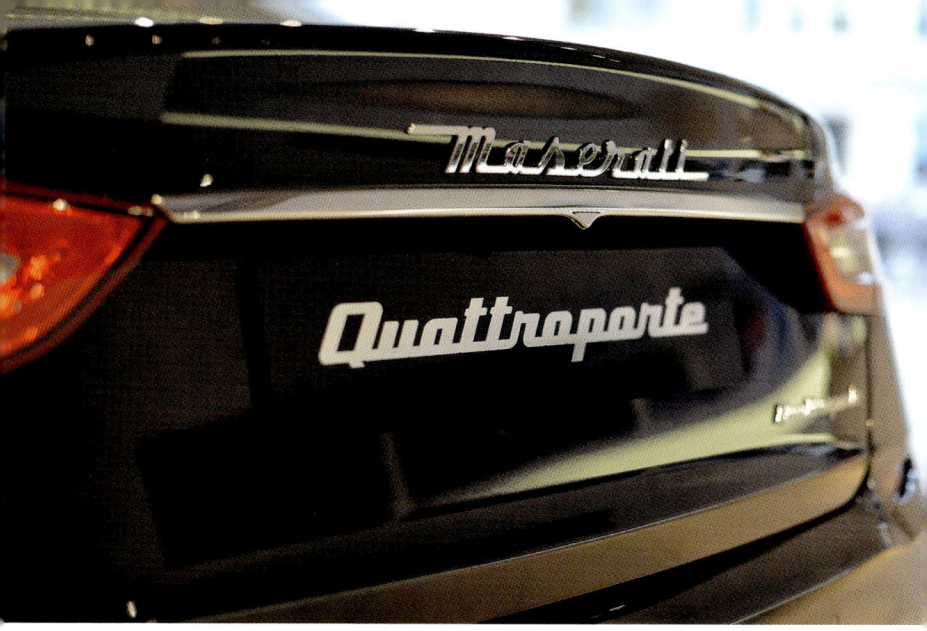

ABOVE: The sixth Quattroporte completed Maserati's transition to in-house styling and was built in the newly refitted ex-Bertone Grugliasco plant near Turin.

While it was known that Maserati was also evaluating a launch into the SUV segment – one which accounted for a substantial element of the US market and which was increasingly popular in the US – it would not happen on Kalbfell's watch. In September 2006 he abruptly departed, replaced by Fiat's head of fleet car sales, Roberto Ronchi. The cycle of executive churn continued as Ronchi enjoyed just under two years in the hot seat before making way for Harald Wester, who dovetailed this role with his existing one of Chief Technical Officer for the entire Fiat Group.

Regardless of developments in the boardroom, in 2007 Maserati had made a profit for the first time since Fiat had acquired it from De Tomaso. Sales of 7,496 units, driven by strong European demand for the Quattroporte and GranTurismo, were a new record even if they fell short of the 10,000 target announced in 2005. Under Wester, Maserati

BELOW: Based on Jeep Cherokee mechanicals, the Kubang show car was an exercise in seeing if the world was ready for a Maserati SUV.

would take more steps towards the mainstream, revealing the Kubang concept car at the 2011 Frankfurt Show. The name was an explicit throwback to an earlier Giugiaro-designed concept shown at Detroit eight years previously and based on the mechanicals of an Audi A8. That car, the Kubang GT, was a putative co-production with Audi which fell through the cracks in the dog days of the De Tomaso ownership. Though the 2011 Kubang was described as an evolution of that concept it had practically nothing in common with it, based as it was on the Jeep Cherokee platform but powered by the familiar Ferrari-Maserati V8. Here the world got its first glimpse of what a Maserati SUV would look like.

Wester's stated aim was to have a range of six models and reach 70,000 worldwide sales by 2018. An ambitious target but achievable through the adoption of a new rear-wheel-drive

platform, codenamed M156, which would underpin the next generation of Maseratis as well as achieving cost amortization through deployment elsewhere in a Fiat empire which was, against expectations, growing.

Maserati was not the only company in the Fiat Group which had become profitable. In 2009 Sergio Marchionne had achieved the seemingly impossible and returned Fiat Auto's balance sheet to the black. His ambition did not stop there. Across the Atlantic, the Chrysler Group was in dire peril and Marchionne offered the hand of partnership – one which, through a complicated process of financial engineering which involved Chrysler filing for Chapter 11 bankruptcy protection, and the tacit assistance of the Barack Obama administration, would lead to the formation of Fiat Chrysler Automobiles five years later, in 2014.

The partnership and gradual merging of the two enterprises would enable the M156 platform to underpin new Chrysler

ABOVE: Although the Kubang was shown in 2011, it would be another five years until the first Maserati SUV entered showrooms. Though anathema to sportscar purists, this segment is a must for all mainstream car makers.

BELOW: Production of the Quattroporte ceased in 2023 as Maserati began to electrify its model range.

OPPOSITE: When the Levante went on sale in 2016 it featured a diesel option.

models and provide a new engine option for Maserati in the form of Chrysler's Pentastar V6. A twin-turbo three-litre V6 based on the Pentastar was the entry-level engine in the fifth-generation Quattroporte, introduced in 2013 and based on the M156. In the same year Maserati revived the Ghibli name in a new mid-size luxury saloon based on a shortened M156 platform. Both cars were built in a new factory near Milan, formerly owned by Bertone.

Wester handed over to new CEO Reid Bigland in 2016, having expanded sales to over 36,000 units per year. Among his last acts was to unveil the Levante, the definitive Maserati SUV, named after the easterly wind that blows through the Strait of Gibraltar. Purists, naturally, were aghast – there was a diesel engine option, too. But this was not the most significant development in the Italian car industry that year: in January Marchionne announced that Ferrari would be split

off from the larger group and floated on the New York Stock Exchange to bankroll a larger investment programme across FCA. As part of this Ferrari would ultimately cease to supply engines to Maserati.

In the summer of 2018 Marchionne unexpectedly resigned from all his positions within Fiat Chrysler Automobiles. On 25 July he died. It subsequently emerged he had been treated for cancer for over a year. Naturally the immense power vacuum created by his absence led to further boardroom tumult and Maserati would have two more CEOs – Tim Kuniskis and Davide Grasso – before FCA merged with Peugeot–Citroën to form the Stellantis Group in 2021. After decades apart, Maserati and Citroën would enjoy family ties again.

In 2022, Maserati returned to single-seater competition 65 years after Adolfo Orsi reluctantly closed the company's factory racing team. This, at least, was the marketing gloss. The reality was somewhat more nuanced: Maserati entered a naming and powertrain partnership in Formula E, the FIA's top-level electric racing championship, with the Monaco-based MSG team which had previously run under the Venturi banner. Thus it was more akin to Maserati's brief late-1960s reappearance as an engine supplier to Cooper.

Formula E has proven itself as a technology incubator as well as a focus for marketing high-performance electric vehicles. In its first year it was purely a branding exercise since the cars and powertrains were standardized but, while the chassis and batteries remain identical, manufacturers have been able to construct their own electric motors and gearboxes since the second season. Maserati's arrival coincided with the debut of the third-generation FE car, featuring four-wheel drive and capable of reaching 200mph. The deal with MSG not only enabled Maserati to have title

OPPOSITE: While Formula E is largely a branding exercise, it offers Maserati a marketing platform for its bold plans to go all-electric by 2030.

BELOW: The MC20 two-seat sportscar introduced the company's last internal combustion engine, a twin-spark V6 related to the one used in the Alfa Romeo Stelvio.

ABOVE: The Grecale SUV slotted in below the Levante in the range and is assembled alongside its Alfa Romeo Stelvio sibling at the Stellantis-owned Cassino plant.

branding for the entire project, it also enabled it to badge the car the Tipo Folgore, a moniker which combined an antique Maserati naming convention with the new title for the company's electric road car offerings.

Folgore – Italian for a bolt of lightning – would distinguish the all-electric models from their petrol-powered brethren. In 2023 Maserati unveiled the Grecale, a new small SUV which slotted in under the Levante, initially with a turbocharged inline-four engine in a choice of two power outputs, plus a performance-oriented Trofeo model.

For the 2024 model year it added a fully electric Folgore model alongside a new GranTurismo with a twin-turbo V6, plus a Folgore-badged variant in which three electric motors combined to deliver the equivalent of 818bhp to all four wheels. Capable of accelerating from rest to 60mph in a claimed 2.7 seconds, the GranTurismo Folgore comprehensively outperformed its conventional counterparts, the most powerful of which mustered 542bhp.

While keen drivers may struggle to adjust to the absence of the familiar sounds of internal combustion, high-end performance cars can mitigate this through responsiveness and brutal acceleration. In the GranTurismo Folgore one motor drives the front axle while the other two individually drive the rear wheels, allowing for a torque-vectoring feature claimed to replicate the characteristics of a limited-slip differential.

These new models were acting as a symbolic passing of the baton. In line with the policy of the rest of the Stellantis Group, Maserati announced another significant development for the company: the gradual phasing out of pure-internal combustion powertrains from the 2025 model year onwards and a commitment to going all-electric in 2030. The arrival of the first electric powertrains in the GranTurismo and Grecale would dovetail with the end of production of the twin-turbo V8.

Electrification represents a problematic necessity for every performance car manufacturer except those vanishing few who enjoy a client base for whom money is no object. But the fact is fossil fuels are running out and synthetic fuels are yet to be produced at scale. Maserati's bold plunge into total electrification is an unusual move in this space, but not at all out of character for a marque which has gone to the edge of extinction more than once and survived – and thrived.

INDEX

(Key: *italic* refers to photos/captions)

A

Aga Khan 107
Agnelli, Gianni 115, 119, 123, 131
Alfa Romeo 16, 29, 34, 47, *52*, 56, 74, 140, 143
    158 60, 62
    P2 48, 50
    P3 *21*
    Stelvio *153*, *154*
    Tipo B *52*
Alfieri, Giulio 40, *88*, 89, 93–5, 99
Aliprandi, Marquis Diego de Sterlich 17
American Automobile Association (AAA) 31
Andreani, Pierangelo 109
Appleton, John *46*
Ards TT *46*
Argentine Grand Prix *65*, 74
Arnold, Billy 32
Ascanelli, Giorgio 131
Ascari, Alberto 61
Association Internationale des Automobile Clubs Reconnus (IAIACR) 46–9, 53
Atkinson, Rowan 144
Audi 146
Auto Avio Costruzione, 815 35
Auto Union 31, 53, *53*
Autocostruzioni Diatto 16
Automobile Club de France (ACF) 46, 73

B

Behra, Jean 74, 76, *76*
Belgian Grand Prix 50
Bellentani, Vittorio 37, 62, 74
Benelli 99
Benz, Carl 45
Berger, Gerhard 131
Bertocchi, Guerino *15*, 19, 95, 99
Bertolini, Andrea 135
Bertone 97, *145*, 148
Bertone Grugliasco factory *145*, 148
Bigland, Reid 148
Biondetti, Clemente ('The Wolf of Tuscany') 29
BMW 109, 140
Borzacchini, Baconin 31, 47
Boyle, Michael ('Umbrella Mike') 32, 34
Brickyard 31–2
British Grand Prix *30*, *58*, 61
British Racing Drivers' Club (BRDC) 56, *58*
Buell, Temple 77
Buenos Aires 1000km 76
Bugatti *21*, 49, *52*
    Type 35 48

C

Camoradi 79
Campari, Giuseppe 51, *51*
Caniato, Alfredo 47
Car 144
Caracciola, Rudolf 58
Carrozzeria Drogo 81
Casner, Lloyd ('Lucky') 79, 81, 123
Cassino factory *154*
Castriota, Jason 143
Cesare Isotta 13
Chicago Mob 32
Chilometro Lanciato (Flying Kilometre) 19
Chiron, Louis *57*, 62
Chrysler 112–13, 147–8, 151
Circuito de Modena 29
Citroën 41, 87–99, *90*, 104, *106*, 107, 151
    DS 87–8, 91
    SM *87*, *89*, 91–2, *93*, 96, *97*, 98, 98–9, 106
    Traction Avant 87
    2CV 87, 88
Collins, Peter 67
Colombo, Gioacchino 37, 56, 64, *64*, 67
Concours d'Elegance 130
Cooper 67, 92
Coppa Acerbo *16*
Coppa di Messina 20
Coppa Florio 13
Cortese, Franco *53*
Costin, Frank 77
Coupes de Paris 59
Credito Italiano 40
Crispi, Francesco 12
Crystal Palace *34*
Cucinotta, Letterio 31
Cunningham, Briggs 79–80

D

Dallara 134
Dallara, Gianpaolo 104
De Tomaso 95, 99, 103–15, 120, 123, 145, 146
Demel, Herbert 139, 140
Diatto 18, *18*, 46
    4DC *12*
    20S 17
Dodge 112
DOHC 62
Dreyfus, René *21*

E

Eldorado 123
Elkann, John 131
ERA 31
Étancelin, Philippe *62*
European Grand Prix 31
European Type Approval 106

F

Fangio, Juan Manuel 40, 60, 65, *65*, *67*, 74–6
Fantuzzi 79
Farina 35
Farina, Battista ('Pinin') 35
Fédération Internationale de l'Automobile (FIA) 46, *132*, 135, 144, 151
Ferrari 20, 35, 41, 47–53, 50, *52*, 57, *62*, *64*, 67, 79, 87, 93, 104, 106, 109, 115, 119–35, 139–40, 146, 148–50,

156 INDEX

750 Monza 74
D50 65–6
Enzo *131*, 134
F149 California 142
Fiorano test track 135
Ferrari, Enzo 15, 21, 35, 45, 47, 48, 50, 51, 62, 87, 94
Fesetics, Count Erno *48*
FIA GT Championship 135
FIA GT4 series 144
Fiat 13, 15, 34, 87, 115, 119–55
Fiat Chrysler Automobiles 147
Filippini, Corrado 27–9
Filippis, Maria Teresa de 67, *67*
Florio, Vincenzo 73
Flying Kilometre (Chilometro Lanciato) 19
Ford 93, 104
Formula 1 60, *62*, 64, 65, 67, *67*, 73, 119, 131, 140
Formula 2 *45*, 62, 65, 67
Formula A 60
Formula E 151, *151*
Formula Libre 47, 60
Franco Tosi Meccanica 14
Frankfurt Motor Show 130, 146
French Grand Prix 51, *62*
Frua, Pietro *40*, 107

G

Gandini, Marcello 97, *98*, 113, 115, 120

General Motors (GM) 139, 143
Geneva Motor Show 35, 91, 93, *95*, *98*, 120, 142, 143–4
GEPI 103, 115
German Grand Prix *53*, *67*, 74
Ghia 99, 104
Giugiaro, Fabrizio 134
Giugiaro, Giorgetto 92, 95, *99*, 107–8, 125, 134
Graffenried, Toulo de *59*
Grand Prix de l'ACF 46, 73
Grand Prix d'Elegance 35
Grand Prix des Voiturettes *9*
Graziano Trasmissioni 144
Great Depression 27
Great War 14, 17, 33
Gregory, Masten 77, 79, 123

H

Hansgen, Walt *81*
Hawthorn, Mike 67, 74
Hill, Phil 74
Hispano-Suiz 14, 16
Horn, Ted 34
Howe, Countess *58*
Howe, Earl 56, *58*
Hudson, Rock *36*
Hulman, Tony 33

I

Imperia factory *52*
Imperial Trophy *34*
Indianapolis 500 (Indy 500) 27, *27*, 31, 32, 33, *33*, 59, 76
Indianapolis Motor Speedway 31, 33
Innocenti 40, 110, *110*, 114, 115
International Brotherhood of Electrical Workers 32
Isotta Fraschini *9*, 13, 16, 21
Istituto per la Ricostruzione Industriale 50
ItalDesign 107, 127–30, *130*
Italia '90 119
Italian Grand Prix *12*, 17, *88*
IVA purchase tax 106, 109

J

Jaguar *76*
D-type 74
Jeep 146, *146*
Jersey Road Race *57*
Juan Carlos I, King of Spain 107
Junior Automobiles 13

K

Kalbfell, Karl-Heinz 139, 140, 145

L

Lamborghini 93, 97, 104, *110*
Lampredi, Aurelio *64*
Lancia 65
Lancia, Vincenzo 12–13
Lang, Hermann 53, 58
Le Mans 24 Hours 56, 73, 74, 75, *75*, 76, *76*, 79, 81, *81*, 93
Leach, Martin 139
Littoriale 27
Livorno *52*
Losi, Carolina 9, 10

M

McLaren 131
McLaren, Bruce *81*
Madonie 73–4
Mallaret, Guy 93
Maranello factory 120, 126–7, 135
Marchionne, Sergio 131, 135, 139–40, *140*, 147–51
Marchiso, Onesimo 17
Maserati:
4CL 60–1, 74
4CL ('Linguette') 57–8, *57*
4CLT *30*, *60*, 61, 62
4CLT/48 *59*
4CLT 'Voiturette' *45*
4CM ('Corsa Monoposto') 53
6C-34, 53
6CM *53*, 56–7, *56*, 57, 60, 74
8C 26M 48, *50*, 51
8C 2800 *50*
8CL 59
8CM *21*, *48*
8CM-3000 49–51, *50*, 51, *51*, 53
8CTF *27*, 32, *33*, 53, 60
8RI 32
26B 31
26M *46*
250 GTO 81
250F *62*, *64*, 65–6, *65*, *67*, 74, *79*,

123
300S 77
350S 76
450S 75, *75*, 76–7, *76*, *77*
1100cc engine *46*
3200 GT 124–7, *124*
3500 GT *36*, 40, 124
3500 GT Series II *41*
3500GT 75
A6 35, *35*, 62
A6 ('Extra Lusso') *35*
A6GCM *45*, 62–5, *62*, *64*
A6GCS ('Corsa Sport') 62, 143
Appleton Special *46*
Barchetta 115
Birdcage 75th 143–4
Biturbo 109–15, *115*
Boomerang *94*, *95*
Bora 93, *95*, 96, *96*, 109
Boyle Special 32–3, *33*
Buran 130, *130*
Chubasco 115
Citroën era 87–99, *88*, 104, 107
Coupé 127, 130, 134, 142
EVs (electric vehicles) *148*, *151*
Ghibli *96*, 115, 120, 148
GranCabrio *144*
GranTurismo *142*, 143, 144–5, *144*, 155

Grecale 154–5, *154*
Indy 89, 107
Khamsin 97, *106*, 109
Kharif 113
Kubang 146, *146*
Kyalami 104
Levante 148, *148*, 154, *154*
Longchamp V8 engine 104
M139 130, 142
M139 platform 142
M156 147–8
MC12 131–5, *131*, *132*, 140
MC20 *153*
marketing *104*
Medici I/II *99*, 107–8
Merak 96–7, *97*, 104, 106, *107*
Mercedes *110*
Mistral *39*, 104, 124
Pentastar V6 engine 148
Quattroporte *28*, 40, *40*, 89, 98, *98*, *99*, 104, 106–9, *108*, 112, 120, *120*, 123, 130, 142, 144–5, 145, *145*, 148, *148*
Quattroporte Evoluzione 125, 127, *127*
Sebring 41, 89
Shamal 115, *115*, 121
Spyder *126*, 127, 142
SUVs 145–8, *147*, 154

Tipo 26 18, *18*, 19, *20*, 46, 74
Tipo 60/61 'Birdcage' 40, 73, *73*, 78, *79*, 123
Tipo 63/64/65 79, 81, 94
Tipo 151 81, *81*
Tipo Folgore 154–5
Tipo Speciale 15–16, 17
Topping Special 32
Trofeo 154
V4 engine *23*, 31, 47, 48
V5 engine 48
V6 engine *87*, 88–9, 92, 106, 109, 112, *115*, 120, 143, 148, *153*, 155
V8 engine *40*, 76, 79, 81, 89–90, 95, 98, 108, 115, *115*, 121, 124, 126–7, 130, 143, 144, 146, 154
V8 RI (Ruote Indipendenti) 53
V8RI ('Poison Lil') 60
V12 engine 62, *62*, 67, 79, 123, 134
V16 engine 47
Maserati, Alfieri 9, *12*, 13–14, *15*, 16–17, *16*, 18–21, 27, 29, 31, 35, 45, 49, *50*, 67, 74, 77, 79–80
6C 34 29
6CM 29, *29*, *34*, 35
Boyle Special 34
Maserati, Bindo 10, 14, 21, 30, 34

Maserati, Carlo 10, 12–14
Maserati, Ernesto 10, *10*, 14, 16, 19, 30, 31, 34, 35, *35*, 45, 51, 61, 62
Maserati, Etorre 10, 14, 30, 34
Maserati, Mario 10, 18, *20*
Maserati, Rodolfo 9, 10
Massimino, Alberto 34, 62
Materassi, Emilio 17
Mazjub family *46*
Menditiguy, Carlos 74
Mercedes-Benz 31, *53*, 65, 131
W125 53
W165 58
Michelin 98
Michelotti, Giovanni *41*
Milan Motor Show 56
Mini 134, 140
Minoia, Ferdinando 13
Modena factory 30, 34, 37, 41, 56, 119, 123, 124, 139
Monaco Grand Prix 51, *52*, *59*, 62, *65*
Monte Carlo 35
Montezemolo factory 126–7
Montezemolo, Luca di 119, 123, *123*
Montlhéry *51*
Monza *12*, 17
'Monzanapolis' Race of Two Worlds 123
Moss, Stirling 74, *75*, 76, 77, *88*, 123, 125
Moto Guzzi 99
MSG 151–4

THE STORY OF
Maserati

Text and design copyright © 2025 Headline Publishing Group Limited

First published in 2025 by Welbeck
An Imprint of HEADLINE PUBLISHING GROUP

1

Apart from any use permitted under UK copyright law, this publication may only be reproduced, stored, or transmitted, in any form, or by any means, with prior permission in writing of the publishers or, in the case of reprographic production, in accordance with the terms of licences issued by the Copyright Licensing Agency.

Cataloguing in Publication Data is available from the British Library

Hardback ISBN 978-1-03542-394-1

Printed and bound in China

Headline's policy is to use papers that are natural, renewable and recyclable products and made from wood grown in well-managed forests and other controlled sources. The logging and manufacturing processes are expected to conform to the environmental regulations of the country of origin.

Disclaimer:
All trademarks, images, quotations, company names, registered names, products and logos used or cited in this book are the property of their respective owners and are used in this book for identification, review and editorial purposes only. This book is a publication of Headline Publishing Group Ltd and has not been licensed, approved, sponsored, or endorsed by any person or entity and has no connection or association to Maserati S.p.A.

HEADLINE PUBLISHING GROUP LIMITED
An Hachette UK Company
Carmelite House
50 Victoria Embankment
London EC4Y 0DZ

The authorised representative in the EEA is Hachette Ireland,
8 Castlecourt Centre, Dublin 15, D15 XTP3, Ireland (email: info@hbgi.ie)

www.headline.co.uk
www.hachette.co.uk

CREDITS

The publishers would like to thank the following sources for their kind permission to reproduce the pictures in this book.

ALAMY STOCK PHOTO: CJM Photography 153; P Cox 152; DPPI Media 133; Foto Arena LTDA 131; Goddard Archive 46; Malcolm Haines 154; Horizon International Images 56; Motoring Picture Library 68; Motorsport Archive Images 96; James Moy 100-101, 114, 118; ZUMA Press, Inc. 132

GETTY IMAGES: Ulrich Baumgarten 147; Bettmann 12; Bernard Cahier 11; Paul-Henri Cahier 72; Michael Cooper/Allsport 95; Daily Express Hulton Archive 24; Jerome Delay/AFP 88; Fred Enke/The Enthusiast Network 30; Evening Standard/Hulton Archive 15; GP Library/Universal Images Group 16, 77; Kym Illman 122; Toshifumi Kitamura/AFP 57; John Lamm/The Enthusiast Network 31; Martyn Lucy 155; Clive Mason 119; National Motor Museum/Heritage Images 89; David Phipps/Sutton Images 19, 32, 38, 39, 41, 43, 64, 67, 86-87; Pascal Rondeau/Allsport 58, 74-75; Mark Thompson 80; Jean-Marc Zaorski/Gamma-Rapho 59; Hoch Zwei/Corbis 117

MOTORSPORT IMAGES: 13, 23, 25, 28, 42, 50-51, 66, 71, 84; Ercole Colombo 54, 78; Glenn Dunbar 116; Andy Hone 81; LAT 49, 91, 92, 146; Zak Mauger 134; Rainer Schlegelmilch 8, 20-21, 52, 90; Sutton Images 37, 53, 60, 69, 145; Steven Tee/LAT 99

SHUTTERSTOCK: 115, 150-151; Eric Alonso/DPPI 138, 139; Diego Azubel/EPA 109, 113; Xavi Bonilla/DPPI 136-137; Colorsport 34-35; Carl Court/EPA 112; DPPI 4; Alejandro Garcia/EPA 125; Felix Heyder/EPA 104; Martin Keep/ProSports 130; Adolf Martinez Soler 142; Gerry Penny/EPA 98; Pixathlon 126-127; F Schneider/imageBROKER 148; Sipa 61, 106, 110; Antonin Vincent/DPPI 135; Valdrin Xhemaj/EPA-EFE 129

Every effort has been made to acknowledge correctly and contact the source and/or copyright holder of each picture. Any unintentional errors or omissions will be corrected in future editions of this book.

Porsche 917 35
Portuguese Grand
   Prix *90*, 93
Prodromou, Peter 138
Project 3 50
Project 4 *43*, *50*,
   51–3, 55, *55*
Prost, Alain 40, 55–8,
   55, *56*, 70, *70*, 73,
   86–9, *88*

R

Räikkönen, Kimi 79,
   94, 96–7
Rast, René *135*
Red Bull 86, 98, 112,
   112, 128, 135, 138
Renault 55, 69, 80–1,
   81, 97, 128
Rev-Em Racing team
   30
Revson, Peter 30, *31*,
   34, 35–6
Reynolds Metals
   Company 34
Ricciardo, Daniel 81,
   132, *132*, 135, *135*
Rindt, Jochen 49, *49*
road cars 48, 59, 66,
   114, 143–55, *147*,
   148, 149, 153
Robson, Dave 97
Rondel Racing
   49–50, 50
Rosa, Pedro de la 106
Rutherford, Johnny
   35–6

S

Sebring 13, *13*
Seidl, Andreas 131,
   134, *134*
Sekiya, Masanori *146*
Senna, Ayrton 55–6,
   56, *58*, 60–1, *60*,
   67, 73–6, *73*, 78,
   85–99, *86*, *88*, *89*,
   90, 124, 147, 152
Serenissima 21
Silverstone *56*
Singapore Grand Prix
   98, *106*
Smith, Bill 30
South African Grand
   Prix 32, 36, *67*
Spa-Francorchamps
   23, *66*
Spanish Grand Prix
   22, *38*, 39
sponsorship 36, 53,
   116, 127
Spygate 97, 106–7,
   112
Stella, Andrea 134–8,
   134
Stevens, Peter 144,
   145
Stewart, Jackie 23
Stuck, Hans-Joachim
   50
Suzuka 87–8, *94*
Swedish Grand Prix
   36

T

TAG Heuer *53*, 55
TAG McLaren
   Research &
   Development LTD
   144
Tambay, Patrick *43*
Tasman Series *16*,
   17, 32
Taylor, William 53,
   78, 144
Techniques d'Avant
   Garde (TAG) 55,
   70, 118
Texaco 36
Toleman 85
Toyota 111–12
Triple Crown of
   Motorsport 146
Trundle, Neil 49
Tyrrell Formula
   Junior 31
Tyrrell, Ken 30

U

Ulster Austin Seven
   10
United States Grand
   Prix *13*, 29–30, *30*,
   43, *52*, *98*
USA Formula Junior
   30

V

Vandoorne, Stoffel
   128, 131

Vettel, Sebastian
   112–14, *112*
Villeneuve, Jacques
   94
Vodafone 116

W

Walsh, Paul 130
Watkins Glen track
   43
Watson, John 40, 55
West 79
Whitmarsh, Martin
   60–1, 80, 96, 98,
   105–19, *105*, *108*,
   116
Williams 53, 55,
   58–61, *60*, 67, 70,
   73–6, 89–90, *90*,
   111
Willmott, Wally 17
World Endurance
   Championship 130

Y

Yardley 36
Young, Eoin 18

Z

Zandvoort *25*

THE STORY OF
McLaren

Text and design copyright © 2025 Headline Publishing Group Limited

First published in 2025 by Welbeck
An Imprint of HEADLINE PUBLISHING GROUP

1

Apart from any use permitted under UK copyright law, this publication may only be reproduced, stored, or transmitted, in any form, or by any means, with prior permission in writing of the publishers or, in the case of reprographic production, in accordance with the terms of licences issued by the Copyright Licensing Agency.

Cataloguing in Publication Data is available from the British Library

Hardback ISBN 978-1-03542-396-5

Printed and bound in China

Headline's policy is to use papers that are natural, renewable and recyclable products and made from wood grown in well-managed forests and other controlled sources. The logging and manufacturing processes are expected to conform to the environmental regulations of the country of origin.

Disclaimer:
All trademarks, images, quotations, company names, registered names, products and logos used or cited in this book are the property of their respective owners and are used in this book for identification, review and editorial purposes only. This book is a publication of Headline Publishing Group Ltd and has not been licensed, approved, sponsored, or endorsed by any person or entity and has no connection or association to McLaren Automotive Limited.

HEADLINE PUBLISHING GROUP LIMITED
An Hachette UK Company
Carmelite House
50 Victoria Embankment
London EC4Y 0DZ

The authorised representative in the EEA is Hachette Ireland,
8 Castlecourt Centre, Dublin 15, D15 XTP3, Ireland (email: info@hbgi.ie)

www.headline.co.uk
www.hachette.co.uk

THE STORY OF
McLaren

A TRIBUTE TO AUTOMOTIVE EXCELLENCE

ALEX KALINAUCKAS

Contents

WHERE IT ALL BEGAN 06

MOVING ON 26

TRANSFORMING TIMES 44

AN ONGOING PROBLEM 62

WRITING LEGENDS 82

CLASH OF THE TITANS 102

A NEW START 120

TRANSFORMATION COMPLETE 140

INDEX 156

CREDITS 160

WHERE IT ALL BEGAN

THE GOOD GUY: BRUCE MCLAREN

> "He was the most friendly and unassuming of all the Formula 1 circus."

Renowned motorsport magazine, *Autosport*, reflecting on Bruce McLaren – just two days after his death, aged 32. This story starts with his legend – one that encompassed 100 Grand Prix starts in Formula 1 motor racing, four of which ended in victory; his triumph at the famous 24 Hours of Le Mans sportscar race; and, of course, founding the organization that bears his name to this day. That he did it all with a friendly, humble reputation intact is one thing. That he achieved all that by age 29 is quite another.

OPPOSITE: The man who started it all: Bruce McLaren in 1965's French GP.

Born in Auckland on 30 August 1937 to Les and Ruth, Bruce Leslie McLaren was raised in the Remuera suburb where his father ran a service station and garage. Contracting Perthes' disease aged nine put an end to Bruce's time captaining his school's junior rugby team. He spent months immobile having his legs set in plaster thanks to what were then the methods of treating the disease. It also left him with a left leg one-and-a-half inches shorter than his right (he would wear shoe lifts to compensate) and unable to play contact sports on medical advice.

He initially turned to rowing, but it was with his father's 1929 Ulster Austin Seven that his sporting aptitude returned and his engineering exploits flourished. Hillclimb success as a 15-year-old with a fresh driving licence was soon followed by saloon car racing and eventually his family purchasing a Cooper sportscar raced by Australian Formula 1 driver Jack Brabham. Bruce quickly began writing to Brabham in England, with the latter eventually suggesting he enter a pair of Cooper Formula 2 cars for them to race in the 1958 New Zealand Grand Prix. Gearbox trouble would mean Bruce did not see the chequered flag, but in coming second in the event's first heat race, he had done enough to win a bigger prize: the New Zealand International Grand Prix Association's 'Driver to Europe' scholarship. Two months later, Bruce flew to London – and his career began in earnest.

Upon his arrival in Britain, Bruce lived in a room in a pub near the Cooper factory. He would be racing the team's Formula 2 T45 car for the rest of the year. Success came quickly. During the 1958 German Grand Prix, which at the time permitted the smaller and slower Formula 2 cars to race alongside Formula 1 machinery on the monstrously long Nürburgring Nordschleife, Bruce finished first in class and fifth overall. This "made Bruce's name in Europe", according to acclaimed journalist and author, Doug Nye.

Bruce had sufficiently impressed Charles and John Cooper – father and son founders of the team for which Brabham already raced – for them to offer him regular Formula 1 race time alongside Brabham when they decided to concentrate solely on the top category for 1959.

His close bond with Brabham – Bruce would often visit Jack and his first wife, Betty, for Sunday lunch – shone through the season in which he would finish a creditable sixth in the drivers' world championship. His adaptability, consistency and eagerness to learn served him well as Brabham's understudy.

BELOW: Bruce racing a Cooper-Climax T45 Formula 2 car in the 1958 German GP, a race that forged his reputation in Europe soon after his arrival from New Zealand.

OPPOSITE: Bruce's record-breaking first Formula 1 win came in the 1959 United States GP at Sebring – the race where his friend Jack Brabham clinched his first world title.

BELOW: Bruce and Jack Brabham shared a close bond – the pair are pictured here at the 1959 British GP at Aintree during their time as Cooper teammates.

Bruce scored his best result in the season-ending race at Sebring, Florida. With Brabham on the verge of clinching that year's world title, Bruce had dutifully followed behind early on. But when Brabham ran out of fuel, Bruce initially pulled over – agonizing over how to help his teammate. Brabham waved him on, and the Australian would eventually push his car over the line to seal fourth place and the title. Bruce, meanwhile, took the win. Aged 22, he became the youngest Formula 1 race winner – a record that stood for 64 years until Fernando Alonso's triumph in the 2003 Hungarian Grand Prix.

That victory brought considerable recognition, but Bruce's humble reputation showed no signs of changing – he just did not feel famous. Neither celebrity nor fortune drove him, instead he just wanted to enjoy working hard at motoring and motorsport.

OPPOSITE: Bruce married Patty Broad in 1961. The pair are pictured here at the 1962 BRDC International Trophy meeting at Silverstone, where McLaren was racing for Cooper.

At the time, Bruce lived in a Surbiton bedsit near the Cooper factory, with his childhood friend and future McLaren Managing Director, Phil Kerr. The pair were often unable to afford all their meals, and while success and fame would follow in time, Nye recalled that "for the moment [Bruce] was utterly unspoiled, getting by on margarine" with the prospect of one day replacing it with butter.

Over the European winter of 1959–1960, Bruce returned to New Zealand. There he proposed to Patty Broad – the pair having met at a dance in early 1958. On his return to action for Cooper in Formula 1, he won the 1960 season Buenos Aires opener to double his victory tally. Brabham would ultimately dominate in 1960 to take a second successive title, with Bruce finishing second come the year's end. He failed to add any more wins for Cooper that year, but his impact was being felt elsewhere at the team.

In contrast to most racing drivers today, Bruce was adept at designing parts of the cars he raced. Having studied engineering at Auckland University of Technology, he would either have been a motor or civil engineer had his driving dream not worked out. In a sign of what was to come with his eponymous team – and harking back to the innovative efforts he had put into fixing the Austin Seven's engine – Bruce helped produce the 'Lowline Cooper'. This would race successfully in 1960, with Bruce even drawing some of the parts required when chief designer Owen Maddock was flat out. Brabham would win five successive races in the car.

In Bruce's personal life, things took another upward turn as Patty moved to England to work as a beautician. They married in Christchurch in 1961. Later that year, however, Cooper began to struggle with Formula 1's new engine rules, which required cars to be fitted with smaller, non-supercharged units.

14 WHERE IT ALL BEGAN

BELOW: The 1964 Tasman Series, where the McLaren team began, was an eight-race championship across New Zealand and Australia eventually won by Bruce.

That year, the Cooper-Brabham partnership ended. Jack left to start his own team, which would take its founder to the 1966 Formula 1 world title. Charles Cooper was so upset by Brabham's decision – seeing it as a betrayal – that he initially tried to stop Bruce having any more influence on designing parts for the team's new-for-1962 car, the T60. Soon enough, however, Bruce's persistence with design suggestions, plus that ever-ready smile, won the Coopers over. He was able to contribute ideas once again with the new Type 60 car, which went on to win the 1962 Monaco Grand Prix. But that triumph would be Bruce's last in the world championship for over six years.

Much of this was down to Cooper's decline as a Formula 1 powerhouse. The 1963 season was a disaster, with the team's T66 car proving unable to produce top results. Bruce began to feel frustrated at leading a struggling squad, but, smiling through adversity as he had done through the weeks and months of Perthes' disease treatment, 1963 would become a momentous year in his life. For it was as the season came to a close that Bruce founded McLaren. That too stemmed from his irritation with Cooper.

Bruce had wanted the team to enter a pair of specially designed cars for the new Tasman Series races that would kick off the 1964 motorsport season. Given the championship took place over four rounds in his native New Zealand and a further four races in Australia, Bruce was eager for success. But what he viewed as the Coopers' poor reaction to his suggestion convinced him that he should go it alone.

Across the final months of 1963, Bruce did a deal with Teddy Mayer – brother of rising American driving star, Timmy, who was set to join the Cooper team full-time for 1964 – to supply engines for the special Tasman Series cars. Bruce had decided he would build these without Cooper's assistance in the team's factory. They came together with Bruce's friend and mechanic – Wally Willmott – but it was Bruce's late 1963 alliance with the Mayers that would prove both terrific and tragic.

The Cooper F1-inspired cars produced by 'Bruce McLaren Motor Racing Ltd' were painted dark green, but with added 'Kiwi Silver' stripes. And they were fast. In the first Tasman race at the Levin track, Timmy Mayer finished second with Bruce third, while another New Zealander, Denny Hulme, won the race for Brabham's eponymous team. Next time out, Bruce triumphed in the 'New Zealand Grand Prix'. He won the next two races, but the McLaren cars struggled after heading to Australia. In the final round at Longford, Timmy Mayer was killed – his wayward car colliding with two trees in practice. McLaren was understandably subdued the next day, but nevertheless clinched the championship.

Heading back to Europe for the upcoming 1964 Formula 1 campaign with Cooper, as well as his sportscar exploits that included racing the famed Ford GT40 at Le Mans, Bruce's mind was made up.

"The die was cast," wrote Bruce's friend and later biographer, Eoin Young. "He'd proved he knew enough about racing to run his own team, which made racing exciting again."

Bruce viewed running his own team as a step above the goal his peers had previously viewed as the pinnacle of their careers: becoming a works driver for a team or automotive marque. As he wrote in one of his regular columns for *Autosport*: "now I enjoy nothing better than running my own cars again."

The McLaren project was still fledgling at this point – the squad's early years spent designing cars with a tiny crew. But a family spirit was imbued from the start, in large part thanks to Bruce being the same age or younger than many of his staff. They were all in it together.

Bruce's main job remained racing in Formula 1 for Cooper, plus his duties for Ford. The latter would prove to be pivotal in the story of McLaren's history. Alongside his Ford connection, Bruce earned his team a deal to compete in the 1965 Tasman series using Firestone tyres and then to test the company's racing rubber using McLaren's early single-seater prototype, the M2A.

"That contract plus Bruce's Ford involvement was instrumental in getting our company going," Mayer, by this stage McLaren team manager, would later say.

McLaren also did a did deal to produce designs for the Elva Cars marque and came to a profitable arrangement with Ford

OPPOSITE: Bruce's relationship with Ford helped the McLaren team, but his triumph here in the 1966 Le Mans 24 Hours for the marque burnished his racing reputation as well.

to adapt GT40 sportscars. Bruce, meanwhile, worked on the single-seater design that would later become the famed M2B. This led to tensions with the Coopers, who feared the episode with Brabham was about to be repeated. That proved to be, as Bruce finally left Cooper at the end of 1965. McLaren had finished the M2B and was now about to enter motorsport's big-time.

In the year he would win Le Mans for Ford, Bruce's team took part in its first Formula 1 world championship race at the season-opening Monaco round. There, the M2B turned heads with its raucous engine noise before an oil leak and imminent engine failure put Bruce out. Despite his mounting major

racing achievements, however, Bruce had already realized there was a big problem.

McLaren had picked a Ford V8 engine to power the M2B that had originally been designed for use at the celebrated Indianapolis 500 oval race because Bruce and Mayer hoped the Ford organization would provide financial support to the new team. That was not to be, and the problematic engine was not used again until much later in 1966. In the meantime, McLaren tried out engines built by the Serenissima company, but these too proved troublesome.

The next year, Bruce opted to change his Formula 1 engine supplier – the first such instance in a long history of

BELOW: Bruce racing the first Formula 1 McLaren at the 1966 Monaco GP. The engine was not designed for the car, which attracted attention but proved problematic.

McLaren engine power play. He picked the British Racing Motors marque that was adapting a powerful V12 engine from sportscar racing to use in 1967's M4B. But the engine was not ready until the final four rounds of that campaign, during which Bruce opted to enter three Formula 1 races for the Eagle team instead.

That same year, something important was happening elsewhere at McLaren. Having realized how lucrative sportscar races could be – even though they lacked Formula 1's glamour and fame – McLaren had decided to divert half its resources to the Canadian-American Challenge Cup sportscar series, where it had raced the M1B in the inaugural 1966 championship.

For 1967, the upgraded M6A – the first McLaren to feature a papaya orange colour scheme – made the difference and Bruce swept to the title with two wins. Hulme, meanwhile, won the first three rounds. He had signed to race for McLaren that year after much planning to join forces with Bruce.

Effectively, McLaren could fund its Formula 1 effort with its sportscar achievements – should they continue. Fuel sponsor fees and bonuses, plus selling older cars to privateer racers, also helped the team expand. But another critical choice was heading Bruce's way, one which transformed his team's reputation in Formula 1.

By 1967's end, Colin Chapman's Lotus squad had shown that the Ford-funded Cosworth DFV was the championship's best engine. And when Lotus' exclusivity arrangement concluded ahead of 1968, Bruce made sure his team bought in. The engines were expensive – £7,500 each – but produced 408bhp from a small, lightweight unit.

McLaren's 1968 M7A car made its Formula 1 world championship bow at the Spanish Grand Prix, where Bruce retired having spotted his fuel pressure running low and was unwilling to blow an expensive engine. Crashes and more

ABOVE: The 1968 Belgian GP was the McLaren team's first Formula 1 victory, but Bruce was only informed of his triumph in the paddock afterwards.

unreliability followed in Monaco before the breakthrough moment.

After Hulme led the early stages before retiring with engine damage, Bruce won the 1968 Belgian Grand Prix. He initially did not realize he had done so; Jackie Stewart having pitted from the lead ahead of him before the final lap at the long Spa-Francorchamps circuit.

Further McLaren Formula 1 success followed. Hulme won 1969's season-ending Mexican race – the year Bruce finished third in the drivers' standings after an experiment with a 4WD M9A design proved an expensive early failure. Can-Am continued to provide the cash, as Bruce won the 1969 championship, after Hulme's 1968 triumph had kept up the team's streak.

ABOVE: Bruce scored four Formula 1 wins before his death – three for Cooper between 1959–1962, where he is pictured here at Zandvoort, and one for McLaren.

OPPOSITE: Bruce was just 32 when he was killed. A missing pin for securing the M8D Can-Am's massive tail body meant this section was ripped off.

And so, 1970 started with McLaren on the up. Before a hammer blow fell.

Bruce was killed testing the M8D Can-Am car at the Goodwood testing track. The car's rear bodywork ripped off at high-speed and the resulting jolt to the rear wheels sent Bruce careering into a concrete-reinforced grass bank at over 100mph. There was no saving him.

"Too often in this demanding sport, unique in terms of ability, dedication, concentration and courage, someone pays a penalty for trying to do just that little bit better or go that little bit faster," said Sir Denis Blundell, quoting Bruce's own words on the death of double Formula 1 world champion Jim Clark in his *Autosport* column two years' prior.

The New Zealand High Commissioner was speaking at a memorial service at London's St Paul's Cathedral three weeks after the crash. Bruce had already been buried at St Mary's Cathedral in Auckland.

But McLaren would live on in Bruce's name.

MOVING ON

THE BAD GUY: TEDDY MAYER

> McLaren urgently needed a driver to replace Bruce on the racing front in Formula 1. And Teddy Mayer had finally worked out exactly what to do.

It'd taken a while. Shortly before Bruce's death, Denny Hulme had badly burned his hands in a practice fire ahead of the 1970 Indianapolis 500 – one of Mayer's chief projects as the burgeoning McLaren operation continued to split its interest between top level Formula 1 competition and lucrative American championships.

After the team had missed the 1970 Belgian GP in the aftermath of Bruce's demise and with Hulme absent, McLaren had blended youth with experience in its F1 cars. Four-time grand prix race winner Dan Gurney and rookie Peter Gethin appeared at the Dutch event, before Hulme reappeared in place of Gethin the next time out and the Englishman later replaced Gurney in turn.

OPPOSITE: Mayer and McLaren at the 1968 British GP at Brands Hatch.

ABOVE: Eventual champion Denny Hulme races a McLaren M8D to victory in the 1970 Can-Am event at the Laguna Seca track in California.

Hulme managed to score three podium finishes on his return in 1970, but when he could not the following year, McLaren's points haul dropped significantly. Here, Mayer acted. He installed 1971 McLaren Indy 500 pole-winner Peter Revson to join Hulme. With the 1967 F1 world champion partnering a proven American open-wheel ace, McLaren's expectation in reviving its fortunes was set. Finally, it could move past the pain of Bruce's death.

Mayer had known Revson for well over a decade. With Mayer acting as team manager, Revson had driven for the Rev-Em Racing Team they formed with Timmy Mayer and Bill Smith – a successful businessman. Rev-Em Racing won 15 of 16 races in the 1962 USA Formula Junior championship, with Timmy's success earning an invitation to race for Ken Tyrrell – later a famous F1 team boss – in another Formula Junior series over in England the following year.

The Mayer brothers made the move across the Atlantic in mid-1963. They were from a wealthy family in Pennsylvania – where their father had been a stockbroker and their uncle a state governor. The brothers shared a passion for motorsport. Like Bruce, they'd started out racing an Austin-Healey, and from their first attempts in 1958 around Teddy's law studies, it quickly became clear that the younger Mayer, Timmy, was the superior driver. Teddy felt he was better in a management role anyway.

Teddy joined Timmy in travelling to join the Tyrrell Formula Junior team for three reasons. Aged 26 in 1963, the elder Mayer wanted to have a bit of a holiday and figure out his future career plans, but mainly he wanted to keep his brother company and

BELOW: Can-Am success – such as Peter Revson's here in 1971 at Laguna Seca – helped Mayer fund the McLaren organization while its Formula 1 operation struggled.

BELOW: Denny Hulme's victory in the 1972 South African GP was McLaren's fifth overall in Formula 1, but was the team's first in three years and since Bruce's death. Hulme would score six McLaren F1 wins.

try to further his racing career. Soon enough, Bruce was visiting the Thames Island house where the Mayer brothers were living and planning the trip to the 1964 Tasman Series that would prove pivotal to the founding of McLaren – and would result in Timmy's tragic death in a crash at Longford.

Hit hard by his brother's death, Teddy returned to America. There, the keen skier carried on mulling his options. In the end, he concluded he could either make a go of being a motorsport team manager with Bruce or "go back to being a lawyer".

Bruce's initial response to Mayer's offer to run the fledgling McLaren operation was surprising – he felt Mayer should instead have a smaller role as a US-based team agent. But Mayer insisted and they soon came to an agreement. This had a significant financial element too, as Mayer invested in the team for a 50 per cent stake. Both McLaren owners were treating the team's initial years as rather speculative. Mayer still had his law

degree and family money to fall back on, while Bruce at this stage remained a works Cooper driver.

"I wasn't particularly convinced that it would be an instant success and I certainly wasn't convinced that it was an excellent financial investment," Mayer would later say. "I didn't see it as a large loss either."

And so, Mayer returned to England in late spring 1964. McLaren was embryonic, with several of Bruce's friends working as mechanics. This, allied with its founder's endearing personality, would provide the strength of a familial bond. But Mayer felt it needed discipline too.

"In many ways he shook the tiny team rigid by taking it by the scruff of the neck, imposing discipline and forcing it to run with the accent on efficiency in all things," journalist Doug Nye assessed.

Mayer "hated time-wasters" and wanted McLaren operating with the order of an established manufacturer, even when its works at the time was a dirt-floored workshop in New Malden. He was forceful with suppliers – naturally establishing a 'Bad guy-Good guy' dynamic with Bruce. Nye called him a "short-fused martinet".

"We used the 'Bad Guy-Good Guy' thing occasionally, when it was right for the situation," Mayer explained. "It sure paid dividends too."

The pair complemented each other – Bruce's friendliness softening Mayer, and Teddy's directness hardening Bruce where required. But the arrival of a third key McLaren staffer meant Mayer would concentrate on the team's US ventures after all.

This was how Bruce's good friend Phil Kerr arrived as joint Managing Director in 1968, and it was he who'd be so key in convincing Hulme – another Kiwi – to race for McLaren that same year. Kerr handled most of McLaren's administrative

BELOW: Peter Revson would score two McLaren victories in Formula 1 and finish second in the team's M16 Indianapolis 500 car in 1971. He was killed in 1974 having joined Shadow.

work, then set the team's longer-term strategy and policy, with Teddy, after Bruce's death.

Before this, Teddy had made his mark on the company through the success of the Can-Am programme. With Kerr running the team's new factory in Colnbrook and its F1 efforts, Mayer and co followed the 1967 Can-Am title with a major deal with Gulf Oil for 1968 sponsorship. Another profitable agreement with US metals giant Reynolds followed. The success of the team in North America "kept us afloat and supported the F1 programme," Teddy said.

Gulf's colours would become closely associated with McLaren's Can-Am programme, where its successful 1967 car – the M6A – had become the team's first papaya orange machine. Mayer, inspired by a similar livery on a rival Lola car, had felt the bright colour really stood out on TV and in the mirrors of other cars. It would soon be synonymous with McLaren, as it was used on Bruce and Hulme's cars for the

team's first F1 and Indy 500 wins, plus many more designs.

The success of the M6A and its lineage meant McLaren's Can-Am streak lasted until 1971. Afterwards, its defeat to Penske-Porsche's turbocharged 917 car led to the team pulling out. Mayer felt engine turbo development "priced our kind of Can-Am out of existence". But success elsewhere in the USA soon followed.

McLaren's first entry to the Indy 500 had come because its post-1966 tyre supplier Goodyear had wanted to try and end rival Firestone's long run of success at the famed 500-mile race. But after Hulme's 1970 crash, McLaren's new-for-1971 M16 was a gamechanger.

The Offenhauser-engined car that had huge turbo lag and fearsome top speed finished second from pole in Revson's hands at the first attempt. Then Mark Donohue won in a privateer Penkse M16B the following year. Johnny Rutherford joined Revson for the 1973 running and he took pole too,

OPPOSITE:
Emmerson Fittipaldi celebrates winning the 1974 Brazilian GP – his first for McLaren in the season he would go on to secure the team's first world titles.

before finishing ninth. But Rutherford was victorious in 1974 and 1976 for the McLaren works team – winning the race that provided a "purse of almost $1 million" to the winner, according to Nye. A big boost, after the Can-Am cash had gone.

Although McLaren took sporadic wins in American open-wheel racing to the end of the 1970s, as 1979 concluded the team decided to concentrate solely on F1. By that point, grand prix racing had finally taken over as the main source of the team's prize money income.

Not that things had been easy for Kerr's side of the organization, even with Revson aboard to partner Hulme for 1972 and some success following. In McLaren's M19s with markedly improved rear suspension, Hulme returned to the F1 podium first time out in Argentina, then won in South Africa – McLaren's first F1 win for nearly three years. Revson added three rostrum visits of his own to his teammate's final tally of six, as McLaren finished third in the constructors' championship. In 1973, Hulme triumphed in the Swedish GP, before Revson won twice – in Britain and Canada – and the team repeated its constructors' result from the previous year.

But even as F1's prize money offering was growing; financial pressure came from elsewhere. This was a period of rapid inflation in Britain, and by 1974 McLaren's sponsorship from the Yardley cosmetics company would no longer cover two cars (and the handful of one-off entries McLaren continued to provide).

Yardley was not happy, but the "impossible situation", as Mayer called it, eventually resulted in a deal being struck with Texaco and Marlboro – the latter, a cigarette industry giant, a new but major sponsorship player in F1 – for 1972 world champion Emerson Fittipaldi to replace Revson alongside Hulme for 1974. Yardley continued to sponsor a one-car team within McLaren that shared technical know-how, but raced the main cars competitively on-track for one year only.

BELOW: James Hunt wins the 1976 Spanish GP at Jarama. Hunt was initially disqualified due to his car being deemed too wide, before McLaren successfully appealed two months later.

Hulme won 1974's season-opening round in Argentina, but Fittipaldi's home win in Brazil next time out and further triumphs in Belgium and Canada led to McLaren's biggest breakthrough: the F1 world title double.

But then the team changed comprehensively: Hulme retired from F1 and returned home to New Zealand, something Kerr soon did too. Mayer was therefore left "running the business on my own". And this meant he was in charge when one of McLaren's most revered F1 stories took place.

After finishing third in 1975 with two more wins, Fittipaldi abruptly decided to leave McLaren at the year's end. Mayer felt "we were left high and dry without a number one driver" for 1976. But with Teddy and co "on the phone to James Hunt whose Hesketh team had just recently folded, within minutes of putting the phone down on Emerson", and with Marlboro's blessing, McLaren felt it had a suitable replacement.

ABOVE: Teddy Mayer and James Hunt at the 1976 Japanese GP, where the latter sealed a famous drivers' world title with third place in a race that took place in treacherous wet conditions.

The 1976 season is one of F1's most famous. Fastidious Ferrari driver Niki Lauda – later a McLaren star too – dominated early on, while playboy Hunt grasped his chance at the big time as best he could.

Hunt won in Spain (after being initially disqualified on technical grounds before being reinstated) and France, plus was controversially disqualified from British GP victory for restarting following an early crash. Then, back at the fearsome Nürburgring, Lauda crashed and nearly died, while Hunt won. The British racer took another win in one of the two races Lauda missed before making a sensational return at Monza just six weeks after his crash, while two more Hunt wins meant they went into the Japan finale with Lauda just three points ahead (having been 34 in front before his crash).

In soaking conditions, Lauda withdrew citing safety concerns, while Hunt did enough to finish third around late

OPPOSITE: Mayer and then-McLaren chief mechanic Gary Anderson with John Watson at the 1979 Italian GP at the Monza circuit.

puncture drama and claim McLaren's second drivers' world title. The team took second in the constructors', behind Ferrari.

Mayer said, "James was fantastic for us when he took his championship" and "good again the following year, once we got the M26 sorted out, but it all went bad for James and us in 1978".

That year McLaren struggled with its M26 car – even at one stage taking six different specifications of it to the British GP – and Hunt departed frustrated. Then "one hell of a blow" for Mayer followed, as the driver signed as his replacement, the highly rated Swede Ronnie Peterson, was killed in an horrendous accident at Monza almost as soon as the deal had been concluded.

Having dived down the F1 pecking order in 1978, McLaren could not pull itself up for 1979, even with a new ground-effect design inspired by the previously class-leading Lotus 79. Marlboro therefore brokered a deal with the Project 4 Formula 2 team – run by one Ron Dennis – which took effect in late 1980. That had been a season where McLaren fielded rising star Alain Prost as a rookie and popular British driver John Watson.

When Watson won his home race in McLaren's MP4/1 – one of the team's most famous F1 designs – Mayer "saw the future as quite bright". His feelings were only heightened when Lauda was coaxed out of early retirement to join McLaren for 1982.

But by this point the DFV was finally being overcome – mainly by the rise of turbo engines in F1. These expensive units worried Mayer, given his experience of soaring costs in Can-Am, but it was soon to be someone else's problem.

Mayer's shareholding in what was now McLaren International was bought out in late 1982, along with other smaller investors. With the team entering a new era, there was a new boss running the show.

OPPOSITE: Mayer (left) here with Patrick Tambay's Haas-Lola in the pits at the 1986 Australian GP in Adelaide. Mayer was the short-lived squad's team manager.

RIGHT: Mayer and Dennis pictured here at the 1980 United States GP at Watkins Glen – shortly after McLaren's merger with the Project 4 organization.

TRANSFORMING TIME

THE BOSS: RON DENNIS

> "Staying solely and exclusively a Formula 1 team is almost surely going to lead to extinction. So, I think there is an imperative need to broaden the commercial basis of this company."

These words were uttered in March 2010. In the 30 years that followed Teddy Mayer's exit from McLaren, the team had secured 17 more F1 drivers' and constructors' world titles. And now McLaren was selling its own road-going supercars – a Ferrari with a British base, to some.

All of this had been achieved through the vision and drive of one man: Ron Dennis. No one, save for Bruce himself, can be said to have done more to establish McLaren as the organization it is today.

For Dennis took it from the team with recent memories of dirt-floor working to a major automotive player with F1 superteam status, boasting an enormous £300 million factory

OPPOSITE: Ron Dennis would helm McLaren for 36 years.

opened by Queen Elizabeth II. Dennis, as he outlined above, saw such a McLaren expansion as critical to its survival.

But so too was it vital for his own flourishing – ultimately into one of F1's most successful team bosses and a businessman trusted by the UK government to be an official business ambassador. Not bad for a man who had left school after taking his O-Levels and started out working for the Chipstead Motor Group. This organization came to own the Cooper F1 team when Bruce was still racing for it in 1965. Dennis himself, however, "positively bristles" at such condescending analysis – according to journalist Doug Nye.

"Perhaps because of that background, which is nothing to be ashamed of, he has always tried that bit harder to progress further," Nye continued.

Indeed, this explains much of what McLaren would become on his watch, as well as the way it set each new aim and strove to achieve them. For Dennis, it did not just matter that McLaren won in F1 or ultimately came to sell road cars, it was the manner in which it did so that was important. Shortly after Dennis took control of McLaren by buying out Mayer's shareholding, every team employee was issued with a company document that emphasized this point.

Something else prized fiercely by Dennis was cleanliness. For himself, but for his racing teams' facilities and products too.

"I truly believe that there's nothing clever about an organization which covers you in grease and sends you home stinking," he would say in the mid-1980s. "Striving for this perfection might sound trivial, but it makes for a better environment and certainly helps when we bring sponsors to the workshop. The standards apply right through the company."

Such an approach shone through his early ventures. By 1966, Dennis was working as a mechanic for Cooper in F1

ABOVE: Dennis lifts the nose of Jochen Rindt's Cooper T81 at the 1966 Italian GP at Monza during his time working as a team mechanic.

aged just 18, before leaving to join the Brabham squad along with rising star driver Jochen Rindt for 1968. In the following two years, Dennis's efforts stood out to the point that Jack Brabham felt comfortable enough to leave him in charge of many elements of running the team – including cashing prize cheques and minding money required for F1 events while on the road.

As he lay by an Acapulco pool ahead of the 1970 F1 season finale in Mexico, Dennis came to think "why not do my own thing?" And so, for 1971, he did exactly that. He formed Rondel Racing with another ex-Brabham mechanic, Neil Trundle, which ran Brabham F2 cars in the European championship.

Rondel Racing's cars were "not particularly successful, although they were always impeccably, sparklingly prepared by

BELOW: Hans-Joachim Stuck racing a BMW Procar at the Donington circuit in England for the Project 4 team that had built many of the championship's cars – an important element of its expansion.

Dennis and his men", according to Nye. But just as Dennis had begun to eye a graduation to F1 for 1974, the OAPEC Oil Crisis led to the team ceasing operations.

Here another man critical to McLaren's transformation enters the picture – Marlboro's John Hogan. He oversaw the company's motorsport sponsorship and advertising, and got Dennis to run what would become the Ecuador-Marlboro F2 team after Rondel Racing ended. But when that did not translate into quick success, Dennis was "determined to do my own thing again" from 1975. This became running more F2 machines in the European F2 series, under the banner "Project 3".

Dennis had come up with this name – he felt the practice of naming racing teams eponymously was best left behind – while lying in a bath this time. He viewed it as his third attempt at cracking the motorsport team management business. By 1976, his entity had become 'Project 4 Racing', which was securing interest from various motor racing sponsors – including Marlboro.

In 1979, Dennis partnered with former racing driver Creighton Brown – who would go on to become a McLaren board member – to form ICI Project Four, which ran a British Formula 3 team in addition to its F2 cars backed by Marlboro. The same year, Project 4 won a tender to build 15 cars for

ABOVE: Niki Lauda celebrates winning the 1982 United States GP West at Long Beach – his first victory for McLaren after Dennis convinced him to return to Formula 1. Lauda would score eight McLaren wins and the 1984 world title.

British teams competing in the new BMW ProCar M1 championship that would race on the F1 support bill featuring many star drivers. When Project 4 had completed its cars, the similarly aspirational Osella racing team had only done three of their 15 over in Italy. BMW subsequently got Dennis's organization to build ten more.

Marlboro then sponsored the team to take one of these cars racing, which it did with F1 legend Niki Lauda driving – before he entered self-imposed F1 retirement before the end of the 1979 season and concentrated on running his nascent airline. Lauda won the ProCar title, with Project 4 drivers also winning the 1979 and 1980 British F3 drivers' titles. So, reckoned Nye, "the only way forward was into Formula 1".

Part of how Dennis did this was to convince designer John Barnard to join his organization. Having sounded out successful F1 designers Gordon Murray of Brabham and Patrick Head of Williams, Barnard signed up having turned down an offer from Mayer to join McLaren first.

At the same time, McLaren biographer William Taylor claims Dennis and Marlboro – via Hogan – were already suggesting the two organizations merge. Mayer's squad was by this time in 1979 struggling, but he initially rejected the idea. Marlboro did not want to leave McLaren and its famous name and achievements, but the company also was not yet convinced Project 4 could do it alone. It nevertheless forced Mayer's hand, by threatening to drop McLaren's now critical sponsorship cash influx.

But, although an F1 innovator as famous as Lotus founder Colin Chapman did not think it was safe enough technology, Barnard had plans to revolutionize F1 car design in the MP4/1 – with an all-carbon fibre chassis.

BELOW: Niki Lauda racing in the 1983 Formula 1 season – the last year McLaren would run the Ford DFV engine before its successes were reignited with the TAG-Porsche power unit. Lauda pushed McLaren to test it in 1983.

It was named after the Marlboro-brokered merger between the McLaren and Project 4 organizations that went through in November 1980. McLaren International was thus launched and, having worked together unofficially but to such a degree that McLaren's F1 results began to uptick by the end of 1980, the next year John Watson won the British GP in the MP4/1. This was imperative, as Marlboro had been promised that McLaren would win an F1 race for the first time since 1977 within a year of the union being completed.

Dennis, with his combative style and often needlessly expressive speaking manner, dubbed 'Ronspeak', was soon transforming McLaren. He secured what would become F1's best engine to replace the Ford DFV with the Techniques d'Avant Garde and Porsche organizations for 1984. In 1985, Dennis launched the McLaren Group to oversee the McLaren team, with TAG CEO Mansour Ojjeh as a co-owner, as well as of McLaren's additional subsidiary tech and engine companies.

Dennis's diplomacy and business nous were again on full display when he lured the surging might of Honda from Williams for 1988. At the same time, he had signed Ayrton Senna to race alongside Alain Prost and by this point McLaren had won 30 races under Dennis's control.

Prost had left McLaren after making his debut in 1980 to sign for Renault, before coming back to race alongside Lauda for 1984. Lauda, convinced of McLaren in part by his ProCar success and Dennis's subsequent attempts to convince him to race again, took the title that year, before Prost won the next two championships.

But Senna proved to be something else entirely. Dennis would later claim that Senna "saw the team was very competitive and made it very clear that he wanted to join".

OPPOSITE: Alain Prost (left), pictured at the German GP, returned to race for McLaren in 1984 after making his Formula 1 debut with the team in 1980.

ABOVE: Ayrton Senna on his way to winning the 1988 British GP at Silverstone for McLaren – a race in which Alain Prost decided to park the other MP4-4.

OPPOSITE: Ayrton Senna and Alain Prost walk from their crash at the start of the 1990 Japanese GP, which the former controversially triggered, sealing his second world title.

Dennis also revealed how Senna's "pretty healthy appetite for money" meant they "started to butt heads on money, half a million, and couldn't agree and this got really tense – it was becoming relationship-threatening". At Dennis's suggestion, the result of a coin-flip for what would become Senna's first three-year contract with McLaren – worth $1.5million – "was the only way to break our log jam".

Once that was settled, Senna then immediately made good on his junior and early F1 career promise by winning the 1988 world title – during which Prost blamed Senna for breaking agreements on in-race battling (Dennis felt it went both ways and that each also secretly lobbied Honda for better engines).

In 1989, the ever-rising tensions led to Prost deciding to join Ferrari for 1990, with the controversial fallout from the Japanese GP crash and Senna's subsequent disqualification

ABOVE: Ayrton Senna struggles to hoist the winner's trophy at his home race in Brazil in 1991. He'd suffered muscle spasms while battling a gearbox problem.

leading to McLaren appealing a result that had made one of its own drivers (Prost) world champion again.

For this really was Senna's team now, and although the 1989 result was upheld, he would go on to dominate F1 for McLaren with the 1990 and 1991 world title doubles. Dennis reflected that these results meant by now he felt compelled to "raise my game" on the management front too. Up to this stage, McLaren had won 69 races and 13 championships under Dennis's stewardship. But trouble was ahead.

First, Honda lost its place as F1's best engine, and then Williams's active suspension innovations in 1992 led it to become the championship's top team once again. At the same time, McLaren was pressing ahead with its F1 road car project.

Barnard had been replaced by Murray to head McLaren's design team ahead of 1987, but although it carried on its success drive through the early Honda years, the development of the F1 road car – under Murray's design watch – led to some observers wondering if McLaren's expanding focus would come at a cost to its F1 results.

With these diving anyway as the end of the Honda era approached in 1992, Senna began feeling frustrated.

McLaren having to run a customer Ford engine for 1993 to replace the effective works arrangement it'd had with Honda caused him concern. So too did Prost returning to F1 with Williams that year following a sabbatical and winning

BELOW: Dennis with Norbert Haug (right), the man in charge of Mercedes' motorsport activities. The German automotive giant joined forces with McLaren for the 1995 season.

BELOW: Dennis with Ayrton Senna in early 1994, after the Brazilian driver had made his ill-fated move to join Williams following six years and 35 wins for McLaren.

a championship Senna had led after the one-third mark due to some of his best F1 career victories. That McLaren's funds were restricted by having to pay for the Ford engines only added to Senna's gripes, as this had a knock-on effect on his salary negotiations, as his contract had run out at the end of 1992.

Senna ultimately only confirmed he would be racing for McLaren in 1993 after entering into a deal that worked out at $1 million a race over the 16-event season. He also only agreed to turn up if the money arrived in his bank account in the days leading up to each respective race. Having been left feeling like his time with the team was effectively over – a feeling compounded by Honda's withdrawal in 1992 – Senna spent early 1993 planning what would become his ultimately tragic move to Williams for 1994.

"In 24-and-a-half years I was at McLaren we were profitable in F1 and our other businesses every single year apart from 1992–93," Dennis's protégé, Martin Whitmarsh,

ABOVE:
Formula 1 drivers including Alain Prost and Jackie Stewart (right centre) gather for Ayrton Senna's funeral in Sao Paulo in May 1994.

would be quoted saying by *Autosport* in 2021. "When we lost £1.5million and we were paying Ayrton a million dollars a race…"

Dennis had a plan in place, should Senna not return to race in 1993 – or indeed if he missed one of his $1 million races. He had signed highly rated young Lotus driver Mika Häkkinen to act as either a race or test driver, with Häkkinen eventually being installed as Senna's final McLaren teammate. This was because McLaren dropped the underperforming Michael Andretti before 1993's end.

Senna left McLaren for the 1994 season but would die during just his third race for Williams. Dennis was left devastated.

But as he dealt with his grief, he also had a serious task to complete for McLaren – solving something of a recurring problem in the team's history with F1 engine supplies.

AN ONGOING
PROBLEM

THE POWER: ENGINES

> There is a word in Formula 1's complex and ever-expanding lexicon that encompasses the McLaren story to this point: *'garagistes'*.

It's a term coined by Enzo Ferrari – eponymous titan of motor racing and luxury car selling. Enzo used it to describe the upstart privateer teams that challenged his established manufacturer for Formula 1 supremacy in the world championship's infancy – how they built cars with fewer resources, smaller factories, often without providing production models. It was not a compliment.

McLaren's early glories from Bruce's vision and Teddy Mayer's management were undoubted garagiste successes. How Ron Dennis transformed McLaren into a motoring powerhouse that now rivals Ferrari in the supercar automotive business, all while collecting world titles and building a factory as grand as that in Maranello, shows how the organization grew clear of Enzo's scorn.

OPPOSITE: McLaren's first Formula 1 car with its adapted Ford V8 engine.

BELOW: By McLaren's second Formula 1 race in 1966, here at Spa-Francorchamps in Belgium, Bruce had decided to trial a Serenissima engine.

But linking all of McLaren's growth together is the need for power. Specifically, engine power.

Garagiste F1 squads inevitably had to buy in the products of other manufacturers, which they might tune to their own preferences. But Dennis turned McLaren into a quasi-works operation in the championship, which had the best engines provided by companies seeking a different sort of motorsport glory. Today, it has fallen into a different realm – that of an engine customer squad tied to the strengths and weaknesses of a supplier, without much influence on squeezing extra power within F1's restrictive rules requirements.

After BMW supplied the V12 engine used in the McLaren F1 road car, the Ricardo engineering company has helped McLaren create all the power units on its supercar fleet ever

since. In F1, however, nine engine builders have had their products placed in the back of McLaren machines. Of the current grid, only Williams has had a wider spread of engine suppliers.

Bruce's first F1 McLaren struggled with its Ford V8 engine in three races across 1966. Fast forward another 27 years, McLaren's MP4/8 – the last McLaren Ayrton Senna ever drove – was powered by another Ford V8. The team had signed up with Ford after Honda had departed F1 in 1992, but as it would run engines a development specification behind those used at Benetton (where Ford already had an existing contract) the deal was not viewed as a long-term prospect.

Before this, the Ford Cosworth DFV Bruce had finally been able to fit in 1968 powered 30 McLaren F1 wins – and was

BELOW: Denny Hulme, second, in action at the 1968 South African GP – the last Formula 1 event in which McLaren would race with a BRM engine.

ABOVE: A Lotus 49 from the 1967 Formula 1 season. The British team held an exclusivity agreement to run the Ford Cosworth DFV engine that year.

fitted to the M23 cars that Emerson Fittipaldi and James Hunt took to their world titles. The Nicholson McLaren Engines company (co-founded by McLaren in 1972) tuned the DFVs in these cars to extract more power.

Serenissima and BRM powered McLarens for three and seven F1 events respectively in the team's first two seasons. In 1970, Italian racers Andrea de Adamich and Nanni Galli raced McLarens that were fitted with Alfa Romeo engines after the Italian manufacturer eyed an F1 return and did this toe-dipping deal for its factory drivers. But after it did not yield any notable results (de Adamich failed to qualify five times) it was not repeated.

As Mayer's time running McLaren was ending in 1982, it was becoming clear that turbo engines were going to revolutionize F1. Knowing from his Can-Am experience that this would inflate costs, Mayer cast around for alternatives before he left McLaren. Renault, BMW, various Formula 2 engine builders – all were considered but declared not viable for team designer John Barnard.

It was Dennis who suggested an alternative – a decision that would prove pivotal in his quest to transform McLaren – in Porsche. The very company whose turbos had ended McLaren's Can-Am success story.

After a rapidly arranged meeting at Porsche's Weissach factory, McLaren had found a willing partner for its first turbo F1 project. But there was a problem. At this stage, the team could only afford to pay for the research and development of what would become the new TTE PO1 V6 turbo engine, but not the building and running supply of the race varieties.

BELOW: Emerson Fittipaldi in action during the 1974 Monaco GP for McLaren – racing the team's M23 car with its Ford Cosworth DFV engine.

AN ONGOING PROBLEM 69

Dennis had another plan, however. In the six months of 1983 Porsche would need for development, he would find the required funding to go racing. The eventual solution was already involved in F1 – sponsoring Williams during its world title run between 1980–1981. This was Techniques d'Avant Garde (TAG) and its CEO Mansour Ojjeh.

McLaren gained valuable insight from racing development TTE PO1s in a car for which the engine had not been designed in 1983 – the E iteration of the MP4/1 – after Niki Lauda agitated for such useful race testing. Barnard had been reluctant, but after McLaren discovered it needed to develop better braking technology alongside the additional power coming from the new engine or waste its potential, hopes were high for the start of the TAG-Porsche engine era the following year.

Things remained complicated as the new championship commenced, however.

Alain Prost – now re-signed with the team for which he had made his F1 debut – had his MP4/2 car built on-site at the Brazil season opener. Despite the late-hour car build, Prost won after Lauda had retired from the lead due to an electrical gremlin occurring.

Come the season's end, Lauda beat Prost to the title by just half a point (as half-points had to be awarded at the shortened, rain-affected Monaco GP). To date, this remains the closest points difference between the top two drivers in the world championship's history. Another two titles would follow for McLaren in 1985 – after which Lauda retired – and 1986. Both went to Prost.

Ultimately, McLaren would take the TAG-Porsche power to constructors' titles in 1984 and 1985, with the engine's race victory total hitting 25.

OPPOSITE: Alain Prost on his way to winning the 1984 Monaco GP. The shortened race meant only half-points were awarded – critical to Prost's eventual championship defeat.

But in 1987, Honda had powered Williams back to full double title success in F1 with its own 1.5-litre turbo engine (the naturally aspirated engines at other teams were typically 3.5-litre V8s during this period) after the team had clinched the 1986 constructors' title ahead of McLaren. At the same time, Honda had begun supplying the Lotus team for which Senna was now turning heads. In a mark of his famed shrewdness, the Brazilian had formed close ties with Honda engineers and managers.

Dennis could see all this, while at the same time having to plan ahead around a big upcoming F1 rule change – a return to normally aspirated engines for 1989. In 1988, he tied it all together and created one of F1's first 'superteams'.

Although he already had a double world champion in Prost, Dennis brought in Senna to form their famous partnership. At the same time, he snared Honda from Williams – benefiting from his efforts to learn and understand Japanese management practices to impress the manufacturer's executives. This all combined in a new McLaren factory in Woking business park.

In 1988, despite rule changes aimed at making things harder for turbo-powered cars, Honda's all-new RA168E dominated. Although Lotus had it too, McLaren took 15 from 16 possible wins and Senna clinched his first world title immediately with his new team.

For 1989, Honda's first naturally aspirated V10 – a 3.5-litre engine – again powered McLaren to the F1 world titles. This controversially went to Prost on the drivers' side, as the tension-filled Senna partnership exploded spectacularly at that season's Japanese GP. Things also were not as straightforward in terms of the MP4/5's engine reliability, but Dennis made sure not to criticize Honda in public.

OPPOSITE: Although it was only used by McLaren for one season, Honda's RA168E 1.5 V6 turbo engine went down in Formula 1 history, powering the MP4-4 to 15 wins.

OVERLEAF: During McLaren's one season back using Ford engine power in 1993, Ayrton Senna scored five Formula 1 wins, which are considered amongst his best in the championship.

AN ONGOING PROBLEM 73

After Senna had swept to the 1990 world title, which came with McLaren's third successive constructors' championship, Honda insisted on building a V12 engine for 1991. Although Senna and McLaren won the double again, the engine's unexpectedly increased weight and bulk annoyed Senna.

Another new V12 for 1992 could not match the performance of its predecessor and by this point Williams was on the rise again. As McLaren's F1 fortunes waned in 1992, Honda announced it was exiting F1 exactly five years to the day after it had revealed it would be partnering McLaren for the first time.

During the one-year recoupling with Ford in 1993, McLaren built a test mule MP4/8 car with which it secretly tested a Lamborghini V12 engine. The intention was to agree a supply of new engine power for 1994, but, although the unliveried car set times quicker than the Ford-powered race MP4/8, McLaren felt the limited nature of the Lamborghini test programme meant it was better taking a different path for 1994 and its first season post-Senna.

Lamborghini owner Chrysler was said to be "livid" at McLaren's decision to instead sign with Peugeot, according to team biographer William Taylor. The French manufacturer built a new V10 for the MP4/9, but testing only in cool conditions led to struggles at hotter early race events that year – a season in which McLaren added power steering and steering mounted clutch controls for the first time in F1.

Although Peugeot added power to its V10 as 1994 went on – aided by aerodynamic rule changes following Senna's death at Imola that brought engine temperatures down – Dennis sensed another opportunity to boost McLaren through its latest rebuilding phase.

Mercedes had returned to F1 as an engine supplier for Sauber for 1994 but was not satisfied with the state of the team's finances for 1995. Dennis therefore deftly extricated

OPPOSITE: Martin Brundle races the MP4/9 in the 1994 Formula 1 season, which yielded no McLaren wins for the first time since the 1980 campaign.

McLaren from its Peugeot deal on good terms and forged its famous partnership with Mercedes.

This came to be class leading – as Mercedes extracted ever more power from its V10 programme. By 1997, the first year after McLaren's long-running partnership with Marlboro had expired and a silver livery with new sponsor West meant the return of the 'Silver Arrows' Mercedes nickname to F1, the manufacturer's engines were producing 740bhp at 16,000rpm.

In the first year of the effectively works Mercedes partnership, the compact V10 meant McLaren could make its F1 chassis smaller – too small for the newly signed Nigel Mansell. McLaren's star driver for the 1995 season lasted just four rounds, only two of which he raced in due to the cockpit size issue, before retiring for good. Fortunately, Mika Häkkinen provided the team with stability on the driving front. This developed into a long-term partnership with new arrival David Coulthard for 1996, after which Häkkinen roared to back-to-back McLaren world title doubles in 1998 and 1999.

The Mercedes deal lasted all through the following decade, in which Ferrari and Michael Schumacher (once a Mercedes junior that the manufacturer and Dennis had hoped to entice to McLaren for 1996 before he headed to Italy) initially dominated.

Kimi Räikkönen's near-misses and Lewis Hamilton's 2008 triumph kept McLaren atop F1 billing through a rule-change to mandatory V8 engines, but after the Brawn GP team secured Mercedes engines for 2009, the company decided it was better off fielding its own squad than just relying on McLaren car prowess.

For another five years, Mercedes nevertheless provided McLaren with customer V8 units. But in 2014 yet another major engine rule change – taking F1 back to turbo power for the first time since the late 1980s but with new hybrid

OPPOSITE: A Mercedes FO 110 V10 engine used by McLaren in the 1995 Formula 1 season – here at that year's French GP. Mercedes would develop the engine to be class leading.

ABOVE: After its disastrous first season back using Honda engines in 2015, McLaren made a step forward with the RA616H power unit in 2016, but progress soon stalled.

electrification elements this time – vaulted Mercedes to the head of the pecking order, while McLaren languished.

With Martin Whitmarsh now at the helm, McLaren had already long been thinking it needed another works partnership and so turned, once again, to Honda.

The new alliance – announced in 2013 for a 2015 commencement – hoped to recapture the old magic. As Hamilton was now racking up titles for Mercedes, former Honda and Brawn GP star Jenson Button was to be partnered with another established champion (and controversial former McLaren star), Fernando Alonso.

But Honda's first V6 turbos were beset by problems and McLaren's expected uplift failed to materialize. After three frustrating years, McLaren opted to become a customer engine squad once again – this time doing a deal with Renault that evoked memories of Alonso's two titles in 2005 and 2006 for the French OEM giant.

This too, did not last, and in 2021 McLaren returned to buying in Mercedes engines. This arrangement is set to last until at least 2030 in F1 and well into the championship's upcoming new engine rules era from 2026 – in which hybrid systems will be simplified.

After Daniel Ricciardo's 2021 Italian GP win and McLaren's 2024 successes with Lando Norris and Oscar Piastri, its win total with Mercedes power sits at 81 GPs. Next up is Honda on 43.

BELOW: McLaren used Renault engines for the first time in Formula 1 in between 2018 and 2020, with the partnership yielding three podiums but no victories

WRITING LEGENDS

THE HEROES:
SENNA, HÄKKINEN, HAMILTON

Since the formation of the Formula 1 world championship in 1950, 34 racers have clinched the drivers' title. Seven of them with McLaren.

But of this distinct crop of champions, a trio stands clear. Either for how McLaren became central to their own legend, for securing special status within the team, or for how McLaren helped them commence a unique story of F1 achievement. These drivers are Ayrton Senna, Mika Häkkinen and Lewis Hamilton.

In 1988, Senna joined McLaren from Lotus, where he had taken a pair of victories each year since making his 1984 debut with Toleman. His reputation was of an ace young driver going places fast – and keen to arrive even quicker.

OPPOSITE: Ayrton Senna celebrates winning the 1988 San Marino GP.

ABOVE: Ayrton Senna in the 1988 Japanese GP – a race where he would start on pole, stall at the start and yet race back to win and seal his first Formula 1 world title.

Autosport magazine said, "he made Lotus – virtually from the day he arrived – into his team, but this is out of the question at McLaren", ahead of his first appearance for Ron Dennis's squad.

That year was also the debut of the McLaren MP4/4. In the hands of Senna and teammate Prost, the Honda-powered turbo car would win 15 from 16 races, a win success rate of 93.8 per cent that was only beaten in 2023 by the Red Bull RB19's 95.5 per cent. Had it not been for a clash while overtaking a backmarker at the Italian GP that put Senna out from the lead late on, McLaren would have taken an historic clean sweep.

Senna had been obsessed with winning the 1988 title. As he prevailed with a great drive in the Japanese GP to seal his first F1 career crown, his fight with Prost had been intense but respectful.

The following year, their relationship descended into acrimony. With both challenging once again in the MP4/4's successor, they collided in the closing stages of that year's Japanese GP. As Prost climbed from his MP4/5, Senna got going again after being pushed by track safety marshals and went on to win – but was controversially disqualified soon afterwards. This move, which Senna felt had been politically engineered with officials and was subsequently upheld in court after McLaren appealed, meant Prost regained his crown.

But Prost had already had enough. He moved to Ferrari for 1990, leaving Senna to lead McLaren alongside his friend Gerhard Berger. Once again, Senna and Prost were the title protagonists and again the outcome of their battle was decided at the Suzuka circuit.

ABOVE: Ayrton Senna with Gerhard Berger at the 1991 Brazilian GP. The pair were good friends, following Senna's tempestuous relationship with previous McLaren teammate, Alan Prost.

Although there was a race in Australia remaining, Senna's points lead meant he held a commanding position, but he was left furious by the Suzuka event organizers deciding to keep the pole position grid spot away from the racing line and the extra grip it gave tyres at race starts.

As Prost nipped ahead on that line at the race's start, Senna kept his throttle pinned at the track's first corner – triggering a crash that put both drivers out but secured his 1990 crown. Then McLaren team principal Dennis later told Senna: "I'm disappointed in you".

The following 1991 campaign was arguably Senna's high point with McLaren. He dominated the season with seven wins – including his first triumph at his home race in Brazil, where he won despite suffering severe shoulder cramp battling on with a gearbox problem.

In 1992, the Williams team led by Nigel Mansell knocked McLaren off its perch as F1's dominant team. This was largely thanks to its FW14B car's active suspension system that McLaren lacked, plus Honda's engine that year being delayed and fuel-demanding. Senna nevertheless won three races to Mansell's nine. The following year he took five more victories and finished as runner-up to Prost, who was now leading Williams, which continued to dominate.

The 1993 campaign took in another legendary Senna win – his triumph at Donington in that year's European GP, where he famously charged from fourth to first on the race's opening lap. But McLaren and Senna were headed for a split. Negotiations over money lasted long into the year and the sophisticated MP4/8 nevertheless proved unreliable.

He eventually left to join Williams himself for 1994, and died tragically in May of that year. But Senna's ability to inspire left a memory felt at McLaren to this day.

BELOW: The 1993 European GP at Donington is considered one of Ayrton Senna's finest Formula 1 wins. He even lost a place at the start before charging into the lead.

RIGHT: Ayrton Senna joining Williams for 1994 would later impact Ron Dennis's consideration of his greatest McLaren drivers – Dennis prized loyalty.

OPPOSITE: Mika Häkkinen made a splash when he finally appeared as a race driver for McLaren, qualifying third for the 1993 Portuguese GP ahead of Ayrton Senna.

Dennis would one day pick Häkkinen as the greatest driver he had ever employed – in part because, unlike Senna, he had stuck things out with McLaren even after losing his place atop the F1 pecking order. That was to come against Michael Schumacher and Ferrari in 2000, but Häkkinen's relationship with Dennis went back over a decade earlier, when the Finn applied to join the Marlboro World Championship Team for 1988, which backed young drivers. Dennis was on the judging panel, given his long history with the cigarette company and its sponsor dealmakers.

Häkkinen entered F1 in 1991, where he made his debut with Lotus. He showed promise in a team that was a shadow of its former self – scrapping for positions well down grid. After a second learning year at Lotus, Häkkinen was among the many that hoped to move to the then dominant Williams team.

Ultimately his efforts were thwarted in a contractual wrangling with Lotus, which later led to a deal with Dennis to become McLaren's test driver for 1993, after Senna decided to carry on racing for the team after all.

When Michael Andretti left his position as Senna's teammate with three races remaining, Häkkinen got his big chance – and immediately seized it at the 1993 Portuguese GP. He out-qualified Senna – enraging the famous Brazilian. Häkkinen, however, refused to revel in his accomplishments and quietly set about his task. This became taking over as McLaren's lead driver for 1994.

That year, he scored six podiums in addition to the one he had taken the previous season, but McLaren's MP4/9 again lacked class-leading pedigree, plus reliability in the team's one year using Peugeot power.

The 1995 season was a similar story. McLaren showed promise, now in the first year of its Mercedes engine supply deal, but was frustrated with reliability problems. It all ended in dramatic circumstances for Häkkinen. In Friday qualifying for the season-concluding Australian GP, the Finn crashed hard after suffering a sudden puncture. His impact with the barriers left him with a fractured skull, with an emergency tracheotomy performed to save his life trackside.

Dennis visited him in hospital, shocked that a driver had nearly died in a car for which he had responsibility for the first time in his career. A long, painful recovery followed – including subsequent surgery – but Häkkinen recovered in time to test McLaren's 1996 car just 12 weeks after his Adelaide crash. He was soon lapping quicker than Schumacher – a junior formula rival of Mika's – who had been practising with his new Ferrari team at the same Paul Ricard track.

That season was the first of five tension-filled championships in which Häkkinen led McLaren alongside David Coulthard. Already a race winner, which Häkkinen envied, Coulthard would come to feel Dennis was subconsciously prioritizing his teammate. Dennis later confirmed this was the case because of the lingering trauma of Häkkinen's crash.

OPPOSITE: Mark Blundell with McLaren team staff at the 1995 Australian GP, wishing Mika Häkkinen a swift recovery after his shocking crash in qualifying.

After a solid but unspectacular 1996 season on his return from injury, Häkkinen finally became an F1 race winner at the end of the 1997 campaign, when eventual champion Jacques Villeneuve gifted him victory in the season-concluding Jerez race. Although contrived, it relieved the pressure he had been facing at having started nearly 100 races without winning. Now in 1998 and 1999, Häkkinen's golden era arrived.

Although he was still suffering with regular headaches because of his 1995 injuries, he emerged triumphant in a famous 1998 title fight with Schumacher. This was in the first McLaren – the MP4-13 – designed by the highly rated engineer, Adrian Newey. Häkkinen doubled up in 1999, even as Newey's second McLaren creation proved fast but fragile.

In 2000, Schumacher and Ferrari finally bested McLaren. But that season included Häkkinen's tenacious pass on his great rival either side of a slower backmarker at the Belgian GP. This moment was another reason why Dennis, who had been vindicated in signing and then sticking by the 'Flying Finn' for so long before his titles arrived, rates Häkkinen so highly in his consideration of the best McLaren drivers.

The other is Hamilton, whose F1 legend started with McLaren. He followed Häkkinen as the team's next world champion – following the near-misses of Kimi Räikkönen, another fast, taciturn Finn – in 2003 and 2005. In winning the 2008 world title, Hamilton ended an eight-year championship drought, as McLaren had likewise endured seven between Senna's final title triumph and Häkkinen's first.

Hamilton had also been introduced to Dennis long before he arrived in F1. The Briton attended the 1995 *Autosport* Awards – an annual prize-giving ceremony hosted by the magazine – as a ten-year-old go-kart racer accepting a trophy. There, he "went up to Ron and said I wanted to race his car and be world champion", as Hamilton would recall in 2007. Dennis

OPPOSITE: Mika Häkkinen celebrates winning the 1999 Japanese GP at Suzuka, which sealed his second successive Formula 1 world championship for McLaren.

ABOVE: Lewis Hamilton and Ron Dennis at the Kimbolton Kart Circuit in England. Dennis would promote Hamilton to race in Formula 1 for McLaren in 2007.

initially told Hamilton to get back in touch nine years later, but in 1998 he signed him to McLaren's young driver development programme.

Hamilton duly climbed the ranks. By late 2006, he was giving Dennis and his key lieutenant, Martin Whitmarsh, little choice in fast-tracking his rise to F1. And so, ahead of the 2007 season in which Räikkönen replaced the exiting Schumacher at Ferrari, Dennis made Hamilton McLaren's first rookie F1 racer since 1995's Pacific GP (where Häkkinen was replaced for one race by the Dane Jan Magnussen following an appendectomy). This broke a long tradition of not selecting rookies that had developed during the team's various runs at the pinnacle of the F1 pecking order.

Hamilton made an instant impression – finishing on the podium at the season opener in Australia and in doing so overtaking his teammate, the reigning world champion, Fernando Alonso, who had just arrived from Renault.

Hamilton had been well prepared by McLaren through his time as a junior, when he was entrusted with testing new F1 cars in minor tests, as one of the team's then-race engineers, Dave Robson, recalled in 2021 after Hamilton had become the first F1 driver to score 100 grand prix poles.

"There was that special quality you can't really define," said Robson. "That was obvious right from when he was just a kid and they took him testing at Elvington [airfield] – going up and down the runway – and he was bored stiff after ten minutes.

"Whereas most kids, when you took them to Elvington, they were just chuffed to bits being in an F1 car – even though they were just going up and down the runway. Lewis was different right from the beginning."

Hamilton was soon winning for McLaren – taking his first triumph in the 2007 Canadian GP. But a schism was developing with Alonso, who was later involved in revealing the Spygate scandal that would come to cost McLaren dearly.

Dennis was resolute in backing Hamilton that year, with Alonso soon deciding he would rather leave for 2008 (he rejoined Renault). The pair nevertheless fought hard for the 2007 world title, with Hamilton losing out in large part due to McLaren's strategy of running wet tyres during that year's Chinese GP. He eventually slipped off the road due to his rubber wearing and retired. After gearbox software trouble for Hamilton at the start of the season finale in Brazil, Räikkönen pipped the McLaren pair to the championship crown.

The following campaign was another classic, in which Hamilton this time emerged with the title despite another

ABOVE: Lewis Hamilton wins the 2008 British GP for McLaren – considered one of his best F1 victories.

OPPOSITE: Forced retirements in 2012, such as here in Singapore, contributed to Hamilton's decision to leave McLaren and join Mercedes.

OVERLEAF: Hamilton scored his final McLaren F1 victory in the 2012 United States GP in Texas – featuring novelty podium hats.

dramatic final race in Brazil. Dennis would later insist Hamilton's result in the wet-dry-wet thriller was down to McLaren's disciplined professionalism and not luck.

Disappointing car designs, unreliability and the rise of the Red Bull team would mean Hamilton and the squad, now helmed by Dennis's anointed successor, Whitmarsh, would not win another title post-2008.

But the driver Dennis prized for his speed and uncompromising attitude still has a fondness for his first team, even after leaving it in 2013 to join the Mercedes squad. There he secured the majority of his seven titles and record F1 race victory haul.

"That's my old, original family," Hamilton said after finishing third behind Oscar Piastri and Lando Norris in the 2024 Hungarian GP, where McLaren finished an F1 race with its cars 1-2 in the order for the only the second time in 14 years.

"I'm really happy to see you, all the boys, the whole team, back up front."

CLASH OF THE
TITANS

THE SUCCESSOR:
MARTIN WHITMARSH

McLaren was riding the crest of a wave as the late 2000s unfurled. Ron Dennis's long-held dream of the company becoming a major automotive power was becoming reality and its Formula 1 team was still winning races and competing for championships. In 2007, its promising junior driver Lewis Hamilton was promoted to grand prix racing and made an instant impact. But sparks that would become flames of disaster were already igniting.

Before promoting Hamilton, McLaren had already moved to secure its long-term F1 driver future by signing Fernando Alonso from Renault back in 2005. This was just after the Spaniard had won his first of two world titles for the French marque, with the other coming in 2006, when Hamilton won an eye-catching GP2 title on the F1 support bill.

OPPOSITE: Whitmarsh was announced as McLaren team boss in early 2009.

ABOVE: McLaren's MP4-24 car was a disappointment in 2009, but the team improved its performance enough for Lewis Hamilton to scoop victories in Hungary and Singapore.

Having arrived expecting to be McLaren's star driver, tensions with the politically agitating Alonso soon arose. These came to a head during the 2007 season's Hungarian Grand Prix. There, Alonso blocked Hamilton in the pitlane during qualifying and was later penalized. But the fallout from the incident revealed a much bigger problem.

Dennis was to then discover that Alonso – plus team test driver Pedro de la Rosa – had been discussing confidential data about the Ferrari team's car that year. In what came to be known as the Spygate scandal, it soon emerged that a Ferrari employee had shared a dossier of design details with McLaren chief designer Mike Coughlan and the case was soon in court when motorsport's governing body, the FIA, had been alerted to the story.

McLaren was eventually handed a $100 million fine – at the time declared a record in sport. While Dennis railed against the punishment, FIA president Max Mosley would claim before his death in 2021 that only £5 million of the fine had been for "what you did" and the rest due to a combustible relationship with Dennis.

The McLaren team was made to forfeit its 2007 constructors' championship points – although the drivers, who were given a degree of immunity from the FIA for co-operating with its investigation, were allowed to keep their personal points and wins. Come the season's end, former McLaren racer Kimi Räikkönen beat Hamilton and Alonso by one point to win the drivers' title for Ferrari.

Alonso departed, but far worse was the reputational damage done to McLaren's brand. It soon became clear that the 2008 campaign would be Dennis's last as McLaren's F1 team boss. But he denied the Spygate affair was resulting in his exit – claiming at the time "my personal future has never been in question" and indicating that it simply crystalized his plans for succession once he had helped "steer the company through this very difficult period".

He would hand power in the McLaren F1 team to a man who had been central to its ongoing success since the late 1980s and had long been a key Dennis lieutenant. This was Martin Whitmarsh.

Whitmarsh had joined McLaren in 1989 as operations director. From an engineering background, he had previously worked for defence systems manufacturer British Aerospace. It was there that he learned the system that he would make famous at McLaren. This was a 'matrix' management approach that meant a flat structure with multiple reporting lines instead of a hierarchy arrangement. It was eventually included in McLaren's F1 car design department and later led to the departure of Adrian Newey, who detested the system, in the mid-2000s.

Whitmarsh would climb McLaren's ranks and is credited with making Dennis's wider vision for expanding the organization a reality. In 1997, he was made the team's managing director and in 2004 was appointed chief operating officer of the McLaren Group. In the intervening time, he had played a key role in planning and developing Hamilton's junior career. By 2008, Whitmarsh and Dennis were already sharing many of the jobs an F1 team principal conducts, to ease the eventual handover.

That came in January 2009, when Whitmarsh said he was "massively privileged" to be appointed McLaren F1 team boss – with the target of defending the title Hamilton had won in dramatic circumstances at the 2008 Brazilian GP, plus scoring McLaren's first constructors' championship since 1998. Dennis, meanwhile, would concentrate on launching McLaren's automotive arm as Group chairman and CEO.

Whitmarsh's promotion to team boss coincided with a new era of F1 car design. The regulations for 2009 required the teams to drop many of the aerodynamic parts that had previously made the old cars so fast and complex, as the FIA was concerned about mounting speeds.

McLaren had been involved in drafting the new rules due to its membership of the FIA's Overtaking Working Group, which at the time looked at car design rules to try and improve F1's racing entertainment spectacle. McLaren believed its 2009 design had met the reduction in downforce targets exactly and so would be in a strong position for the campaign.

But, before it discovered this was not the case, Whitmarsh made what has come to be viewed as a major mistake.

This was to allow the McLaren's exclusivity arrangement to run Mercedes' F1 engines – an agreement that had been

OPPOSITE: Future McLaren driver Jenson Button on his way to winning the 2009 Australian GP – the year Whitmarsh gave up McLaren's exclusivity deal to use Mercedes engines.

unbroken since 1995 and continued to be viewed as class-leading even after F1's rules on power units meant they were all V8s from 2006 – to be diluted.

It was a special and famous case. The former Honda works team had been on the cusp of closing when its management – led by team principal and famed F1 engineer Ross Brawn – had stepped in to buy the team and try to save it through 2009. Progress was made, but what was now Brawn GP still needed an engine or it would fold before ever racing.

Here, Whitmarsh was eyeing the chairmanship of the Formula One Teams' Association organization, which opposed the FIA's plans to change F1's rules amid wider renegotiations of its commercial structures. He agreed to help Brawn, and would indeed later go on to helm the Teams' Association.

McLaren insiders now view Whitmarsh's choice as him wanting to be seen as a statesman-like figure in the wider F1 world by helping to save another squad. And while this did maintain the championship's overall sporting health, at the same time many of his staff were suddenly wary about what this might mean for the team's future now Mercedes had had its head turned by a second engine customer.

The Brawn GP car would prove to have 2009's best aerodynamic platform with its infamous double diffuser development. The Williams and Toyota teams also had this device, but its ability to claw back the downforce lost in the rule changes had been dismissed by the teams including McLaren that formed the OWG.

Brawn won both championships that year, while McLaren somewhat saved its season with what Hamilton called "the worst car that I had driven, apart from the engine was good", as he won two races following urgent redesign work. The bigger problem for McLaren was what this all meant for Mercedes from 2010.

OPPOSITE: Lewis Hamilton celebrates winning the 2009 Hungarian GP. After his 2008 world title success, he was unimpressed by McLaren's subsequent chassis design under F1's new rules.

ABOVE: McLaren signed Jenson Button for the 2010 Formula 1 season after he had won the 2009 world title for Brawn GP, creating a strong line-up with Lewis Hamilton.

OPPOSITE: In another disappointing season, despite the novel design of McLaren's MP4-26, Hamilton scored an impressive win in the 2011 Chinese GP ahead of Red Bull's Sebastian Vettel.

The German automotive giant, which had given McLaren "crucial" backing, according to *Autosport* in 2007 during Spygate, decided it would now rather fund its own team and it purchased the Brawn squad. Mercedes then gradually exited the 40 per cent shareholding it had in the McLaren F1 team, with its ownership stake passing to the McLaren Group.

McLaren and Hamilton – plus 2009 world champion Jenson Button, who had been lured from Mercedes in something of a coup for McLaren late in the year that he won his title – challenged for the 2010 and 2012 world titles. But McLaren's star had really started to wane.

The rising Red Bull team was now hoovering up championships ahead of many of F1's long-established squads, while the matrix management style came to be viewed as responsible for successive McLaren cars having disappointing designs. By late 2012, when McLaren's MP4-27 was quick but very fragile, Hamilton decided he had had enough of seeing Red Bull's Sebastian Vettel race to four world titles when he

ABOVE: Jenson Button's victory in the wild 2012 Brazilian GP was to be McLaren's last in Formula 1 for almost nine years, amid the rise of the Red Bull and Mercedes teams.

still only had the 2008 crown. He was convinced to leave the team that had raised him in F1.

After Hamilton decided to join Mercedes for 2013, Button won McLaren the 2012 season-ending Brazilian GP. Its road cars were gaining considerable respect in the automotive world, but now Bruce's team was about to enter its longest-ever silverware drought.

Whitmarsh signed young driver Sergio Pérez to partner Button for 2013 – a year in which McLaren made a bold call that backfired in abandoning 2012's relatively successful design and pursuing a new concept that failed with just one year before the next major rule change arrived in 2014. This shift introduced V6 turbo engines back into F1, although with new hybrid elements. With these engines, Hamilton and Mercedes would go on to dominate the championship. McLaren, as a customer team, could not compete.

But by this point Whitmarsh's time helming its F1 squad was over. He and Dennis had fallen out spectacularly, with Dennis even trying to remove his former protégé from his post on several occasions in the two years running up to 2014. Ironically, these attempts failed because of his similarly strained relations with fellow board members. Mansour Ojjeh was said to have been most upset by Dennis's treatment of Whitmarsh.

After finally acting in January 2014, Dennis said the board had "mandated me to write an exciting new chapter in the story of McLaren, beginning by improving our on-track and off-track performance".

BELOW: Sergio Pérez (right) was signed to replace Lewis Hamilton alongside Jenson Button for the 2013 Formula 1 season. But he lasted only one season in McLaren's line-up.

ABOVE: Whitmarsh on the McLaren team's pitwall stand at the 2013 Brazilian GP, which was to be his last running the Formula 1 team.

Before he left, Whitmarsh had approved a deal with Honda to return as McLaren's engine supplier from 2015, which at the time was billed as an attempt to return to the uber-successful run of the late 1980s and early 1990s. This would continue after his exit (first as team CEO, a role Dennis resumed, then team principal), while McLaren also lost a major sponsor in Vodafone after 2013 that left its F1 cars appearing to lack backing.

Whitmarsh would go on to hold new roles, including CEO of the Ineos America's Cup team – before returning to F1 as group chief executive officer of Aston Martin Performance Technologies, a role he left in late 2024.

Dennis did not go back to running the McLaren F1 team as he previously had. Instead, he installed the former Lotus team principal, Eric Boullier, as racing director, while remaining in

ABOVE: Jenson Button, Whitmarsh and Sergio Pérez (all centre), lead McLaren's celebrations of the 50th anniversary of the team's founding at the 2013 Italian GP.

his McLaren Group roles. But Dennis's issues with his fellow owners were not over.

In late 2014, by which time Dennis had followed through on a plan initially begun under Whitmarsh and sensationally re-signed Alonso, by now racing for Ferrari, even bigger developments at the very top of McLaren were in motion.

Dennis had agreed with his fellow shareholders – at this stage the Bahrain royal family's Mumtalakat investment fund owned 50 per cent of the McLaren Group, having first taken on 30 per cent of the McLaren F1 team backed in 2007, with Dennis and Ojjeh owning 25 per cent each – that he could gain majority control if he could find new investors.

Nearly two years later, however, this had not happened. A deal Dennis thought he had secured with a Chinese consortium apparently worth £1.65 billion fell through. In the meantime,

ABOVE: Fernando Alonso in action for McLaren at the 2015 Japanese GP – a race where the Spaniard would castigate Honda for the poor performance of its Formula 1 engine.

Honda's first attempt at a turbo F1 engine in 27 years had been an embarrassing failure for the manufacturer and McLaren.

Its F1 results nosedived. From finishing third in 2012, it had slipped to fifth (twice) in the final years of its Mercedes customer deal and in 2015 finished ninth of the ten teams – its lowest constructors' ranking since 1980.

For Dennis, a showdown was coming. In November 2016, he sought an injunction from the High Court of England and Wales to prevent his fellow directors from suspending him. This failed and, with Dennis's contract with McLaren concluding in January 2017, his 36-year stint running the organization was over.

He stepped down from his positions, saying, "I am disappointed that the representatives of TAG and Mumtalakat, the other main shareholders in McLaren, have forced through this decision to place me on gardening leave, despite the strong warnings from the rest of the management team about the potential consequences of their actions on the business".

He added. "The grounds they have stated are entirely spurious; my management style is the same as it has always been and is one that has enabled McLaren to become an automotive and technology group that has won 20 Formula 1 world championships and grown into an £850-million-a-year business.

In June 2017, Dennis sold his shareholdings in McLaren Technology Group and McLaren Automotive for £275million and relinquished his directorships of both entities. A new era at McLaren was truly underway.

BELOW: Ron Dennis enacting Whitmarsh's plan to re-sign Fernando Alonso (left) was considered a bold strategy given the pair's difficult relationship at McLaren in 2007.

A NEW
START

THE HEIR: ZAK BROWN

> "We'd become Darth Vader and I wanted us to be Luke Skywalker."

How McLaren changed in the years following Ron Dennis's exit. His successor as Formula 1 team boss, American marketeer Zak Brown, is an irrepressible character. The quote above was spoken in McLaren's giant motorhome in the F1 paddock at the 2024 Italian Grand Prix, painted papaya orange – in contrast to the imposing silver of his predecessor's era – simply because Brown is a McLaren fan.

The day after these words were uttered, McLaren drivers Oscar Piastri and Lando Norris fought for the race victory at Monza – the latter in championship contention and the first McLaren driver to be so since Lewis Hamilton back in 2010. The nadir of the final years of Dennis's reign finally seemed a mere memory.

OPPOSITE: Zak Brown has overseen a resurgence in McLaren's F1 fortunes.

"They were," Brown said in response to the suggestion that the boardroom showdowns through the final months of Dennis's time were dramatic. "I was there."

"The shareholders ultimately had a dispute and it was going to come down to one entity going to need to buy out the other. Because it was clear at that point it was no longer a harmonious relationship and seemed unrepairable."

But Brown claimed he entered the story of McLaren at Dennis's invitation as 2016 wore on.

By this point, Brown was nearly 45. He had started out hoping to make it as an F1 racer himself in the mid- to late-1980s. During McLaren's famously dominant 1988 season, he "fell in love with" the team and Ayrton Senna in particular. Brown won races throughout his time as a go-kart and junior single seater racer and rose as high as competing in the prestigious British Formula 3 series that Senna had won in 1983, as well as IndyCar's Indy Lights series on the other side of the Atlantic. This was 1994, but the following year Brown really started on the journey that led him to running McLaren's F1 squad.

His grand prix driver dream would never be realized – although Brown continued to race on for years, mainly in GT sportscar racing – but in 1995 he started a company that would lead him to the pinnacle of motor racing via another route.

Brown founded Just Marketing, which arranged sponsorship deals for motorsport teams and championships. This started out "of the necessity to just make a living", as well as to continue funding his professional racing ambitions. These finally ended in 2000, but in the meantime, Brown had realized "if I wasn't limited to just selling my own career, I could maybe turn it into something".

"I had no idea it was going to turn into what it did, which was ultimately the world's largest motorsports [sponsorship] agency," he continued.

"I sold the majority of it in 2008 but stayed on as CEO. And then in 2013, we sold the whole thing to Chime Communications, which was a London PLC. They then absorbed the business, put me in as group CEO [of the business then known as CSM] and I ran out my contractual period."

As Dennis was ultimately failing to acquire the funding to buy out his fellow McLaren owners, Brown admitted "Ron had been pursuing me". At the same time, the wider F1 world was changing significantly too, and this nearly altered Brown's career path massively once again.

Liberty Media had taken over the company that owned the championship's commercial rights, Formula One Management, and was starting to flesh out its vision for how F1 would subsequently change. This began with installing its own senior management group to lead FOM after former supremo Bernie Ecclestone was sidelined. Chase Carey was installed as F1 CEO, with Brown heavily linked with the role of commercial

BELOW: McLaren's difficult start to the 2017 Formula 1 season with the MCL32 led Brown and co to end the team's arrangement to run Honda engines.

ABOVE: Jenson Button makes a one-off reappearance for McLaren in Formula 1 at the 2017 Monaco GP, replacing Fernando Alonso, who was competing in the Indy 500.

boss. But with, as he put it, "a view to doing the big boy job at some point".

In late September 2016, Brown resigned as CSM CEO and was poised to join FOM, until McLaren came calling. As a result of "a prolonged wait" to find out the result of FOM's hiring process, Dennis and McLaren had come into the picture. Brown said he was left with "the opportunity to go to either Formula 1 or McLaren" and "ultimately picked McLaren because I felt it gave me the thrill of deal making, which I love".

"But what McLaren then also had was going racing," he added. "And I haven't looked back since."

Indeed, first as executive director of the McLaren Technology Group, Brown made an impact by reviving

McLaren's iconic papaya orange livery on its 2017 F1 car. This decision made headlines, as Dennis had resisted changing the team's colours even after Mercedes had departed as co-owner, much to the frustration of many McLaren supporters.

"That was what the fans wanted," Brown explained. "The car was dark [in 2015 and 2016], we weren't a very inclusive team, we weren't very approachable. But in today's day and age, I wanted the team to have a lot more inclusivity, be very warm, engaging, fan friendly."

But other wins were harder to find. Behind the scenes, Brown found a team where "there were a lot of ghosts being seen on the shop floor – morale was terrible". And so, he set off with a two-pronged strategy. First, to make a series of commercial deals that would increase sponsorship numbers

OPPOSITE: Fernando Alonso waves farewell at the 2018 Abu Dhabi GP – his final race for McLaren before he entered a sabbatical period from racing in Formula 1.

considerably (Brown claimed the team had 10 per cent of the sponsors it does in 2024 when he arrived), while at the same time learning and understanding the workforce to improve McLaren's working culture. With a happier squad and more money coming in, results would follow.

Except they did not. The 2017 F1 season had started with much expected from Honda's reshaped V6 turbo hybrid engine – particularly with more power promised from its internal combustion engine element. But McLaren's results were disastrous again, as the MCL32 car proved to be slow and unreliable.

"We could barely finish a race," Brown said of a year in which Fernando Alonso and Stoffel Vandoorne raced McLaren's first car without an MP4 moniker in 36 years.

Change was inevitable. McLaren ended its Honda partnership after just three years and did a new deal to run Renault customer units in F1 from 2018 – in part to convince Alonso to stay on board. The decision, Brown said, meant they "left a lot of money on the table". Honda soon teamed up with Red Bull and has since made good on the turbo hybrid programme that will switch to Aston Martin's team for 2026.

"But we felt, ultimately, it's a results-based business and if we weren't going to get results, then you're leaving this money on the table, but you're not going to get this money," Brown adds. "Your prize money, your sponsors aren't happy, and things of that nature."

Still, though, all was not right. McLaren's 2018 car – the MCL33 – was a regular points scorer, which was an improvement over its predecessor, but it was still far from leading a class that was by now dominated by its former partner Mercedes.

Alonso grew frustrated and opted to leave McLaren for an F1 sabbatical in 2019 – after Brown and co had allowed him

ABOVE: Lando Norris makes his Formula 1 debut at the 2019 Australian GP for McLaren. The Briton had previously been a junior driver for the team.

to make extra-curricular forays into IndyCar and sportscar racing's World Endurance Championship.

The problem was McLaren's F1 chassis was not as good as the team had previously assumed around Honda's engine issues.

"We were of the view," said Brown, "it was all their fault. And when we put another power unit in the back, we saw we were definitely not where we needed to be. It was a wake-up call."

Again, Brown's McLaren acted. He was by now working as McLaren Racing's CEO and reporting into the McLaren Group chairman role Paul Walsh has held since 2020, alongside the twin CEO of McLaren Automotive. These days, Mumtalakat owns 100 per cent of the McLaren Group, which owns 71 per cent of Racing, with the rest owned by MSP Sports Capital.

In mid-2018, Eric Boullier was ousted as McLaren's F1 racing director. The leadership of the team's technical department was also heavily revised. For 2019, Boullier was replaced by a new McLaren team principal: Andreas Seidl.

At the same time, big change had arrived on the driving front. To replace Alonso and former McLaren junior Vandoorne, another driver the team had invested in – Norris – and Carlos Sainz Jr came in. Via the latter, and with its car design now improving, McLaren scored its first podium since 2014 in the 2019 Brazilian Grand Prix.

Here the results began to pick up, as Brown and Seidl – a Le Mans-winning team principal for Porsche – also agreed a major investment programme was required at the McLaren Technology Centre. This meant building an expensive new wind tunnel critical to getting the best F1 car designs. By 2019's end, McLaren also had decided to do another engine deal and resume as a Mercedes customer from 2021.

BELOW: Carlos Sainz Jr's podium finish at the 2019 Brazilian GP was McLaren's first in F1 for five years. He was boosted to third after Mercedes' Lewis Hamilton was penalized.

ABOVE: McLaren returned to racing in the IndyCar championship in the United States for the 2020 season in partnership with the Arrow Schmidt Peterson Motorsports team.

OPPOSITE: Daniel Ricciardo ended McLaren's near nine-year F1 win drought with his emotional victory in the 2021 Italian race ahead of Lando Norris.

From scoring two more podiums with Norris and Sainz in 2020 – the year the team finished third in the constructors' championship, having made steady progress since being ninth again in 2017 – McLaren finally became an F1 race winner again in 2021. This came via Daniel Ricciardo, who had been signed to replace Sainz when the Spaniard joined Ferrari.

F1 then began a new technical rules era in 2022, with a move back to cars using the ground-effect principle as the main driver for aerodynamics. This was such a dramatic departure from the previous rules – and done because these types of cars can overtake each other more easily – it raised expectations that finally McLaren might vault its way back to challenging for F1 titles for the first time since 2008.

This was not to be at first. And when a major car upgrade package introduced at the 2022 French GP did not work as expected, Brown decided he had to act again regarding the team's leadership.

ABOVE: Brown would replace Andreas Seidl as McLaren's Formula 1 team principal with Italian engineer Andrea Stella ahead of the 2023 season.

"That can happen," Brown said. "What I didn't like was the lack of response, and urgency and concern, that it didn't work."

By this stage, Seidl had received an offer to head up Audi's new F1 programme from 2026 at the end of his McLaren contract. But Brown decided "'you can go now'" at the end of 2022 and then revived a plan he had originally had back in 2018. This was to make Andrea Stella – McLaren's latest racing director, albeit in a less senior position than Boullier – run the show. Stella had worked as a vital engineer to Michael Schumacher at Ferrari during the German driver's world title run in the early 2000s and held a similar role with Alonso before following him to McLaren in 2015.

"I actually wanted to appoint Andrea before we appointed Andreas," Brown revealed. "I wanted to promote Andrea, but he felt he wasn't ready yet. So, I brought in Andreas. That didn't work out, at all."

In Stella's first season as McLaren team boss in 2023, the squad began running Piastri as Norris's teammate. Ricciardo's results had been too inconsistent and the decision had been made the previous summer to pay him off from the rest of his contract. Piastri was so highly rated that McLaren had gone to court over his 2023 services, after it signed him from the Alpine squad where he had been a rising star.

The 2023 F1 season started with McLaren off the pace because of the previous year's design failings, but by mid-year the MCL37 was pushing the now-dominant-again Red Bull team for victories.

In 2024, further improvements to its car design package led to McLaren's first multi-win season in 12 years. Brown

BELOW: Lando Norris's impressive results contributed to the team deciding to replace Daniel Ricciardo with his compatriot Oscar Piastri for 2023.

OVERLEAF: Since 2022, McLaren has fielded a team in the all-electric Formula E championship. Here with Jake Hughes (centre) and René Rast.

credited Stella for "unleashing" talented engineers, such as aerodynamics chief Peter Prodromou – a former key colleague of Adrian Newey at both McLaren in the 1990s and Red Bull in the late-2000s to mid-2010s – with new responsibilities.

With McLaren now firmly on the up again, Brown has big hopes for its future, yet ones that evoke memories of the team's past achievements, as well as Bruce's own.

"Probably the one thing I'd like to get done here is get us in Le Mans," he explained. "And if we can, at one point, win Le Mans, F1's Monaco GP and the Indy 500 as one group, [that] would be cool. If we wanna get really greedy, it would be fun to do it all in one year."

But what would ending McLaren's long F1 title drought mean to Brown?

"Everything…"

BELOW: Lando Norris (left) and Oscar Piastri celebrate McLaren winning the 2024 Hungarian GP, which was the latter's first F1 grand prix victory.

OPPOSITE: Lando Norris crosses the finish line to win the 2024 Miami Grand Prix. It was the British driver's first Formula 1 victory after 110 GP starts.

**TRANSFORMATION
COMPLETE**

THE CARS: AUTOMOTIVE

> The story of McLaren is not just about motorsport. Although these days it is active in a wider range of motor racing championships than it had been for a long swathe of its history, its Automotive road car production corps is world-renowned.

Tying these various strands together is the company's headquarters: the McLaren Technology Centre. Opened in 2004 after six years of construction on the site of a former ostrich farm, the MTC was designed by Wembley stadium architect Norman Foster. The impetus for this move was Ron Dennis wanting to improve overall efficiency within McLaren by providing staff with state-of-the art facilities in which to work.

The MTC moved the company and its Formula 1 race division from nearby Woking town's business park – following on from their previous factory site in Colnbrook. The MTC sits at 63,000m² – beside a man-made lake that dissipates heat from a wind tunnel below. A huge glass façade provides McLaren employees with views over the surrounding Surrey countryside, while in front of the lake a boulevard stretch of

OPPOSITE: The 1969 McLaren M6GT (right) was designed by Bruce.

the interior regularly hosts historic examples of McLaren's racing designs, just feet from where the current F1 racers are assembled and serviced.

In 2021, Zak Brown and his fellow senior managers authorized McLaren to make a £170 million sale and leaseback deal with the Global Net Lease company for the MTC, as the company faced serious cashflow issues during the COVID-19 pandemic.

"Why have all this money tied up in real estate?" Brown said at the time. "We're not a real estate company. We're a racing team and an automotive company."

The sprawling site includes the McLaren Production Centre. Also designed by Foster, and opened in 2011 by then UK prime minister David Cameron and featuring a subterranean walkway to connect with the MTC's main building, here the models from the McLaren Automotive range are assembled. Certain additional bodyshell parts are produced at a separate composites facility in Sheffield.

The history of McLaren's road car offerings can be traced back to Bruce's M6GT design. This was a "genuinely street legal road car" with "Can-Am cousins", according to McLaren biographer William Taylor, that Bruce designed himself in 1969. The project was ultimately shelved – bar the prototype built for Bruce to use and fettle as his personal car. Any ambitions he had for one day still selling the M6GT *en masse* died with him, but Denny Hulme later bought the prototype car and shipped it home to New Zealand.

In 1989, Dennis formed McLaren Cars from another related company – TAG McLaren Research & Development LTD. This produced the world-famous McLaren F1.

Designed by Gordon Murray and Peter Stevens, it was at the time the world's fastest production car, with a launch at the 1993 Monaco GP. Featuring an unusual three-seat cockpit and central driving position, the F1 was the first supercar with an all-carbon fibre monocoque, which was allied to active aerodynamics to achieve enhanced corner handling around what was at the time conceived as the highest power-to-weight ratio of any production car.

The F1 cost £634,500 at the time of its release (£1,323,000 today) and had a top speed of 240mph. It was noted as being able to reach 150mph quicker than most sportscars of the time could reach 60mph by *Autocar* magazine. Its 627bhp came

BELOW: McLaren's F1 supercar was launched at the 1993 Monaco GP. It featured a rare three-seat cockpit layout and was designed by Gordon Murray and Peter Stevens.

ABOVE: The Kokusai Kaihatsu-entered McLaren F1 GTR wins the 1995 Le Mans 24 Hours. It was driven by Yannick Dalmas, Masanori Sekiya and JJ Lehto.

from a BMW-designed V12 engine. Just 70 F1s were made (including prototypes), with extremely limited edition F1 LM and F1 GT varieties built in 1996 and 1997 respectively.

In 1995, a McLaren F1 GTR (which inspired the LM edition) entered by the Kokusai Kaihatsu team won the Le Mans 24 Hours endurance sportscar race – 29 years after Bruce's triumph in the same legendary event for Ford. McLaren had only decided to adapt the F1 for racing to boost flagging sales and was not confident the modified design could even last a 24-hour test.

Through this success, McLaren can claim the 'Triple Crown of Motorsport' – a prestigious title awarded to those who have won the F1 world title, Indianapolis 500 and 24 Hours of Le Mans (an alternative interpretation swaps the F1 championship for victory in the Monaco GP). The only racer to lay claim to a Triple Crown was Bruce's contemporary, Graham Hill, with the accolade generally only applying to drivers. Although McLaren's F1 titles and 15 Monaco GP wins (the most of any team, with five coming via Ayrton Senna) certainly count towards such a consideration, the unofficial, semi-works status of the Kokusai Kaihatsu squad (which was nevertheless put together by McLaren) also detracts from the company's claim.

But there can be no denying the McLaren F1's impact on the supercar sphere upon its release. It was declared "not simply the fastest mid-engined supercar ever built, but the most practical (it had space for luggage in its flanks)" by renowned magazine *Motor Sport*. Its celebrity owners include Rowan Atkinson and Jay Leno.

For 16 years, however, the F1 remained McLaren's sole road car offering, as the McLaren Cars division lay effectively dormant between 1994 and 2010. Not that this stopped the marque's name from appearing in the automotive business in the decade following the F1's release.

As part of its close collaboration with Mercedes, the two companies joined forces on a Grand Touring supercar – with a far greater production volume than that of the F1. This became

BELOW: The Mercedes-Benz SLR McLaren was launched at the 2003 IAA Frankfurt motor show, as McLaren and Mercedes took their partnership into road cars.

BELOW: The Mercedes-Benz SLR McLaren Stirling Moss was around 200kg lighter than the SLR Roadster and featured a longer, lower nose, no roof or windows.

the Mercedes-Benz SLR McLaren, which was introduced to the world at the 2003 IAA Frankfurt motor show. The SLR – 'Sport-Leicht-Rennsport' or 'Sport-Light-Racing' – honoured Mercedes' success in the 1955 Mille Miglia 1000-mile road race that went from Brescia to Rome and back again.

Powered by a supercharged 5.4 litre AMG Mercedes V8, the SLR produced 626bhp. It could do 0–62mph in 3.8 seconds, 0–125 mph in 10.6 seconds, and had a top speed of 207mph. The car was mid-engined, but to achieve the stated aim of a 49:51 front to rear weight distribution, it was placed ahead of the driver and as far back as possible. The bonnet was made long enough to incorporate this aspect, along with side exit exhaust pipes.

Here came McLaren's main contribution – producing a dedicated carbon composite tub that had high torsional

rigidity, as inspired by its many racing designs since the MP4/1. The SLR also featured a separate carbon fibre crash structure that was styled to look like the nose cone of an F1 racer. The SLR's aerodynamics were derived from McLaren's motorsport exploits, too. It featured a flat floor that combined with a rear diffuser to add downforce, with an initial asking price of £315,000 (£560,000 in 2024). As the SLR's production run went on, Mercedes tasked McLaren with producing a soft-top Roadster version, plus a final iteration – the SLR Stirling Moss. This was a 75-model run of a special version of the SLR, which nodded to famed 1950s–1960s racing driver Moss's Mille Miglia success for Mercedes.

The value of the Mercedes SLR collaboration was measured in different ways to just total car sales and income. McLaren claimed ahead of its milestone relaunch of McLaren Cars in 2010 – rebranded as McLaren Automotive that year – that having been able to produce a maximum of three F1 road cars a month during its production run, the experience gained with the SLR meant that it was then capable of making up to four cars a day.

With the expansion of the MTC to include greater road car production facilities just around the corner, McLaren announced in 2010 that, after five years of planning, the car sales from the Automotive arm would "support the long-term future of McLaren and our people".

McLaren Automotive's first car was the MP4-12C. Named in homage to McLaren's old F1 car designations, it was released in 2011.

Dennis said it realized "a long-held dream of mine to launch high-performance sports cars that set new standards in the industry". The MP4-12C is powered by a bespoke McLaren-built V8 twin-turbo engine that put out 600hp. It was followed by a Spider roadster version in 2012, after the MP4 part of the name had been dropped.

BELOW: The MP4-12C was McLaren Automotive's first design when it launched in 2011 and its name referenced McLaren's old F1 car model designations.

BELOW: The McLaren P1 on display at the Geneva Motor Show in 2013. The model, of which 375 were produced, was McLaren's first high-performance hybrid supercar.

In 2013, McLaren released its first high-performance hybrid supercar, the P1, which debuted at the previous year's Paris Motor Show. This twin-turbo engine car, of which 375 were made, combined with an electric motor to produce 903bhp and a top speed of 217mph. Next came 2014's 650S. Its S stands for 'Sport', with coupé and Spider roadster models offered from the start of its production run. The 650 refers to its calculated horsepower output (641bhp), as do the names of similar later McLaren models.

By 2015, McLaren had structured Automotive's offering so that it covered three distinct lines: the Sports, Super, and Ultimate series.

The 2015-released 675LT echoed the 'longtail' design added to the F1 GTR back in 1997, while in 2017 the McLaren Senna was named after the celebrated F1 champion. In 2018, the McLaren Speedtail was introduced – considered something of a successor to the McLaren F1 because of its similar three-seat cockpit layout.

In 2019, McLaren altered Automotive's structure again to incorporate a fourth offering: GT. The McLaren GT was then released that year. Since 2012, certain McLaren designs – starting with the MP4-12C GT3 – had also been adapted for use in the GT category of sportscar racing via the company's dedicated McLaren GT division. In 2024, the GT's successor – the GTS – was introduced to McLaren's fleet.

The McLaren Elva of 2020 pays homage to the deal with the now-defunct British manufacturer that Bruce made in the early days of the company's existence. Today, McLaren offers the Solus GT, which also traces the Ultimate series lineage back to the F1 road car. This track-only car was originally designed as a concept in the *Gran Turismo* video game series.

But the McLaren name can also be found elsewhere. McLaren Applied – first formed as McLaren Applied Technologies as part of an amalgamation of various subsidiary companies in 2003 – is actually no longer owned by the McLaren Group. The company, which since 2008 has supplied

BELOW: A McLaren GT at the 2019 Goodwood Festival of Speed. A dedicated GT division has adapted McLaren supercars for use in sportscar racing since 2012.

ABOVE: A McLaren Elva on display at the 2020 Salon Privé Concours d'Elegance event held at Blenheim Palace in England in the year it was released.

the standard ECU (electronic control unit) that processes all the data and command functions on all F1 cars, plus other components made for teams across the current grid, has been owned by the Greybull Capital investment company since 2021.

Throughout its history, McLaren Applied worked on projects including performance management systems for Team GB's sailing, rowing, canoeing and cycling squads at the 2012 Olympics, improved production efficiency for pharmaceutical giant GSK, and made the S-Works+ McLaren Venge for bicycle company Specialized. Separately, the McLaren group also had a short-lived partnership with the Bahrain-Victorious professional cycling team.

McLaren is now active in new and emerging motorsport disciplines as well. After the Applied division had produced the spec electric motor for the first season of the all-electric Formula E championship, and the spec battery for its Gen 2 era between 2018–2022, McLaren entered its own team in the series. Since 2022, McLaren has also fielded a team in the related Extreme E off-road electric racing series.

And in bringing McLaren's racing story to intertwine again in a manner of which Bruce would no doubt approve, the company recently opted to rejoin the American racing scene, where it enjoyed so much success right back at its roots in the 1960s and 1970s.

After two dedicated attempts to win the Indy 500 with former F1 driver Fernando Alonso (in 2017 in collaboration with the Andretti Autosport organization), Brown's McLaren Racing re-entered Indycar racing full-time in 2020. It partnered with the Sam Schmidt Motorsports squad at the time, then wielded the controlling stake in the team, with Brown acting as its chairman, since 2022.

Papaya orange liveries are racing on both sides of the Atlantic and all around the world as the 2020s unfurl. McLaren's story continues, exactly as Bruce had begun it.

BELOW: A McLaren Solus GT is presented at the 2024 Goodwood Festival of Speed. Only 25 models will be produced, with the car originally a gaming concept.

INDEX

(Key: *italic* refers to photos/captions)

A

Abu Dhabi Grand Prix *128*
Adamich, Andrea de 68
Aintree *13*
Alfa Romeo 68
Alonso, Fernando 13, 80–1, *81*, 97, 105, 106–7, *118*, *126*, 128, *128*, 131, 155
AMG Mercedes 149
Anderson, Gary *40*
Andretti Autosport 155
Andretti, Michael 61, 93
Argentine Grand Prix 14, 36, 38
Arrow Schmidt Peterson *132*
Aston Martin Performance Technologies 116
Atkinson, Rowan 147
Austin-Healey 31
Austin Seven 14
Australian Grand Prix *43*, 88, 93, 97, *108*, *130*
Autocar 145
Autosport 9, 18, 25, 61, 86, 94, 112

B

Bahrain-Victorious 154
Barnard, John 53, 59, 69–70
Belgian Grand Prix 23, 23, 29, 38, *66*
Benetton 67
Berger, Gerhard 87, *88*
Blenheim Palace *154*
Blundell, Sir Denis 25, *93*
BMW 52, 66, 69, 146
BMW ProCar M1 50, 52, 55
Boullier, Eric 116, 130–1
Brabham 49, 53
Brabham, Jack 10, 11, 13–14, *13*, 16, 17, 49
Brawn GP 111–12, *112*
Brawn, Ross 111
Brazilian Grand Prix *36*, *58*, 70, 88, 88, 98, 108, 114, *116*, 131, *131*
BRDC International Trophy 14
British Aerospace (BAe) 107
British Grand Prix *13*, *28*, 36, 39, 40, *50*, 55, *56*, 98
British Racing Motors (BRM) 22, *67*
Brown, Creighton 51
Brown, Zak 123–35, 144, 155
Bruce McLaren Motor Racing Ltd 17
Brundle, Martin 76
Button, Jenson 80, *108*, *112*, 114, *115*, *117*, *126*

C

Cameron, David 144
Can-Am 22, 25, *25*, *30*, *31*, 34, 35–6, 40, 69
Canadian Grand Prix 36, 38, 97
Carey, Chase 125
Chapman, Colin 22, 53
Chime Communications/ CSM 125–6
Chinese Grand Prix 97, *112*
Chipstead Motor Group 48
Chrysler 76
Clark, Jim 25
Colnbrook factory 34, 143
Cooper 10–14, *11*, *13*, 17, 18, *25*, 33, 48, *49*
'Lowline Cooper' 14
T60 *14*
T66 17
Cooper, Charles 11, 16, 20
Cooper, John 11, 20
Cooper, John and Charles 11, 16
Cosworth 22, 67, 68, *69*
Coughlan, Mike 106
Coulthard, David 79, 93
covid-19 144

D

Dalmas, Yannick *146*
Dennis, Ron 40, *43*, 47–61, *49*, *52*, *59*, *60*, 65–6, 69–70, 73–9, 86, 88, 90, *90*, 93–8, *96*, 105–8, 115–19, *118*, 123–8, 143, 149
Donington *50*, 89, *89*
Donohue, Mark 35
'Driver to Europe' scholarship 10
Dutch Grand Prix *25*, 29

156 INDEX

E

Eagle 22
Ecclestone, Bernie 125
ECU (electronic control unit) 154
Ecuador-Marlboro 50
Elizabeth II 48
Elva Cars 18
European Grand Prix 89, *89*
EVs (electric vehicles) *135*, 154–5
Extreme E 155

F

Federation Internationale de l'Automobile (FIA) 106–7, 107, 108, 111
Ferrari 56, 87, 90, 94, 96, 106, *117*, 132, 134
Ferrari, Enzo 65
Firestone 18
Fittipaldi, Emmerson 36, *36*, 38, 68, *69*
Ford 18, 18–20, 18, 21–2, *53*, 55, 59, 65, 67, *68*, *69*, *73*, 146
Formula 2 10, *11*, 49, 50, 69
Formula 3 52, 124
Formula E *135*, 154
Formula One Management (FOM) 125
Formula One Teams' Association (FOTA) 111
Foster, Norman 143, 144
Frankfurt Motor Show *147*, 149
French Grand Prix *79*, 132
FW14B 89

G

Galli, Nanni 68
garagiste 65, 66
Gen2 cars 154–5
Geneva Motor Show *152*
German Grand Prix 10, *11*, 39, 55
Gethin, Peter 29
Global Net Lease 144
Goodwood Festival of Speed *153*, 155
Goodyear 35
Gran Turismo 153
Greybull Capital 154
GSK 154
Gurney, Dan 29

H

Haas-Lola *43*
Häkkinen, Mika 61, 79, 85–99, *90*, *93*, *94*
Hamilton, Lewis 85–99, *96*, *98*, 105, 106–7, 108, *111*, 112–15, *112*, 123, *131*
Haug, Norbert *59*
Hill, Graham 146
Hogan, John 50, 53
Honda 55, 56–60, 67, 73–6, *73*, 80, *80*, 86, 116, *118*, *125*, 128, 130
Hughes, Jake *135*
Hulme, Denny 17, 22, 23, 29, *30*, *32*, 34, 35, 38, *67*, 144
Hungarian Grand Prix 13, 98, 106, *106*, *111*, *138*
Hunt, James 38–40, *38*, *39*, 68

I

ICI 51
Indianapolis 500 (Indy 500) 21, 29, 30, *34*, 35, *126*
Indy Lights series 124
IndyCar 124, 130, *132*, 155
International Grand Prix Association 10
Italian Grand Prix 39, 40, *49*, 81, 86, *117*, 123, *132*

J

Japanese Grand Prix *39*, 56, *56*, 73, 86–7, *86*, *94*, *118*
Jarama *38*
Jerez 94
Just Marketing 124

K

Kerr, Phil 14, 33–4, 36–7
Kimbolton *96*
Kokusai Kaihatsu 146, *146*

L

Laguna Seca track *30*, *31*
Lamborghini 76
Lauda, Niki 39, 52, *52*, *53*, 55, 70
Le Mans 24 Hours 9, 18, *18*, 138, 146
Lehto, JJ *146*
Leno, Jay 147
Levin 17
Liberty Media 125

Lola 34
Long Beach *52*
Lotus 22, 40, 53, *68*, 73, 85–6, *86*, 90

M

McLaren Applied/McLaren Applied Technologies 153–4
McLaren Automotive 118, 130, 144, 149, *151*, 152
McLaren, Bruce 9–25, *9*, *11*, *14*, 25, *25*, 29, *29*, 30, 33, 34, 47, 65–7, *66*, 138, *143*, 146, 153, 155
McLaren Cars 144, 147, 149
675LT 152
M1B 22
M2A 18
M2B 20, 21, *21*
M4B 22
M6A 22, 34–5
M6GT *143*, 144
M7A 22
M8D 25, *25*, *30*
M9A 23
M16 35
M23 68, *69*
M26 40
MCL32 *125*, 128
MCL33 128
MP4 128
MP4/1 40, 53, 55, 70, 149
MP4/2 70
MP4/4 56, *73*, 86–7
MP4/5 73, 87
MP4/8 67, 76, 89
MP4/9 *76*, 78, 93
MP4-12C 149, *151*
MP4/13 94
MP4-24 *106*
MP4-26 *112*
MP4-27 112
P1 152, *152*
Solus *155*
Speedtail 152
McLaren Group 55, 108, 112, 117, 130, 153–4
McLaren International 40, 55
McLaren, Patty (née Broad) 14, *14*
McLaren Production Centre (MPC) 144
McLaren Racing 130, 155
McLaren Senna 152
McLaren Technology Centre (MTC) 131, 143–4, 149
McLaren Technology Group 118, 126
Maddock, Owen 14
Magnussen, Jan 96
Mansell, Nigel 79, 89
Marlboro 36, 38, 40, 50, 51–4, 79, 90
Mayer, Teddy 17, 29–43, *29*, *39*, *40*, *43*, 47, 65, 69
Mayer, Timmy 17, 18, 21, 30–1, 32
Mercedes *59*, 79, 79–80, *79*, 98, *98*, 108, *108*, 111, 114–15, 118, 131, *131*, 147, *147*, 149
Mercedes-Benz SLR McLaren *147*, 148
Mercedes-Benz SLR McLaren Stirling Moss *148*, *149*
Mercedes FO 110 *79*
Mexican Grand Prix 23, 49
Miami Grand Prix *138*
Mille Miglia 149
Monaco Grand Prix 16, *21*, *69*, 70, *70*, *126*, 138, 144, *145*, 146
Monza 39, *49*, 123
Mosley, Max 107
Moss, Stirling 149
Motor Sport 147
MSP Sports Capital 130
Mumtalakat 117, 118
Murray, Gordon 53, 58–9, 144, *145*

N

New Zealand Grand Prix 10, 17
Newey, Adrian 94, 108, 138
Nicholson McLaren Engines 68
Norris, Lando 81, 98, 123, *130*, 131, 132, *132*, 135, *135*, *138*
Nürburgring 10, 39
Nye, Doug 10, 14, 33, 36, 48, 50, 52

O

OAPEC Oil Crisis (1973) 50
Offenhauser 35
Ojjeh, Mansour 55, 70, 115, 117
Olympics, London 2012 154
Osella 52
Overtaking Working Group (OWG) 108, 111

P

Pacific Grand Prix 96
Paul Ricard track 93
Penske M16B 35
Penske-Porsche 35
Pérez, Sergio 114, *115*, *117*
Peterson, Ronnie 40
Peugeot 78–9, 93
Piastri, Oscar 81, 98, 123, 135, *135*, *138*
Porsche *53*, 55, 69–70, 70, 131